"Lhara is a passionate advocate for neurodivergent children and their families and presents a lived experience voice to the field of practitioner education. This book is a must-read for those aiming to practice from a truly individualized and informed perspective, which empowers and enables neurodivergent children and their families."

Paula McGowan, OBE, *founder of The Oliver McGowan Mandatory Training in Learning Disability and Autism*

Supporting Neurodivergent Children and Families

Supporting Neurodivergent Children and Families presents an innovative blueprint using academic literature, research and theory, to provide a best practice approach in equipping practitioners to support neurodivergent children and their families.

The knowledge and insight provided in this book allows practitioners to effectively create supportive environments and plan appropriate practice responses, whilst never changing the child. By altering the system perspective and transcending the physical boundaries of space where the interaction occurs, a supportive environment is created, thus providing more positive outcomes. The blend of practice experiences, tangible case studies and theory prompts the reader to critically reflect on their practice and potentially integrate new, innovative changes into their approach.

This comprehensive and thought-provoking read is not only ideal for students and professionals who interact with neurodiverse families, but also practitioners and educators looking to alter their practical approach to understanding neurodivergent children and their families.

Dr. Lhara Mullins is a lecturer at the University of Galway in Ireland, has a PhD in health promotion and an MA in social work. Her own experiences as a neurodivergent academic, with a background in social work, and 17 years of experience interacting with health, social care and education services with her three neurodivergent children acts as a foundation for her writing.

Supporting Neurodivergent Children and Families

A Practitioner's Guide

Lhara Mullins

Routledge
Taylor & Francis Group

NEW YORK AND LONDON

Designed cover image: RobinOlimb © Getty Images.

First published 2024
by Routledge
605 Third Avenue, New York, NY 10158

and by Routledge
4 Park Square, Milton Park, Abingdon, Oxon, OX14 4RN

Routledge is an imprint of the Taylor & Francis Group, an informa business

© 2024 Lhara Mullins

ISBN: 978-1-032-59697-6 (hbk)
ISBN: 978-1-032-59394-4 (pbk)
ISBN: 978-1-003-45586-8 (ebk)

DOI: 10.4324/9781003455868

Typeset in Galliard
by Apex CoVantage, LLC

Contents

Figures

Tables

Preface

A supportive environment is about so much more than the physical class-room, clinic or therapy suite. It's about communicating before you even meet a child and their family that you accept them, they are welcome and will be included. A supportive environment is one within which the neuro-divergent child and their family are confident in your knowledge and un-derstanding of their child's diagnosis/diagnoses and that you are practicing from an informed perspective. When families are struggling, every interac-tion can feel so much more potent. That kind word, or that space to allow silence . . . for a moment of reflection, can make a monumental difference.

This text will present a unique and novel approach to supporting neu-rodivergent children and their families, via a blend of health promotion concepts and practical strategies, for constructing and maintaining spaces of inclusion and belonging. As a lecturer in health promotion and qualified so-cial worker, I truly value the wealth of literature and insight both disciplines present, in terms of the factors which influence the health and wellbeing of neurodivergent children and their families. My 20 years of experience engaging with services as a parent of three neurodivergent children, affords me an inimitable perspective from which to discern best practice approaches and strategies for supporting families like my own. As a neurodivergent person myself, I am further uniquely placed to present the reality of neu-rodivergence and encapsulate within a learning format how best the needs of neurodivergent children and their families can be addressed. The inter-generational element of neurodivergence is further acknowledged within the strategies proposed in this book and is fundamental to consider within practice, which aims to create and maintain truly supportive environments.

Creating supportive environments is about constructing and maintaining a metaphorical space of openness to the child's unique needs, while simultane-ously acknowledging the broader impact of the child's disability on their whole family. A supportive environment recognises the power of each interaction between the practitioner and the family, as an opportunity to build supportive relationships and offer unconditional support and genuine care. A supportive environment is one where children and families don't have to change or conform to engage and they know that you as the practitioner will meet them where they're at. It's an environment where the wellbeing of each member of the family is valued, while the practical issues affecting the child and their family directly impact the practitioner's approach to their care and support.

A supportive environment is one where there's an inherent acknowledgement and acceptance that everyone needs a support network, and that social networks are instrumental for neurodivergent children and their families. The practitioner respects the child's and family's preferences and values intrinsically, and aims to form a strong partnership with parents/caregivers. A supportive environment is based upon reflective practice and continual critical consideration of one's approach, to effectively and holistically support neurodivergent children and their families.

A focus on creating supportive environments both appreciates and acknowledges the broader factors which impact the neurodivergent child and their family, and tailors practice which is focused to meet their unique needs. This book will present insightful and tangible practice examples and case studies, which will enable the application of theory to practice, based on the lived reality for neurodivergent children and families.

My inspiration for writing this book stems from my extensive experiences as a parent interacting with educational, medical and social care providers, in my efforts to meet my children's needs. The aim of this book is to present an insider perspective and a view from across the table, concerning practice, in effectively supporting neurodivergent children and their families. The impact of both educators and health and social care professionals on the lives of families like mine are momentous. We've had the most profound and life-changing interactions with practitioners, who have demonstrated reflective and knowledgeable insight concerning our children and an appreciation for the wellbeing of our whole family. We've also had less positive experiences, which have further contributed to my comprehension and insight in terms of what works and what doesn't work. Although this may seem counterintuitive, establishing what strategies and methods don't work is equally as insightful as establishing what does.

Creating supportive environments encompasses strategies, actions and intent, both inside and outside of the clinic or classroom. It communicates a wish to establish and address the issues which really matter to and impact the child and their family, based on their unique and individual circumstances. No one-size-fits-all approach is sufficient. This book will share specific principles and catalysts for creating supportive environments for neurodivergent children and their families, which can be employed across settings, sectors and contexts. These principles and catalysts of creating supportive environments present tangible values and ideologies from which to inform practice, with neurodivergent children and their families.

Writing this book has been a journey in itself. My review of the literature has further substantiated my wish to build upon the existing evidence base regarding neurodivergence, and populate this with more neurodivergent voices and reflections concerning effective vs. ineffective practice. I'm always a work in progress, and that's okay! I learn every day from my children and their unique perspectives and interactions with the world around them, while my professional practice insight and expertise is consistently evolving, through my own critical reflection and the integration of new ideas, insights and experiences.

My hope is that this book will prompt practitioners and future practitioners to think outside the box, question their practice and reflect on ways to truly positively impact the lives of neurodivergent children and their families, via creating supportive environments.

Structure of This Book

This book presents a unique and novel practice approach to supporting neurodivergent children and their families, based upon the concept of creating supportive environments. Yet understanding and awareness of what neurodivergence means for children and their families is a vital prerequisite for contextualising the application of new ideas and concepts to practice. The emergence of neurodivergence as a concept is further significant to the broader context within which your practice occurs. The three key neurodivergent presentations of autism, ADHD and dyspraxia further present completely uniquely for each child. Consequently, this book will commence with an exploration of the discourse development surrounding neurodiversity, in Chapter 1, and will explore the individual neurodivergent presentations of autism, dyspraxia and ADHD, in Chapters 2, 3 and 4.

Chapter 5 will introduce the concept of creating supportive environments and explore the role of health promotion, within every facet of practice with neurodivergent children and their families. This chapter places in context the significance of creating supportive environments specifically, as it pertains to neurodivergent children and their families. Key principles to underpin practice aimed at creating supportive environments and catalysts for action will be presented within this chapter. This cornerstone chapter will enable the reader to consider such principles and catalysts intrinsic to creating supportive environments for families of neurodivergent children, in the context of their own practice role and concerning each key subsequent chapter presented in this text.

Specific practice issues pertinent to creating supportive environments with neurodivergent children and their families, such as communication, making each contact count and managing conflict with parents, will be explored within Chapters 6, 7 and 8. Chapters 9, 10 and 11 will examine evidence-based practice, parental wellbeing and the role of advocacy, in the context of creating supportive environments. Family support, reflective practice and practitioner self-care will be presented within Chapters 12, 13 and 14, and will further facilitate learning and development pertaining to the medley of fundamental factors which can be employed to create truly supportive environments for neurodivergent children and their families.

Acknowledgements

First and foremost, I would like to thank my editor at Routledge New York, Ms. Amanda Savage. Amanda shared my excitement and enthusiasm for writing this book and valued from the outset my unique insight from both sides of the table. I love that Amanda appreciated and reciprocated my use of exclamation marks! I would also like to thank Ellie Broadhurst, editorial assistant at Routledge. Thank you, Ellie.

To each of my children, thank you for sparking my passion for transforming practice with families like ours. Each of you teaches me daily about what really matters. Your brutal honesty and humour make me unbelievably proud to be your Mom.

To my husband, Kenneth, I'm so grateful to have you in my corner always and for your acceptance of my perpetual state of always being a work in progress.

Thank you to my aunties Carmel, Alice, Maureen and Martina, who are my biggest cheerleaders and share my accomplishments wherever they go.

To Emma, Hazel, Ellen, Sharon, Jean and Jim: You are my people.

Chapter 1

An Introduction to Neurodiversity

Abbreviations

ADHD: Attention Deficit Hyperactivity Disorder
APA: American Psychiatric Association
DSM: Diagnostic and Statistical Manual of Mental Disorders
UN: United Nations
WHO: World Health Organisation

Introduction

Neurodiversity as a concept appears relatively recent. Yet the disability move-ment has long advocated for the reframing of disability in terms of how this is perceived and acknowledged within society and within the medical field. The previous dominant and traditional medical model identified disability as a deficit or defect and not within the normal or typical range of health. This evolution in terms of understanding now focuses on disability as a variation or difference, as opposed to atypical or unhealthy. The disability movement has reframed disability and placed acceptance and inclusion firmly on the global agenda. The neurodiversity movement adopts a similar outlook and contends that varied neurotypes are not abnormal or defective, yet are based on divergence and variation within the continuum of neurotypes.

This chapter will introduce the concept of neurodiversity and discuss the paradigm shift which has culminated in our current understanding of varied neurotypes. This chapter will explore the terminology used within the neu-rodiversity discourse, alongside the social construction of both childhood and neurodivergence. Chapter 1 will engage learners in critical reflection and prompt them to develop new insights and understandings concern-ing neurodivergence. Such understanding will be instrumental in laying the theoretical and practical foundations, for creating supportive environments, for neurodivergent children and their families.

DOI: 10.4324/9781003455868-1

Learning Outcomes

On completion of Chapter 1, learners should demonstrate an enhanced understanding concerning:

- The development of neurodivergence as a concept
- The language/terminology surrounding neurodiversity
- The impact of social constructions of childhood and neurodivergence
- The ability to articulate, based on reflection, the meaning of neurodiversity

What Is Neurodiversity?

The term *neurodiversity* was initially coined by Judy Singer in the 1990s, within her sociology thesis. Singer (2017) herself is autistic, and she sought to destigmatise variations of neurotypes. Singer (2017) reports that the label "Autistic Spectrum Disorder" manifested in society, marginalising those diagnosed and dismissing them as people with psychiatric problems. Singer (2017) argues that during the early days of autism diagnoses, there were no grey areas concerning the stigma attached to this disorder: people were either deviant from the norm/autistic or normal. However, specific diagnoses which exist within the neurodiversity umbrella also include ADHD, dyspraxia, dyscalculia and dyslexia, in addition to autism (Stenning & Bertilsdotter Rosqvist, 2021). Neurodiversity refers to previously labelled neurodevelopmental disorders and reframes these as divergences or differences which should be embraced.

Rotella (2022) argues that traditionally neurodivergence was viewed and responded to as a psychiatric issue and that the inclusion of autism and ADHD within the *Diagnostic and Statistical Manual of Mental Disorders* (DSM) further clouds understanding of the needs of neurodivergent individuals. Neurodivergent refers to an individual whose neurocognitive function presents as different from that considered within societal norms (Shah et al., 2022). The core foundation of the neurodiversity movement is concerned with enhancing awareness and acceptance and embracing variations in neurotypes.

Neurodiversity at its simplest means that people's brains are different and that such differences do not equate to deficits (Lorenz, Reznik, & Heinitz, 2017). Masataka (2017) argues that approaching practice from a neurodiversity perspective prompts practitioners to consider the strengths of the individual, rather than focusing on their deficits. Stenning and Bertilsdotter Rosqvist (2021) argue that neurodiversity should not be limited to specific conditions or diagnoses, and instead should be non-prescriptive to remain inclusive. They contend that as our understanding of neurodivergence is still quite novel, the door should remain open to encompass additional presentations of neurodiversity as they emerge and evolve (Stenning & Bertilsdotter Rosqvist, 2021).

Dr. Temple Grandin is a notable figure within the neurodiversity movement and is an author and autistic advocate (Grandin, Barron, & Zysk, 2017). Dr. Grandin, a professor at Colorado State University, speaks all over the world about her journey as an autistic person (Grandin, 2023). Dr. Grandin advocates that autism impacts each person completely differently, with some autistic children requiring round-the-clock support, and others with lower levels of support need perhaps engaging well in mainstream school. However, Dr. Grandin suggests that each autistic person possesses abilities and unique attributes, which may not be identified or nurtured within a neurotypical environment. For example: using standardised academic testing will often not enable and empower autistic children to demonstrate their full potential. Yet autism is not a deficit, but rather a difference in ability and how the autistic child's brain functions (Grandin, 2023).

Author Reflection Point!

As I research and write this chapter, almost all of the literature about neurodiversity and autism (as most of this research discusses autism specifically) is still steeped in deficit terminology. The language use very much approaches neurodivergence from a medical or scientific lens, which reverts consistently to describing neurodivergence as disordered and deviant from expected norms, in terms of development and function.

The Development of Neurodiversity

The development of neurodiversity as a concept stems from the idea that just as society has adapted to be more inclusive for people with physical disabilities by building ramps and making entrances accessible, such accommodations should be employed for people with varied neurotypes (Baker, 2011). Barker contends that traditionally society has aimed to embrace differences which are visible, such as race, gender and sexual orientation. Invisible differences are now emerging as equally warranting of accommodations to promote inclusion, as our understanding of hidden disabilities and neurodivergence is evolving (Baker, 2011).

Krcek (2013) argues that the neurodiversity movement adopts a social rather than a medical perspective of disability and advocates for difference, as opposed to viewing disability as a disorder. Equally, the emergence of neurodiversity as a concept acknowledges that disability is socially constructed and consequently, can and should be reconstructed as a difference, rather than assuming a deficit (Kreck, 2012). In essence, this means that when and where a neurodivergent person lives and is socialised will impact the familial and societal response to their needs. For example: in Ireland, neurodivergence is much more widely recognised than it was 20 years ago, which reduces stigma, increases early identification and promotes inclusion. Yet neurodiversity in developing countries is underdiagnosed, and this has been partially attributed to cultural stigma surrounding disability (Shibli & Hamdoun, 2019). Ahmed and colleagues (2019) argue that in poorer countries the response to communicable disease often dominates the public health system, rather than a focus on neurodivergence. A lack of awareness and understanding surrounding neurodivergence further contributes to underdiagnoses (Ahmed et al., 2019).

The medical model of health approaches health and wellness in terms of the absence of disease. A defect or disorder is identified and treated accordingly, based on a medical approach (Thompson, 2018). This biological-medical model has worked well for centuries, in treating physical illness such as infection and immunising to prevent the spread of disease. The medical model of health was initially questioned by George Engel in the 1960s, who argued that this approach to health was limited and failed to consider the social and environmental factors which contributed to health and wellness (Engel, 1977).

Thompson (2018), who writes from an experiential perspective having worked in the mental health field as a social worker, argues that mental well-being is not a case of being present or not present. The absence of a mental health diagnosis does not necessarily render one mentally well. Conversely, a diagnosed mental health condition such as depression or anxiety should not render someone unwell or not healthy (Thompson, 2018). Farre and Rapley (2017) contend that understandings of health and wellness shape the practitioner's response to the needs of the person/patient. Haegele and Hodge (2016) expand on this notion and add that understandings surrounding disability and the language attached to these influence people's expectations of and interactions with people living with disabilities. For example: describing someone as a paraplegic as opposed to a Paralympian or a professor. Or introducing a child as having communication deficits/challenges, as opposed to a child who communicates amazingly well via their assistive communication device!

In contrast to the medical model of health, the social model of health recognises the collective societal responsibility for health and wellness (Schoeb, 2016). The social model of health approaches health from the perspective that the person's environment, community and support network directly impact their health and opportunity to be healthy (Schoeb, 2016). This approach is further supported via the World Health Organisation's (WHO, 2017) assertion that health is strongly influenced by social and environmental determinants such as: housing, sanitation, access to healthcare, food availability, employment, education and the economy. For example: individuals who grow up in poverty, and lack access to education or clean water, are much more likely to face the burden of illness, when compared to someone who grows up in an affluent area, with all of the resources they need to thrive.

The society within which neurodivergent children are born and live will further impact how their neurodivergence is viewed and how their needs are responded to. Taha and Hussein (2014) argue that much of the research to date surrounding autism has been undertaken in Western countries. A study by Memari and colleagues in 2012 found that autistic children in Iran were being overprescribed medication. Of the 345 children who participated in their study, all with a diagnosis of autism, 97% had been prescribed psychotropic medication in the previous year. In comparison to the use of psychotropic medication in developed countries, a 2010 study in the US found that 35% of autistic children were being prescribed psychotropic medication (Rosenberg et al., 2010). It should be noted that there is no medication which treats autism specifically, but rather medication is used to manage some of the challenges which may present due to autism, such as violent behaviours, hyperactivity or self-injurious behaviours (Posey, Stigler, Erickson, & McDougle, 2008). Memari et al. (2012) cite potential reasons for the high rate of psychotropic medication use for autistic children in Iran as largely related to the lack of non-pharmaceutical alternatives in the form of therapeutic and behavioural supports. Hence medication for some autistic children may be the only option offered, even if this is not the most appropriate response to their needs (Memari et al., 2012).

Reflection Point!

How do you think the evolution of neurodiversity has impacted neurodivergent people? How do you think the concept of neurodiversity has impacted medicine and the medical response to neurodivergent children and adults? How do you think enhanced understanding of neurodiversity influences education/classroom settings?

Language Surrounding Neurodiversity

Language surrounding neurodiversity remains a contentious issue, particularly concerning autism. Debate and discussion continue concerning descriptions of autism, such as high functioning, which was included in the now-defunct diagnosis of Asperger's Syndrome (Alvares et al., 2020). Autistic individuals who are labelled high functioning are said to require less support to engage in tasks of everyday living. Yet both Den Houting (2019) and Alvares et al. (2020) argue that functioning capacity varies greatly for autistic individuals, with someone labelled as high functioning experiencing substantial difficulties depending on a multitude of variables, while people labelled as low functioning can be restricted in terms of expectation of need and perhaps restricting their opportunities for achievement. Although descriptions concerning functioning have been deemed as unhelpful and potentially damaging for autistic individuals, they appear to remain frequently used by professionals in their descriptions of autistic people.

Person-first language is another source of much discussion regarding accepted and appropriate language, when describing neurodivergent individuals. Again, this is particularly the case pertaining to autism (Shah et al., 2022). Many autistic adults prefer being referred to as autistic, which is their identity, as opposed to a person with autism (Taboas, Doepke, & Zimmerman, 2023). "With autism" suggests that autism is separate from the person, rather than inherent to who they are (Grandin, 2023). Person-first language would be using person with autism or person with hearing loss or diabetes, etc., while identity-first language would mean referring to the person as autistic. I find myself more recently using identity-first language pertaining to autism, yet not when referring to another condition, largely because the majority of autistic adults prefer this. Yet it's important to use language the child and their family are comfortable with and identify as respectful and representative of how they view themselves and neurodivergence. Always ask a child or family what their preference is in terms of language and terminology. Interestingly, at the time of this writing, autism and ADHD are still diagnosed via the use of the *Diagnostic and Statistical Manual* (DSM-5) and are categorised as disorders, based on specific deficits (American Psychiatric Association, 2013).

Table 1.1 provides a glossary of terms relevant to neurodiversity.

Table 1.1 Glossary of terms in neurodiversity (Shah et al., 2022)

Neurodivergent	An individual with a neurocognitive function different from that of previously considered typical societal norms. The opposite of neurotypical.
Neurodiversity	A range of varied neurocognitive functioning expected across a population and encompassing both neurodivergent and neurotypical individuals.
Neurotypical	An individual with neurocognitive function within the parameters of expected societal norms. The opposite of neurodivergent.
Person-First Language	Using the person before the condition, e.g. person living with autism or ADHD.
Identity-First Language	Using the person's identity first, e.g. blind person, hearing impaired person, autistic person.

Social Constructions of Childhood

Social constructions of childhood shape societal expectations concerning child development, behaviour, policy and legislation. Social constructionists believe that people and things in society are created and understood, based on how they are interpreted and constructed by people (Norozi & Moen, 2016). In essence, children and childhood exist, based on the social understandings and ideas people have created around this (Norozi & Moen, 2016). The society within which the child exists and the culture within which they are born will shape views and perspectives on what being a child means and how this is viewed.

Reflection Point!

How would you describe a child? What makes a child different from an adult?

Based on such social constructions, laws are created to protect the rights of the child regarding protection and the right to education (United Nations, 1989). Legislation is further created based on this social construction of childhood concerning the legal responsibility of parents to meet their child's needs physically and emotionally. Social constructions of childhood are further evident within legislative measures to protect children from labour (International Labour Organisation, 2023). Such legislative instruments recognise and aim to protect the social constructions of childhood as a time of dependence and a child's need for protection (UN, 1989; International Labour Organisation, 2023).

More recent social constructions of childhood view the child as having agency in their own right and not merely as adults in the making, or members of a family. This evolution in social understandings of childhood has prompted the development of specific research concerning the needs of children in their own right (not only within their familial context). The idea of children possessing agency is now reflected within policy and legislation, aimed specifically at meeting the distinctive needs of them as a group within society (UN, 1989).

It is only within the consideration of these social constructions and expectations surrounding childhood that we recognise and respond to variations or divergence, compared to these typical constructions. When a child presents with needs or development outside of the socially constructed norms for their age, this catalysts examination or the cause and intervention to mitigate the challenges they face. For example: neurodivergent children may display language and communication which is considered atypical before the age of 3 years old. Some children may communicate non-verbally, have problems with speech, issues with social interaction, or may use language at an exceptionally advanced level for their age.

Social Constructions of Neurodivergence

Neurodevelopmental conditions are socially constructed, to attribute understanding to diversities in ways of being and interacting. These social constructions of neurodiversity signify the evolution in understanding differences and accepting variations from the typical or norm. For example: from the medical model of disability which identifies autism as a syndrome or condition and a deviation from normal or typical development (Thompson, 2018), to a perspective which appreciates variations in ways of interacting with the world as different, as opposed to deficits or abnormal (Lorenz et al., 2017; Singer, 2017). Yet social constructions of neurodivergence initially were met with a search for a cure and connotations of dependence and impairment (Ortega, 2009). Such initial constructions of childhood neurodevelopmental disabilities profoundly influenced how practitioners, families and neurodivergent people themselves acted and lived (Ortega, 2009).

Leveto (2018) argues that children have presented with a need for sameness and communication difficulties for centuries, yet autism has only been identified in recent years. Leveto (2018) contends that what may appear at first glance as an autism epidemic is in fact a shift in understanding, the evolution of policies and systems, and a greater awareness of neurodivergence. The neurodiversity paradigm shift has culminated in parents and practitioners identifying differences in child development, rather than deviations or deficits, and exploring ways of mediating the environment to meet the child's unique needs.

Chiri, Bergey and Mackie (2022) propose that government policy and legislation represents social constructions of disability and the evolution of views concerning neurodivergence. They contend that social constructions of neurodiversity are further shaped by their classification within psychiatry and diagnostic criteria (Chiri et al., 2022). Such framing within psychiatry via the DSM-5 medicalises autism and essentially presents this as symptoms and deficits. Such medicalisation promotes policy development aimed at treatment and symptom management, as opposed to inclusion or belonging, while policy further shapes and informs societal understanding of neurodivergence and the professional response to the needs of neurodivergent children and their families. Social constructions of neurodiversity are consistently being re-evaluated to encompass the progressing acceptance of diversity and difference as part of a spectrum of "normal", rather than atypical (Krcek, 2013).

Reflection Point!

Think about when you first heard about autism, ADHD or dyspraxia . . .
    What has changed in your understanding of this diagnosis since
then? What are the key misconceptions about neurodivergent
conditions?

Krcek (2013) argues that the label attributed to the child/person is a
powerful mechanism for invoking judgement, support and entitlements.
The neurodivergent community constructed their own identity as simply
a difference or variation from the typical, much like a variation in sexuality
or race (Jaarsma & Welin, 2012). The neurodiversity movement aims for
people previously labelled with neurodevelopmental disabilities to now be
identified as neurodivergent (Jaarsma & Welin, 2012). In essence, neurodivergence is considered a difference, rather than a deficit, disability or medical condition (Jaarsma & Welin, 2012; Lorenz et al., 2017).

Self-Assessment

What is neurodiversity?
    Name two diagnoses within the neurodiversity umbrella.
    What was the initial rationale for the emergence of neurodiversity
as a concept?
    How can understanding of neurodiversity impact professional prac-
tice with neurodivergent individuals?

Chapter Summary

This chapter has introduced the concept of neurodiversity and explored
its development to date. Neurodivergence encompasses previously labelled
neurodevelopmental disorders and reframes deficits as variations of typical development. The neurodiversity movement contends that neurodivergence is akin to race or sexuality and is merely a divergence from the socially
constructed norms within society. By viewing autism, ADHD and dyspraxia
via the lens of neurodiversity, society aims to create supportive environments and opportunities for inclusion. Understanding of neurodiversity and
the development of this concept to date equips practitioners and educators
with the knowledge and awareness, from which to effectively support neurodivergent children and their families.

References

Ahmed, N., Raheem, E., Rahman, N., Khan, M.Z.R., Mosabbir, A.A., & Hossain, M.S. (2019). Managing autism spectrum disorder in developing countries by utilizing existing resources: A perspective from Bangladesh. *Autism*, *23*(3), 801–803. https://doi.org/10.1177/1362361318773981

Alvares, G.A., Bebbington, K., Cleary, D., Evans, K., Glasson, E.J., Maybery, M.T., Pillar, S., Uljarević, M., Varcin, K., Wray, J., & Whitehouse, A.J. (2020). The misnomer of 'high functioning autism': Intelligence is an imprecise predictor of functional abilities at diagnosis. *Autism*, *24*(1), 221–232. https://doi.org/10.1177/1362361319852831

American Psychiatric Association. (2013). *Diagnostic and statistical manual of mental disorders: DSM-5*. Washington, DC: American Psychiatric Association.

Baker, D.L. (2011). *The politics of neurodiversity: Why public policy matters*. Boulder, CO: Lynn Rienner Publishers.

Chiri, G., Bergey, M., & Mackie, T.I. (2022). Deserving but not entitled: The social construction of autism spectrum disorder in federal policy. *Social Science & Medicine*, *301*. https://doi.org/10.1016/j.socscimed.2022.114974

Den Houting, J. (2019). Neurodiversity: An insider's perspective. *Autism: The International Journal of Research and Practice*, *23*(2), 271–273. https://doi.org/10.1177/136236131882076

Engel, G. (1977). The need for a new medical model: A challenge for biomedicine. *Science (American Association for the Advancement of Science)*, *196*(4286), 129–136.

Farre, A., & Rapley, T. (2017). The new old (and old new) medical model: Four decades navigating the biomedical and psychosocial understandings of health and illness. *Healthcare (Basel)*, *5*(4), 88. https://doi.org/10.3390/healthcare5040088

Grandin, T. (2023, June 5). *Temple grandin PhD*. Retrieved from www.templegrandin.com/

Grandin, T., Barron, S., & Zysk, V. (2017). *Unwritten rules of social relationships: Decoding social mysteries through the unique perspective of autism* (new edition with author updates). Arlington, VA: Future Horizons.

Haegele, J.A., & Hodge, S. (2016). Disability discourse: Overview and critiques of the medical and social models. *Quest*, *68*(2), 193–206. https://doi.org/10.1080/00336297.2016.1143849

International Labour Organisation. (2023). *International labour standards on child labour*. Retrieved from www.ilo.org/global/standards/subjects-covered-by-international-labour-standards/child-labour/lang--en/index.htm

Jaarsma, P., & Welin, S. (2012). Autism as a natural human variation: Reflections on the claims of the neurodiversity movement. *Health Care Analysis*, *20*, 20–30. https://doi.org/10.1007/s10728-011-0169-9

Krcek, T.E. (2013). Deconstructing disability and neurodiversity: Controversial issues for autism and implications for social work. *Journal of Progressive Human Services*, *24*(1), 4–22. https://doi.org/10.1080/10428232.2013.740406

Leveto, J. (2018). Toward a sociology of autism and neurodiversity. *Sociology Compass*, *12*(12), E12636. https://doi.org/10.1111/soc4.12636

Lorenz, T., Reznik, N., & Heinitz, K. (2017). A different point of view: The neuro-diversity approach to autism and work. *InTech.* https://doi.org/10.5772/65409

Masataka, N. (2017). Implications of the idea of neurodiversity for understand-ing the origins of developmental disorders. *Physics of Life Reviews, 20,* 85–108. https://doi.org/10.1016/j.plrev.2016.11.002

Memari, A., Ziaee, V., Beygi, S., Moshayedi, P., & Mirfazeli, F. (2012). Overuse of psychotropic medications among children and adolescents with autism spectrum disorders: Perspective from a developing country. *Research in Developmental Dis-abilities, 33*(2), 563–569. https://doi.org/10.1016/j.ridd.2011.10.001

Norozi, S., & Moen, T. (2016). Childhood as a social construction. *Journal of Educational and Social Research, 6*(2), 75. https://doi.org/10.5901/jesr.2016. v6n2p75

Ortega, F. (2009). The cerebral subject and the challenge of neurodiversity. *BioSoci-eties, 4*(4), 425–445. https://doi.org/10.1017/S1745855209990287

Posey, D.J., Stigler, K.A., Erickson, C.A., & McDougle, C.J. (2008). Antipsychot-ics in the treatment of autism. *Journal of Clinical Investigation, 118*(1), 6–14. https://doi.org/10.1172/JCI32483.

Rosenberg, R., Mandell, D., Farmer, J., Law, J., Marvin, A., & Law, P. (2010). Psychotropic medication use among children with autism spectrum disorders en-rolled in a national registry, 2007–2008. *Journal of Autism and Developmental Disorders, 40*(3), 342–351. https://doi.org/10.1007/s10803-009-0878-1

Rotella, J. (2022). No one brain is the same: A neurodivergent clinician's approach to caring for the neurodivergent patient in the emergency department. *Emergency Medicine Australasia, 34*(4), 613–615. https://doi-org.nuigalway.idm.oclc. org/10.1111/1742-6723.14039

Schoeb, V. (2016). Healthcare service in Hong Kong and its challenges: The role of health professionals within a social model of health. *China Perspectives,* (4), 51–58. https://doi.org/10.4000/chinaperspectives.7118

Shah, P., Boilson, M., Rutherford, M., Prior, S., Johnston, L., Maciver, D., & For-syth, K. (2022). Neurodevelopmental disorders and neurodiversity: Definition of terms from Scotland's National Autism Implementation Team. *The British Jour-nal of Psychiatry, 221*(3), 577–579. https://doi.org/10.1192/bjp.2022.43

Shibli, A., & Hamdoun, O. (2019). Autism spectrum disorders. Is it under reported in third world countries? *The American Journal of Biomedical Science and Re-search, 4*(4). https://doi.org/10.34297/AJBSR.2019.04.000818

Singer, J. (2017). *Neurodiversity. The birth of an idea.* Washington, DC: Kindle ebooks.

Stenning, A., & Bertilsdotter Rosqvist, H. (2021). Neurodiversity studies: Mapping out possibilities of a new critical paradigm, *Disability & Society, 36*(9), 1532–1537. https://doi.org/10.1080/09687599.2021.1919503

Taboas, A., Doepke, K., & Zimmerman, C. (2023). Preferences for identity-first versus person-first language in a US sample of autism stakeholders. *Autism, 27* (2):565–570. https://doi.org/10.1177/13623613221130845

Taha, G.R.A., & Hussein, H. (2014). Autism spectrum disorders in develop-ing countries: Lessons from the Arab world. In V. Patel, V. Preedy & C. Mar-tin (Eds.), *Comprehensive guide to autism.* New York: Springer. https://doi. org/10.1007/978-1-4614-4788-7_98

Thompson, N. (2018). *Mental health and wellbeing. Alternatives to the medical model.* New York: Routelege.

United Nations. (1989, August 4). *Convention on the Rights of the Child.* Retrieved from www.ohchr.org/en/instruments-mechanisms/instruments/convention-rights-child

World Health Organisation. (2017, June 6). *Determinants of health.* Retrieved from www.who.int/news-room/questions-and-answers/item/determinants-of-health

Chapter 2

The Autistic Child and Their Family

Abbreviations

ADHD: Attention Deficit Hyperactivity Disorder
ADI-R: The Autism Diagnostic Interview – Revised
ADOS: The Autism Diagnostic Observational Schedule
APA: American Psychiatric Association
CDC: Centers for Disease Control and Prevention
DSM: Diagnostic and Statistical Manual of Mental Disorders
UK: United Kingdom

Introduction

Autism is a neurodevelopmental condition, which impacts the child in terms of communication, executive functioning, sensory processing and the need for sameness. Yet how does this impact the child in terms of their day-to-day life? How does autism impact the family as a whole? This chapter will discuss, using case studies and practice examples, the practical, emotional and social difficulties autism presents for children and families. The influence of autism and caregiving on the family's functioning will illuminate the unique needs of families as they interact with professionals in various community, medical and educational settings. This chapter will discuss autism assessment, the impact of autism across the lifespan and the extent to which broader systemic factors influence autistic children and their families.

Understanding of this context, background and impact of autism can empower practitioners to practice from an informed and critical lens, when supporting autistic children. Knowledge and understanding of autism is a fundamental prerequisite to creating supportive environments for autistic children and their families.

DOI: 10.4324/9781003455868-2

Learning Outcomes

On completion of Chapter 2, learners should demonstrate an enhanced understanding concerning:

- Autism and how this impacts the child in their daily life
- Autism assessment and diagnosis
- The impact of autism on the family
- The lifelong implications of an autism diagnosis
- How systemic factors and the societal response to autism affect the autistic child and their family

What Is Autism?

Autism is a neurodevelopmental condition which manifests in difficulties navigating, interpreting and interacting with the world. Autism is a disability which affects communication, the need for sameness and executive functioning (Hodges, Fealko, & Soares, 2020; Salari et al., 2022; American Psychiatric Association, 2013). Autism can also affect sensory processing (Kojovic, Ben Hadid, Franchini, & Schaer, 2019). However, initially and from the outset, it's important to emphasise that autistic children are so unique and no two children will present with the same needs. Even when two children both struggle with verbal language or find loud noises distressing, how they interpret this and how their needs should be met will contrast completely. This chapter on autism will provide an overview and background, yet spending time with the child and conducting a detailed and holistic individual assessment, is the most appropriate way to gauge the needs of an autistic child within your practice.

There is a wealth of information, literature and research available which explains autism from a diagnostic perspective, some of which will be referred to in this book. However, this chapter will describe autism from a day in the life perspective, based on the less-researched ways this presents and how this translates into needs and behaviours. This chapter will prompt you to critically reflect on what you see, but also on what you don't see.

Author Reflection Point!

Of my three autistic children, the key issue they all present with in exactly the same way is . . . nothing!

Autism presents completely differently for each of them, and their other co-occurring conditions (ADHD/dyspraxia) further contribute to their unique needs. Although all three struggle with the need for sameness and sensory issues, each communicates this completely differently. All three found socialising difficult, but again this was expressed entirely distinctively for each of them.

Communication

Communication and social and interactional difficulties are common for autistic children, yet they often present completely differently for each child. An autistic child may not communicate verbally, may communicate verbally, yet may struggle with language use, may miss nuances in communication and be unable to interpret body language, while social stressors and anxiety can further impact the child's capacity to communicate in different settings. This can manifest in selective (situational) mutism.

Example 1: Jenny is 7 years old and communicates verbally. Yet when she's in school, she is unable to speak. She doesn't respond when spoken to, but follows the teacher's instructions and doesn't display any behavioural difficulties. Jenny has started to have toileting accidents in school, as she is unable to ask the teacher if she can use the restroom. Although her teacher has assured Jenny she can use the restroom and doesn't need permission, Jenny won't do this. She comes home from school most days in pain, from needing to use the restroom.

Example 2: Liam is eager to make friends and tries to speak to the other boys at his basketball group. He tends to be a bit louder than he intends to be and is quite blunt in how he communicates. Liam screeches when he is excited and attempts to high-five his teammates when he scores a basket. His peers think Liam is weird and avoid communicating with him where possible, even ignoring him when he attempts to join their conversations. Their body language communicates that they are uncomfortable and don't want to engage with Liam. However, Liam does not notice these nuances and continues to try to become part of the group. He is oblivious to the rejection he is experiencing.

Executive Functioning

Executive functioning refers to the ability to plan and carry out tasks (Akbar, Loomis, & Paul, 2013). It is further associated with memory, organisation, time management and self-control (Leung, Vogan, Powell, Anagnostou, & Taylor, 2016). When a child struggles with executive function, they may need prompts, reminders and continued support to stay on task and complete activities. Executive functioning difficulties can present challenges and stressors for the child at home, at school and when engaging socially with their peers.

Example 1: Alisha misplaces and forgets items she needs for school on a daily basis. When the school bell rings, Alisha feels rushed and tries to pack her bag quickly. This results in her forgetting books, papers and her homework diary almost every day. Alisha has lost two coats, a school sweater and five lunch boxes in one semester.

Example 2: Jax struggles with completing tasks that have more than one action required. When instructed to take off his shoes and sit at the table, he becomes overwhelmed. As he starts to complete the first task, he forgets the second task and gets frustrated. Jax finds school very difficult and needs constant prompting and one-to-one support to complete his schoolwork. This frustration can lead to emotional distress and behavioural outbursts.

Need for Sameness

A change in routine or expectations can feel catastrophic for an autistic child. A teacher out sick or a general practitioner changing offices, an unplanned visit or a last-minute change of plan, can prevent an autistic child from being able to continue with their planned activity or can prompt a complete meltdown. Routines, structure and knowing what to expect, increases certainty for autistic individuals and reduces anxiety.

Example 1: Leah is collected by the school bus every morning at 7 am. One morning, the bus doesn't come. She waits and waits and eventually her Dad calls the bus company who advise him that the driver is off sick today. Leah's Dad tells her he will drive her to school, but she begins screaming and stimming, repeating over and over that the bus comes at 7 am and this is how she goes to school. She is so distressed at this change that it takes two hours for her to be calm enough to be able to go to school. The plan, routine and certainty she had for the day ahead has been removed. Leah feels worried, anxious and afraid. She doesn't know what to expect, how she will get to school, where her Dad will park, which door she will enter the school from, or what to expect when she gets there. Leah cannot adjust to this unexpected change and is distressed for the remainder of the day.

Example 2: It's 90°F outside but Joe still wears his winter coat. He remembers a time five years ago when he couldn't find his coat and now wears it every single time he leaves the house, regardless of the weather. This presents certainty for Joe, it comforts him and is a staple part of his everyday routine. This is more important to him than his comfort (he's sweating profusely) or what other people think (everyone he meets queries why he is wearing his coat and he often smells of body odour).

Sensory Processing

Sensory processing is about how we process and respond to the five senses of sight, sound, taste, touch and smell. Sensory processing issues are estimated to be prevalent for 90% of autistic individuals (Ben-Sasson et al., 2019; Balasco, Provenzano, & Bozzi, 2019). Autistic children respond to sensory stimuli atypically via hyper-responsiveness, hypo-responsiveness or sensory seeking (Foss-Feig, Heacock, and Cascio (2012).

In reality, this means that a shirt can feel like having fire ants on your body and a car starting can sound like a jet taking off. Shoes can feel like your toes are being ripped from your body with a wrench. Other children talking amongst themselves in the classroom can sound like they are screaming and their voices are getting louder and louder inside your head. A smell no one else notices can feel overpowering and be so consuming that you feel nauseous and unable to focus on anything else.

Example 1: Ben wraps his fingers around his mother's hair and rubs it against his lips. He seeks out people with long hair and finds comfort and enjoyment from feeling hair between his fingers and on his lips.

Example 2: Rebecca is hyper-sensitive to sounds and is profoundly distressed at the noise of dogs barking. Rebecca screams and runs away from any environment when she hears a dog barking. Her parents have stopped bringing her to the park as they frequently meet dogs there. Rebecca is experiencing social isolation as other children are frightened by her screaming and tend to not want to play with her. Rebecca worries constantly about hearing a dog, and this wakes her at night frequently.

Author Reflection Point!

When we go to grocery stores, my son often covers his eyes. He explains that the light is extremely bright and he needs to leave. Once my child communicates this I can see it, yet often I may not notice before this. I find myself looking at the world differently through the lens of autism, which my children give me a glimpse of as I try to support them to navigate their world.

Autism Assessment and Diagnosis

The Centers for Disease Control and Prevention (CDC) argue that diagnosing autism can be challenging, as there is no blood test or definitive testing method. Rather, autism is diagnosed based on behavioural observation, reviewing the child's developmental history and the use of specific screening tools (CDC, 2022). The DSM-5 categorises autism in terms of communication deficits and restrictive and repetitive behaviours (Hyman, Levey, & Myers, 2020). Very specific criteria such as hypo-/hyper-sensitivity to sensory stimuli, extreme distress at changes in routine and poor social ability, must be present for a diagnosis of autism to be confirmed (Hyman et al., 2020). The behaviours must have been present or emerging within the child's early development and must further be consistent across settings, for an autism diagnosis to be concluded (APA, 2013).

Two specific screening tools are used to assist clinicians in assessing and diagnosing autism: the Autism Diagnostic Interview – Revised (ADI-R) and the Autism Diagnostic Observational Schedule (ADOS) (Gray, Tonge, & Sweeney, 2008; Wiggins et al., 2019). Wiggins et al. (2019) caution that no screening tools should replace the level of clinical skill and practitioner expertise required to comprehensively assess and diagnose autism in children.

A broad range of professionals are qualified to assess and diagnose autism based on the specific screening tools listed here and utilising their clinical expertise and professional judgement. The CDC (2022) contend that paediatricians, child psychologists and psychiatrists, speech-language pathologists and occupational therapists often deliver autism assessments. However, it is frequently during developmental checks or in the family physician's office that professionals and parents initially identify the need for an autism assessment, via discussion of parent concerns or developmental delays.

Additional Autism-Specific Presentations

Comorbidities are common for children with a diagnosis of autism and will influence the level and type of supports the child may need. Autism may be accompanied by anxiety disorder, ADHD, bipolar, depression, intellectual disability, sleep disorder, oppositional defiant disorder, psychosis or obsessive compulsive disorder (Mutluer et al., 2022). Mutluer et al. (2022), in their analysis of research studies regarding comorbidities associated with autism, estimate that ADHD impacts 26% of autistic children, while they estimate the prevalence of intellectual disability in 22% of this population. Percentages regarding the prevalence of comorbid conditions in autistic children will vary from study to study and country to country (Skwerer, Joseph, Eggleston, Meyer, & Tager-Flusberg, 2019; Simonoff et al., 2008). Simonoff et al. (2008) report that 70% of autistic children present with at least one comorbid condition. They surmise that social anxiety disorder is the most prevalent of these comorbid conditions, which they estimate at 29% within their study, while ADHD is the subsequent most likely concurring condition, which they estimate at 28%.

Concerning intellectual disability prevalence for autistic individuals, Shenouda et al. (2023) estimate this at 33% of autistic children, based on their study undertaken in New York and New Jersey. Postorino et al. (2016), within their Italian study, estimate the prevalence of intellectual disability in autistic children at 47%. Nonetheless, such statistics and estimations should not lead to practitioners assuming that an autistic child will present with a comorbid condition, and their support should be tailored to meet individual needs. Further assessment should be undertaken if an autistic child experiences challenges which may be associated with a comorbid condition.

Autism-Specific Presentations

Meltdowns, masking and stimming are three presentations largely associated specifically with autism. Understanding what each means will enable educators and practitioners to respond in an informed and knowledgeable perspective, to the needs of autistic children and their families.

A *meltdown* has been defined by Khullar, Singh, and Bala (2021) as an intense explosion of challenging behaviour. A meltdown is involuntary and stems from feelings of being overwhelmed, stressed or a need to escape the situation they find themselves in (Bedrossian, 2015). A meltdown has no logical end or no solution, which will satiate the child experiencing this feeling. It's a loss of control where emotions overflow and reach a point where the child can't communicate in any other way how they are feeling. It may manifest in screaming, shouting, being aggressive or violent, throwing objects or slamming doors, crying uncontrollably, hurting themselves, stimming, and repeating words or phrases. Meltdowns are often the result of an unmet need, a frustration the child is unable to communicate, or a response to feeling overwhelmed. A meltdown can further be prompted by feelings which are difficult to cope with such as embarrassment or fear (Mullins, 2022). An unexpected change in routine can cause a meltdown, as the child grapples with managing the change and the adjustment from what they expected would happen. Routines and rituals present certainty and safety for autistic children, so when a change occurs, particularly an unexpected change, the emotions this prompts can be all-consuming.

Masking is associated with behaviours an autistic child or adult engages in to hide their autistic traits from the world around them. Masking is in essence wearing a mask which is neurotypical, in order to feel included and not be identified as different or face stigma and judgement. Parents often discuss masking experienced by their autistic children in school. Children will work extremely hard in some settings to appear neurotypical and not react outwardly to the challenges and triggers presented by the environment around them. For example: a child may not react outwardly to being completely overwhelmed by the proximity of other children and the volume of other children in the classroom (Mullins, 2022). The child still feels this stress, distress and even anxiety within this situation, yet outwardly does not display these feelings in any way. Often after masking, the child is completely emotionally and physically exhausted or may display challenging behaviour or a meltdown, when they reach an environment where they feel more comfortable and safe (usually at home).

Masking within the literature is described as social camouflaging and is associated with an autistic person actively concealing autistic behaviour or traits (Allely, 2019; Alaghband-rad, Hajikarim-Hamedani, & Motamed, 2023). Hull et al. (2017) explain that masking is a coping strategy for autistic people and occurs when they suppress their autistic traits, in an effort to portray themselves as neurotypical. Masking is associated more so with autistic girls and is said to be a causal factor in missed diagnoses and late diagnoses of autistic girls, compared to autistic boys (Cook, Ogden, & Winstone, 2018; Hull et al., 2017). Girls tend to mask in an effort to make and maintain friendships and fit in socially (Cook et al., 2018).

Stimming is a repetitive behaviour the autistic child may engage in when they are distressed, frustrated, excited or to make them feel more comfortable, within a situation they are unfamiliar with (Mullins, 2022). Stimming may present as rocking back and forth, clicking fingers, walking or running in circles, spinning on the spot or any other repetitive behaviour which presents comfort for the child (Mullins, 2022).

Reflection Point!

Think of a time when you felt self-conscious or embarrassed. Perhaps you fell over really awkwardly in a room full of people? Or called someone by the wrong name repeatedly? Or maybe you felt extremely uncomfortable giving a presentation to your classmates or team?

Now multiply this feeling by 100, and this will give you a brief insight into the discomfort, anxiety and fear many autistic children live with every day.

Impact of Autism on the Family

When a family consists of a child who is autistic, autism impacts every facet of the family's life. The autistic child's unique needs will often shape the family's social lives, interaction within their community and even their daily routine. The stigma associated with autism, combined with potentially challenging behaviour or difficulty within social settings, means that some families of autistic children are socially isolated.

Employment and Childcare

Parents of children with a diagnosis of autism are more likely to miss work, reduce working hours or stop working, due to their child's care needs (Dovgan & Mazurek, 2019). Employment opportunities for parents are impacted by childcare availability and suitability. The availability of childcare is impacted by issues presented by autism such as challenging behaviour, communication need, and the training and experience of the childcare provider. Some parents are unable to source appropriate childcare for their autistic child and cannot work as a result. While parents who do work often need to leave work early or take time off to cope with their child's needs or when childcare placements break down (Mullins, 2022).

Relationships

Having an autistic child impacts parental relationships/marriages (Hirsch & Paquin, 2019). Hirsch and Paquin (2019) found that parents reported the need for working as a team when parenting an autistic child and that relationships are impacted by the time and level of care their child requires. Parenting one or more autistic children can mean that family life is dictated by frequent medical appointments, the necessity of a much greater level of parental supervision and perhaps a lack of sleep. Such stressors often permeate even the strongest of romantic relationships. Equally, the stressors and challenges of parenting an autistic child can bring partners or spouses together, as their commitment to their child strengthens their relationship.

Siblings

Siblings of autistic children can be negatively impacted emotionally and in terms of parental presence and availability (Mullins, 2022). Autistic children often require substantially greater emotional, practical and supervisory support compared to their siblings, which can manifest in siblings feeling left out. Siblings can be exposed to aggressive or violent behaviours from their autistic sibling and may miss out on social opportunities and events, due to their autistic sibling's needs. Garrido, Carballo, and Garcia-Retamero (2020) argue that having an autistic sibling, negatively impacts a sibling's quality of life. They contend that autism severity and the challenges this presents for the autistic sibling are further relevant in terms of impact on the non-autistic sibling (Garrido et al., 2020).

Alexandra, Thompson, and Freeth (2020) contend that siblings can find themselves in a caring, parental-like role, concerning their autistic brother and sister. Non-autistic siblings may provide support relating to schoolwork, socially and with personal care tasks, which can negatively impact their own wellbeing (Alexandra et al., 2020). Yet equally, having an autistic sibling can develop empathy and care skills in siblings and manifest in feelings of protectiveness. Siblings may feel a strong sense of positive responsibility regarding including their autistic sibling and providing them with social support.

Autism in Adulthood

Autism is a lifelong condition. Autistic adults may struggle to cope with the communication, sensory and executive function demands placed on them by society. Although the current title relates specifically to neurodivergent children and their families, awareness and understanding of the impact of autism into adulthood, places practitioners and educators in a more informed position from which to provide appropriate care and support. Mason et al. (2018) suggest that quality of life for autistic adults is positively impacted by being in a relationship, being in employment and receiving adequate support. Autistic adults may be coping with trauma from childhood and experiences of stigma, exclusion or unmet need. Such trauma can manifest in self-isolation and an unwillingness or inability to access support when needed.

Mental Health Issues

Autistic people are at an increased risk of mental health problems (Camm-Crosbie, Bradley, Shaw, Baron-Cohen, & Cassidy, 2019). In a study by Mason et al. (2018) involving 370 autistic adults, 70% reported a current diagnosis of at least one mental health condition. Yet Rydzewska et al. (2018) propose that 33% of autistic adults present with mental illness. Kirsch et al. (2020) argue that depression, anxiety and bipolar disorder occur at a higher incidence for autistic adults, with 54% of their study participants having a diagnosis of depression.

Suicide rates are substantially higher for autistic adults, compared to people in the general population (Hirvikoski et al., 2016). Camm-Crosbie et al. (2019) argue that less than half of autistic adults with mental health problems, access mental health services. Malik-Soni et al. (2022) contend that autistic people face multiple barriers when attempting to access health services, such as stigma and misconceptions about autism, long waiting lists and cost to access services privately.

Employment

Autistic adults may further be impacted by unemployment. In the UK, autistic adults have the lowest rates of employment of all disabled people (e.g. hearing impaired people, people living with mental illness or progressive illness) (Office for National Statistics, 2021). The Office for National Statistics (2021) report that just 22% of autistic adults in the UK are in employment. In the US, just 15% of autistic adults with a college degree are employed (Sparrow, 2018). Sparrow (2018) contends that unemployment for autistic adults is impacted by stigma, the comorbidities associated with autism and restrictive social security rules and parameters.

Autistic adults are more likely to work part-time, work reduced hours and work in roles they are overqualified for (Harvery, Froude, Foley, Trollor, & Arnold, 2021). Yet Harvery et al. (2021) argue that appropriate workplace supports and adjustments enhance employment opportunities and experiences for autistic adults. Employment, or indeed lack thereof, influences financial stability, social opportunities, independence and a sense of identity. Consequently, employment opportunities and experiences can have a momentous effect on the lives of autistic adults.

Family and Relationships

Parents and siblings of autistic adults often provide emotional, social and practical support to their autistic family member throughout adulthood. Support need will vary from one autistic adult to the next, and comorbid diagnoses will further influence the level of support required. Some autistic adults may lack any form of familial support and may consequently require significant formal support. Yet Anderson, Sosnowy, Kuo, and Shattuck (2018) argue that formal supports decrease for autistic adults. Social isolation and loneliness are further more likely for autistic adults, as the social opportunity provided by school is no longer available (Umagami, Remington, Lloyd-Evans, Davies, & Crane, 2022).

Author Reflection Point!

It's always been innate for me to speak about autism and how this impacts my children. It also permeates every single facet of our lives as a family. My son who is neurotypical has been substantially impacted by having three autistic siblings. When you love someone who is autistic and want them to be happy, included and understood, autism becomes part of your journey too. You can't separate autism from the child; it's who they are. Consequently, you can't separate autism from the child's family (Mullins, 2022).

Societal Response to Autism

Systemic factors and the societal response to autism, profoundly impact both autistic children and their families across the lifespan. Governmental responses to the financial hardships of families of autistic children, alongside access to and availability of services, considerably influences families in their capacity to meet their child's needs. While autistic children and families are impacted by broader societal understandings, and indeed misconceptions, surrounding autism.

Misconceptions

Misconceptions about autism in society further permeate the lives of autistic children and families. Social media has opened a door for anyone with an opinion to share this, which can culminate in misinformation spreading and damaging stereotypes surrounding autism. In fact, some members of society possess only the information provided by the media about autism, and hence their understanding is largely shaped and moulded by this.

The societal environment within which the child and family live will impact how they view autism and how they feel they will be viewed by other people. For example: what most people consider as a positive attribute of autism is the child's exceptional ability or talent in one specific area. Indeed, autistic children can excel in an area of special interest or fixation, but not all autistic children will demonstrate exceptionality or a special interest which they have harnessed to the point of excellence (e.g. mathematics, playing an instrument or counting cards!). Another common misconception is that autistic people lack empathy, when in fact the opposite can be true. Autistic people can be overly empathetic, but they may not express or communicate empathy in the same way as neurotypical people do.

Case Study

Dylan is 8 years old, autistic and in mainstream school. Dylan tries very hard to make friends. The other children find Dylan immature and can't understand why he gets so upset if they break the rules or speak out of turn. Dylan is often the subject of his friend's jokes and doesn't notice when someone is being mean or pretending to be nice. Dylan tells his parents every day about his friends in school and how great they play together. Zack is his best friend, and Dylan is so excited for his upcoming birthday party. However, one day Dylan comes home and locks himself in his room, extremely distressed. Dylan eventually shares that Zack's party happened a few days before, and he wasn't invited.

What factors could have contributed to this situation?

Should Dylan have done anything differently to impact this situation?

What could change within the classroom environment to make Dylan feel more included?

What other actions could create a more supportive social environment for Dylan?

One study undertaken with professionals responsible for autism assessments and treatment of autistic children in Kazakhstan, found that misconceptions are common, even among this group (Somerton, Stolyarova, & Khanin, 2022). Participants included psychologists, paediatric neurologists and psychiatrists, and Somerton et al. (2022) found that some participants understood that autistic children could not feel empathy and "cannot feel happiness". A 2022 study undertaken in Germany examined psychotherapists' understanding of autism and found that misconceptions were further common within this group (Lipinski et al., 2022). Forty-three percent of participants in this study (n498) thought that autism could be caused by vaccinations, and 52% asserted that autistic individuals had special talents. Finally, 72% of participants reported that autism is an emotional disorder (Lipinski et al., 2022).

Financial Supports

The societal response to autism and how this impacts children and families, is further influenced by financial supports available and stipulated within government policy. In the United States (US), families of autistic children may qualify for Supplemental Security Income (SSI) (Social Security Administration, 2023). The Social Security Administration (2023) states that SSI is subject to assessable income eligibility criteria and the condition that the child's disability substantially impairs the child's activities.

In 2021, 214,771 autistic children were in receipt of SSI in the US (Office of Retirement and Disability Policy, 2021). Romig (2017) describes SSI as a lifeline for children with disabilities, yet argues that just 1.2 million, out of 11 million children living with disabilities in the US, are receiving SSI. Stringent eligibility criteria in terms of income limits and severity of disability, means that SSI is approved for less than half of child applicants (Romig, 2017). Those who are awarded SSI may have this removed upon regular reviews, if their child's condition has improved (Romig, 2017).

Medicaid waivers for autistic children are another economic measure undertaken by both federal and state governments in the US (Shea, Koffer

Miller, Verstreate, Tao, & Mandell, 2021). Shea et al. (2021) contend that Medicaid 1915c waivers provide for the medical, health and social care needs of autistic children to be met by the state, with an increase in the number of states providing autism-specific waivers increasing consistently in recent years. Yet similar to SSI eligibility, Medicaid waivers for autistic children are dependent on family income, and further vary from one state to the next (Holingue, Jang, Azad, & Landa, 2022).

Access to Services

Access to health, social care and education services for autistic children and their families profoundly impacts on the overall wellbeing of the family and outcomes for children. Long waiting lists for assessment, diagnoses and therapeutic intervention, alongside access to appropriate education placements, result in substantial stress for the families of autistic children. In Ireland, the current wait time for an autism assessment via the public system, is one to three years (Mullins, 2022). Private autism assessments are further difficult to obtain, and the cost associated mean that many families are not in a position to avail of these. Time spent waiting results in unmet need, and appropriate and necessary resources and suports not being made available to the child (Mullins, 2022).

Successfully accessing the services needed, means that the child and their family can move forward in terms of identifying effectively and actively working towards meeting the child's goals. Time spent waiting presents a pause in this process and can mean the child and their family feel stuck or at an impasse in terms of how to help their child. For example: therapies, assistive communication methods and appropriate educational placements are crucial resources for empowering and enabling an autistic child to thrive, via meeting their unique needs.

Access to healthcare in the US can also be problematic in terms of waiting times, according to Lindly, Zuckerman, and Kuhlthau (2019). Fong, Lee, and Iarocci (2022) suggest that barriers to accessing services include language and communication issues, stigma and a lack of clarity concerning navigation of the system of services. System navigation is an issue I have written extensively about and appears to be a collective problem experienced by autistic children and families. There is often no clarity or consistency concerning how and where families should seek and access autism assessment and support (Mullins, 2022).

Living rurally can present additional challenges concerning access to services for autistic children (Antezana, Scarpa, Valdespino, Albright, & Richey, 2017). Antezana et al. (2017) argue that the distance between families and service providers reduces the frequency of access. This distance can further result in autistic children with lower support needs not having their autism recognised or diagnosed (Antezana et al., 2017). Fong et al. (2022)

contend that professional knowledge and insight pertaining specifically to autism, can act as a barrier to access for autistic children and their families. Autistic children living in rural locations may face disadvantage educationally with the range of educational options available and if school staff lack appropriate knowledge and awareness to inform their practice (Antezana et al., 2017).

Recent Research

Havdahl et al. (2021) argue that specific genes which increase the likelihood of autism have been identified. Pellicano and Stears (2011) propose that developments within autism research can cause conflict within both the autism community and society more generally. Research is evolving to detect the gene differences which cause autism and demonstrates what could be perceived as a breakthrough in autism research. Yet autistic advocates argue that such findings could culminate in eugenics, potentially removing the autism gene and autistic people from society (Austin, Byres, & Morris, 2022). Austin et al. (2022) found through their research involving autistic adults that the majority express reservations about genetic testing for autism and contend that this should only be undertaken if the child or adult can consent.

In contrast, autism researchers counter that genetic research and advancing of understanding concerning the biological factors which cause autism, can enable earlier testing and subsequently earlier intervention and more positive outcomes for autistic children (Hens, Peeters, & Dierickx, 2016). Hens et al. (2016) argue that genetic testing can help prepare parents for their child's needs and planning for their care. Arnett, Trinh, and Bernier (2019) suggest that genetic research on autism can mean more precision in diagnoses.

Self-Assessment

What are the key ways in which autism impacts the child?
How is autism assessed and diagnosed?
Explain what masking is and how this impacts the autistic child.
How can access issues affect the autistic child and their family?

Chapter Summary

This chapter introduced autism and explored what this means for the autistic child and their family. Autism is a neurodevelopmental condition which impacts the child concerning communication, executive functioning, the need for sameness and sensory processing. Autism impacts each child completely differently. Some autistic children will require some support to navigate the world around them, while other autistic children, and particularly those with comorbidities, may need significant and substantial support in their daily lives. This chapter discussed the impact of autism on the family, from parental relationships to siblings and the social engagement of the whole family. Autism is a lifelong condition and some autistic individuals will require support across their lifespan. Autistic children and their families are greatly influenced by systemic factors such as access to and availability of support services, financial supports and societal understandings of autism. Practitioner knowledge, insight and awareness concerning autism is a vital prerequisite for facilitating the provision of adequate information and support, to autistic children and their families.

References

Akbar, M., Loomis, R., & Paul, R. (2013). The interplay of language on executive functions in children with ASD. *Research in Autism Spectrum Disorders*, *7*(3), 494–501. https://doi.org/10.1016/j.rasd.2012.09.001

Alaghband-rad, J., Hajikarim-Hamedani, A., & Motamed, M. (2023). Camouflage and masking behavior in adult autism. *Frontiers in Psychiatry*, *14*. https://doi.org/10.3389/fpsyt.2023.1108110

Alexandra, T.L., Thompson, A.R., & Freeth, M. (2020). A thematic synthesis of siblings' lived experiences of autism: Distress, responsibilities, compassion and connection. *Research in Developmental Disabilities*, *97*. https://doi.org/10.1016/j.ridd.2019.103547.

Allely, C.S. (2019). Understanding and recognising the female phenotype of autism spectrum disorder and the "camouflage" hypothesis: A systematic PRISMA review. *Advances in Autism*, *5*(1), 14–37. https://doi.org/10.1108/AIA-09-2018-0036

American Psychiatric Association. (2013). *Diagnostic and statistical manual of mental disorders: DSM-5*. Washington, DC: American Psychiatric Association.

Anderson, K.A., Sosnowy, C., Kuo, A.A., & Shattuck, P.T. (2018). Transition of individuals with autism to adulthood: A review of qualitative studies. *Pediatrics*, *141*(suppl. 4), S318–S327. https://doi.org/10.1542/peds.2016-4300I

Antezana, L., Scarpa, A., Valdespino, A., Albright, J., & Richey, J. (2017). Rural trends in diagnosis and services for autism spectrum disorder. *Frontiers in Psychology*, *8*, 590. https://doi.org/10.3389/fpsyg.2017.00590

Arnett, A.B., Trinh, S., & Bernier, R.A. (2019). The state of research on the genetics of autism spectrum disorder: Methodological, clinical and conceptual progress. *Current Opinion in Psychology*, *27*, 1–5. https://doi.org/10.1016/j.copsyc.2018.07.004

Austin, J., Byres, L., & Morris, E. (2022). 64. Exploring autistic adult's perspectives on genetic testing for autism. *European Neuropsychopharmacology*, *63*, E80. https://doi.org/10.1016/j.euroneuro.2022.07.151.

Balasco, L., Provenzano, G., & Bozzi, Y. (2019). Sensory abnormalities in autism Spectrum disorders: A focus on the tactile domain, from genetic mouse models to the clinic. *Frontiers in Psychiatry*, *10*, 1016s

Bedrossian, L. (2015). Understand autism meltdowns and share strategies to minimize, manage occurrences. *Disability Compliance for Higher Education*, *20*, 6. https://doi.org/10.1002/dhe.30026

Ben-Sasson, A., Gal, E., Fluss, R., Katz-Zetler, N., & Cermak, S.A. (2019). Update of a meta-analysis of sensory symptoms in ASD: A new decade of research. *Journal of Autism and Developmental Disorders*, *49*(12), 4974–4996. https://doi.org/10.1007/s10803-019-04180-0

Camm-Crosbie, L., Bradley, L., Shaw, R., Baron-Cohen, S., & Cassidy, S. (2019). 'People like me don't get support': Autistic adults' experiences of support and treatment for mental health difficulties, self-injury and suicidality. *Autism*, *23*, 1431–1441. https://doi.org/10.1177/13623613188160

Centers for Disease Control and Prevention. (2022, July 13). *Screening and diagnosis of autism spectrum disorder*. Retrieved from www.cdc.gov/ncbddd/autism/screening

Cook, A., Ogden, J., & Winstone, N. (2018). Friendship motivations, challenges and the role of masking for girls with autism in contrasting school settings. *European Journal of Special Needs Education*, *33*(3), 302–315. https://doi.org/10.1080/08856257.2017.1312797

Dovgan, K., & Mazurek, M.O. (2019). Impact of multiple co-occurring emotional and behavioural conditions on children with autism and their families. *Journal of Applied Research in Intellectual Disability*, *32*, 967–980. https://doi.org/10.1111/jar.12590

Fong, V.C., Lee, B.S., & Iarocci, G. (2022). A community-engaged approach to examining barriers and facilitators to accessing autism services in Korean immigrant families. *Autism*, *26*(2), 525–537. https://doi.org/10.1177/13623613211034067

Foss-Feig, J.H., Heacock, J.L., & Cascio, C.J. (2012). Tactile responsiveness patterns and their association with core features in autism spectrum disorders. *Research in Autism Spectrum Disorders*, 6, 337–344. https://doi.org/10.1016/j.rasd.2011.06.007

Garrido, D., Carballo, G., & Garcia-Retamero, R. (2020). Siblings of children with autism spectrum disorders: Social support and family quality of life. *Quality of Life Research*, *29*, 1193–1202. https://doi.org/10.1007/s11136-020-02429-1

Gray, K.M., Tonge, B.J. & Sweeney, D.J. (2008). Using the autism diagnostic interview-revised and the autism diagnostic observation schedule with young children with developmental delay: Evaluating diagnostic validity. *Journal of Autism and Developmental Disorders*, *38*, 657–667. https://doi.org/10.1007/s10803-007-0432-y

Harvery, M., Froude, E.H., Foley, K.-R., Trollor, J.N., & Arnold, S.R.C. (2021). Employment profiles of autistic adults in Australia. *Autism Research*, *14*(10), 2061–2077. https://doi.org/10.1002/aur.2588

Havdahl, A., Niarchou, M., Starnawska, A., Uddin, M., Van der Merwe, C., & Warrier, V. (2021). Genetic contributions to autism spectrum disorder. *Psychological Medicine*, *51*(13), 2260–2273. https://doi.org/10.1017/S0033291721000192

Hens, K., Peeters, H., & Dierickx, K. (2016). Genetic testing and counselling in the case of an autism diagnosis: A caregivers perspective. *European Journal of Human Genetics, 59*, 452–458. https://doi.org/10.1016/j.ejmg.2016.08.007

Hirsch, K.H., & Paquin, J.D. (2019). The stress of the situation has changed us both: A grounded theory analysis of the romantic relationship of parents raising children with autism. *Journal of Child and Family Studies, 28*, 2673–2689. https://doi.org/10.1007/s10826-019-01448-y

Hirvikoski, T., Mittendorfer-Rutz, E., Boman, M., Larsson, H., Lichtenstein, P., & Bölte, S. (2016). Premature mortality in autism spectrum disorder. *The British Journal of Psychiatry, 208*(3), 232–238. https://doi.org/10.1192/bjp.bp.114.160192

Hodges, H., Fealko, C., & Soares, N. (2020). Autism spectrum disorder: Definition, epidemiology, causes, and clinical evaluation. *Translational Pediatrics, 9* (Suppl. 1), S55–S65. https://doi.org/10.21037/tp.2019.09.09

Holingue, C., Jang, Y., Azad, G., & Landa, R. (2022). Key stakeholder perspectives on obstacles to an autism-specific Medicaid waiver service delivery model. *Journal of Applied Research in Intellectual Disabilities, 35*(1), 205–216. https://doi.org/10.1111/jar.12940

Hull, L., Petrides, K.V., Allison, C., Smith, P., Baron-Cohen, S., Lai, M., & Mandy, W. (2017). "Putting on my best normal": Social camouflaging in adults with autism spectrum conditions. *Journal of Autism and Developmental Disorders, 47*(8), 2519–2534. https://doi.org/10.1007/s10803-017-3166-5

Hyman, S.L., Levey, S.E., & Myers, S.M. (2020). Council on children with disabilities. Section on developmental and behavioral pediatrics. Identification, evaluation, and management of children with autism spectrum disorder. *Pediatrics, 145*(1). https://doi.org/10.1542/peds.2019-3447

Khullar, V., Singh, H., & Bala, M. (2021). Meltdown/tantrum detection system for individuals with autism spectrum disorder. *Applied Artificial Intelligence, 35*(15), 1708–1732. https://doi.org/10.1080/08839514.2021.1991115

Kirsch, A.C., Huebner, A., Mehta, S., Howie, F.M., Weaver, A., Myers, S., Voigt, R., & Katusic, S. (2020). Association of comorbid mood and anxiety disorders with autism spectrum disorder. *JAMA Pediatrics, 174*(1), 63–70. https://doi.org/10.1001/jamapediatrics.2019.4368

Kojovic, N., Ben Hadid, L., Franchini, M., & Schaer, M. (2019). Sensory processing issues and their association with social difficulties in children with autism spectrum disorders. *Journal of Clinical Medicine, 8*, (10) 1508. https://doi.org/10.3390/jcm8101508

Leung, R.C., Vogan, V., Powell, T.L., Anagnostou, E., & Taylor, M.J. (2016). The role of executive functions in social impairment in Autism spectrum disorder. *Child Neuropsychology, 22*(3), 336–344. https://doi.org/10.1080/09297049.2015.1005066

Lindly, O.J., Zuckerman, K.E., & Kuhlthau, K.A. (2019). Healthcare access and services use among US children with autism spectrum disorder. *Autism, 23*(6), 1419–1430. https://doi.org/10.1177/1362361318815237

Lipinski, S., Boegl, K., Blanke, E.S., Suenkel, U., & Dziobek, I. (2022). A blind spot in mental healthcare? Psychotherapists lack education and expertise for the support of adults on the autism spectrum. *Autism, 26*(6), 1509–1521. https://doi.org/10.1177/13623613211057973

Malik-Soni, N., Shaker, A., Luck, H., Mullen, A.E., Wiley, R.E., Lewis, S.M.E., Fuentes, J., & Frazier, T.W. (2022). Tackling healthcare access barriers for individuals with autism from diagnosis to adulthood. *Pediatric Research*, *91*, 1028–1035. https://doi.org/10.1038/s41390-021-01465

Mason, D., McConachie, H., Garland, D., Petrou, A., Rodgers, J., & Parr, J.R. (2018). Predictors of quality of life for autistic adults. *Autism Research*, *11*(8), 1138–1147. https://doi.org/10.1002/aur.1965

Mullins, L. (2022). *It takes a village. Navigating the journey of parenting your autistic child*. Dublin: Orpen Press.

Mutluer, T., Aslan Genç, H., Özcan Morey, A., Yapici Eser, H., Ertinmaz, B., Can, M., & Munir, K. (2022). Population-based psychiatric comorbidity in children and adolescents with autism spectrum disorder: A meta-analysis. *Frontiers in Psychiatry*, *13*, 856208. https://doi.org/10.3389/fpsyt.2022.856208

Office for National Statistics. (2021, August 3). *Outcomes for disabled people in the UK: 2020*. Retrieved from from www.ons.gov.uk/peoplepopulationandcommunity/ healthandsocialcare/disability/articles/outcomesfordisabledpeopleintheuk/2020

Pellicano, E., & Stears, M. (2011). Bridging autism, science and society: Moving toward an ethically informed approach to autism research. *Autism Res*, *4*, 271–282. https://doi.org/10.1002/aur.201

Postorino, V., Fatta, L., Sanges, V., Giovagnoli, G., De Peppo, L., Vicari, S., & Mazzone, L. (2016). Intellectual disability in autism spectrum disorder: Investigation of prevalence in an Italian sample of children and adolescents. *Research in Developmental Disabilities*, *48*, 193–201. https://doi.org/10.1016/j.ridd.2015.10.020

Romig, K. (2017, July 14). SSI: A lifeline for children with disabilities. *Center on Budget and Policy Priorities*. Retrieved from www.cbpp.org/research/ social-security/ssi-a-lifeline-for-children-with-disabilities

Rydzewska, E., Hughes-McCormack, L.A., Gillberg, C., Henderson, A., MacIntyre, C., Rintoul, J., & Cooper, S.A. (2018). Prevalence of long-term health conditions in adults with autism: observational study of a whole country population. *BMJ Open*, *8*, e023945. https://doi.org/10.1136/bmjopen-2018-023945

Salari, N., Rasoulpoor, S., Rasoulpoor, S., Shohaimi, S., Jafarpour, S., Abdoli, N., Khaledi-Paveh, B., & Mohammadi, M. (2022). The global prevalence of autism spectrum disorder: A comprehensive systematic review and meta-analysis. *Italian Journal of Pediatrics*, *48*, 112. https://doi.org/10.1186/s13052-022-01310-w

Shea, L.L., Koffer Miller, K.H., Verstreate, K., Tao, S., & Mandell, D. (2021). States' use of Medicaid to meet the needs of autistic individuals. *Health Services Research*, *56*(6), 1207–1214. https://doi.org/10.1111/1475-6773.13671

Shenouda, J., Barrett, E., Davidow A.L., Sidwell, K., Lescott, C., Halperin, W., Silenzio, V.M.B., & Zahorodny, W. (2023). Prevalence and disparities in the detection of autism without intellectual Disability. *Pediatrics*, *151*(2), e2022056594. https://doi.org/10.1542/peds.2022-056594.

Simonoff, E., Pickles, A., Charman, T., Chandler, S., Loucas, T., & Barid, G. (2008). Psychiatric disorders in children with autism spectrum disorders: Prevalence, comorbidity, and associated factors in a population-derived sample. *Journal of the American Academy of Child & Adolescent Psychiatry*, *47*, 921–929. https://doi. org/10.1097/CHI.0b013e318179964f

Skwerer, D., Joseph, R., Eggleston, B., Meyer, S., & Tager-Flusberg, H. (2019). Prevalence and correlates of psychiatric symptoms in minimally verbal children and adolescents with ASD. *Frontiers in Psychiatry*, *10*, 43. https://doi.org/10.3389/fpsyt.2019.00043

Social Security Administration. (2023, July 14). *Supplemental Security Income (SSI) for children*. Retrieved from www.ssa.gov/benefits/disability/apply-child.html

Social Security. Office of Retirement and Disability Policy. (2021, July 14). *SSI annual statistical report, 2021*. Retrieved from www.ssa.gov/policy/docs/statcomps/ssi_asr/2021/sect04.html#table20

Somerton, M., Stolyarova, V. & Khanin, S. (2022). Autism and the knowledge and beliefs of specialists in Kazakhstan. *The Journal of Autism and Developmental Disorders*, *52*, 1156–1168. https://doi.org/10.1007/s10803-021-05021-9

Sparrow, M. (2018, August 3). Why is the autistic unemployment rate so high? *Thinking Person's Guide to Autism*. Retrieved from https://thinkingautismguide.com/2018/02/why-is-autistic-unemployment-rate-so.html

Umagami, K., Remington, A., Lloyd-Evans, B., Davies, J., & Crane, L. (2022). Loneliness in autistic adults: A systematic review. *Autism*, *26*(8), 2117–2135. https://doi.org/10.1177/13623613221077721

Wiggins, L.D., Rice, C.E., Barger, B., Soke, G.N., Lee, L., Moody, E., Edmondson-Pretzel, R., & Levy, S.E. (2019). DSM-5 criteria for autism spectrum disorder maximizes diagnostic sensitivity and specificity in preschool children. *Social Psychiatry and Psychiatric Epidemiology*, *54*, 693–701. https://doi.org/10.1007/s00127-019-01674-1

Chapter 3

The Dyspraxic Child and Their Family

Abbreviations

ADHD: Attention Deficit Hyperactivity Disorder
APA: American Psychiatric Association
DCD: Developmental Coordination Disorder
DSM: Diagnostic and Statistical Manual of Mental Disorders

Introduction

Dyspraxia, also known as developmental coordination disorder (DCD), is a developmental condition which impacts coordination and organisation. Yet how does this impact the child in terms of their day-to-day life? How does dyspraxia impact the family as a whole? This chapter will discuss, using case studies and practice examples, the practical, emotional and social difficulties dyspraxia presents for children and their families. Each child will present completely uniquely, and no broad definition or understanding of a developmental condition can paint an accurate picture of an individual child's or family's needs. This chapter will consider the range and scope of dyspraxia in terms of the extent to which it can impact the life of a child and their family. How dyspraxia is assessed and diagnosed will be explored, and the influence of dyspraxia in adulthood will further be discussed. As both dyspraxia and DCD are accepted terms used to describe this developmental condition which impacts coordination and organisation, both terms will be used interchangeably throughout this chapter.

Learning Outcomes

On completion of Chapter 3, learners should demonstrate an enhanced understanding concerning:

- How to define dyspraxia/DCD and explain how this is assessed and diagnosed

DOI: 10.4324/9781003455868-3

- How dyspraxia impacts the child in their daily life
- The impact of dyspraxia on the family
- The implications of dyspraxia in adulthood

What Is Dyspraxia?

Dyspraxia is diagnosed in children who present with motor and coordination problems, which are not attributable to any other condition (Blank et al., 2019). Dyspraxia manifests in poor spatial awareness, resulting in bumps and falling over, in addition to movement which appears awkward (Dyspraxia Foundation, 2023a). Dyspraxia is a developmental disorder which impacts the child in terms of performing motor tasks and presents coordination difficulties (Colley, 2006). Interestingly, a study by Farmer, Echenne, and Bentourkia (2016) found that children with dyspraxia were more likely to be left-handed or ambidextrous, which was evident within 47% of their total sample of 129 children. They further identified that slow movement in undertaking tasks was present for 100% of the children who participated in their study (Farmer et al., 2016).

Reflection Point!

What tasks do you use fine motor skills for? What activities do you use gross motor skills for?

The National Institute of Neurological Disorders and Stroke (2023) defines dyspraxia as "an impairment in the ability to plan and carry out sensory and motor tasks". This may impact the child regarding balance, perception difficulties, memory and posture (National Institute of Neurological Disorders and Stroke, 2023). The American Psychiatric Association (APA) describes dyspraxia as a developmental condition which affects coordination and movement, which is present from birth, whereas acquired dyspraxia occurs after a brain injury (usually a stroke) and is resultant of this injury (APA, 2013).

Dyspraxia means that the child uses a considerable amount of effort and focus to undertake everyday tasks (Dyspraxia Foundation, 2023a). Yet Meachon, Melching, and Alpers (2023) report that many professionals lack awareness and understanding about dyspraxia/DCD. They conducted a survey with 346 healthcare clinicians participating, across the UK and Germany. They found that 42% of clinicians had not heard of DCD, and overall clinicians were much more informed and aware about ADHD, compared to dyspraxia (Meachon et al., 2023).

Dyspraxia was previously known as "clumsy child syndrome", as it was characterised by children who fall over frequently (Missiuna & Polatajko, 1995). Gibbs, Appleton, and Appleton (2007) argue that clumsy child syndrome was replaced with the term dyspraxia and subsequently developmental coordination disorder (DCD). Nonetheless, dyspraxia and DCD are often used interchangeably within medical, community and school settings. Research to date surmises that dyspraxia is more common in boys compared to girls, with a ratio estimated between 1.7:1, up to 3:1 (Nowak, Gnitecka, & Romanowska-Tolloczko, 2015; Farmer et al., 2016; Dyspraxia Foundation, 2015, Lingam et al., 2009).

Comorbidities are estimated in up to 50% of children with neurodevelopmental disorders (Smits-Engelsman, Jover, Green, Ferguson, & Wilson, 2017). The most common comorbidities for children living with dyspraxia are ADHD, autism and dyslexia (Dyspraxia Foundation, 2023b). Yet the dearth in the literature to date is problematic, concerning appropriate interventions to support dyspraxic children with comorbid conditions (Smits-Engelsman et al., 2017).

Reflection Point!

Had you heard of dyspraxia or DCD before now? How would your level of awareness concerning dyspraxia compare to your awareness of autism or ADHD?

How Does Dyspraxia Impact the Child?

Dyspraxia impacts the child in terms of their ability to be independent and their need for support to complete everyday tasks. Some children may need help with personal care, such as showering and brushing teeth, or could need help with feeding themselves (cutting up food, getting food on to their fork, etc.). Tasks which require planning and sequencing can be challenging. For example: getting dressed may seem instinctive for a neurotypical child. They just know what to do and in what order. For a dyspraxic child, this task can seem daunting, as in reality, it consists of multiple tasks which must be undertaken in a specific order to be successful. Some children may forget to put on items of clothes, may put underwear on over outer clothing, sweaters back to front, and even leave home with no shoes on.

The difficulties that dyspraxia presents in terms of balance can further impact the child as they perform their daily tasks. Some children may fall over frequently, causing injuries, and find maintaining their balance while undertaking motor tasks challenging. For example: when putting trousers or shoes on and lifting one foot off the floor, some children will lose their balance and fall over. While running or playing outside and the juggling of motor and social tasks simultaneously (looking at or for another child/ friend, chasing or running in a game of tag, avoiding hazards and other children, while socialising/interacting, possibly while being given instructions) can culminate in regular trips, falls and accidents.

Children living with dyspraxia may struggle socially and appear younger than their neurotypical peers, due to their support needs regarding everyday tasks. For example: a 12-year-old who needs help to fasten their coat buttons or to cross the road. Or requiring support to undertake tasks such as tying shoes or having a shower at age 12 or 13. Such support needs can make dyspraxic children acutely aware of their differences compared to their neurotypical peers. This can culminate in social exclusion.

Dyspraxic children often perform poorly at sports, due to the level of motor planning, organisation and coordination that most sports require. Couple this with the peer pressure to perform well within a team environment (even within physical education class games), and this can culminate in negatively influencing the child's self-esteem and self-belief. Children living with dyspraxia report feeling excluded when playing sports at school (Zwicker, Suto, Harris, Vlasakova, & Missiuna, 2018). Zwicker et al. (2018) report that children feel blamed for their performance when playing team sports and further that they are often not passed the ball/given an opportunity to engage. Other social activities such as swimming and cycling require planning, sequencing, movement and execution simultaneously, making each activity particularly challenging for children living with dyspraxia. Being unable to swim or ride a bicycle without support can further cause feelings of inadequacy.

Handwriting difficulties are common for children with DCD, and they tend to have a lower volume of writing output compared to their typical peers (Barnett & Prunty, 2021). Barnett and Prunty (2021) contend that handwriting requires both motor skill and planning, sequencing and organisation, presenting multiple difficulties for the child. Handwriting difficulties can make academic endeavours (both at home and in school) particularly challenging for children with dyspraxia and taking considerably more time. This can lead to frustration and feelings of inadequacy, as the child tries very hard, yet their efforts may not be commensurate to their output.

Children with DCD lack the ability to problem solve and correct errors within their motor function (Schoemaker & Smits-Engelsman, 2015). Intuitively and via imitating others and following instruction, neurotypical children learn to perfect their motor skills and master motor tasks such as running, jumping or riding a bicycle (Schoemaker & Smits-Engelsman, 2015). However, children with dyspraxia do not improve in their motor function, without specific intervention aimed at addressing this (Schoemaker & Smits-Engelsman, 2015).

UNESCO (2023) contends that dyspraxia can impact the child's ability to communicate and form speech. The child may have difficulty with pronouncing certain words and regarding their ability to plan and deliver speech, which represents what they wish to say (UNESCO, 2023). Difficulties with speech arising from dyspraxia can further impact the child socially and contribute to feelings of inadequacy when compared to their peers. Speech challenges can subsequently culminate in social exclusion.

Assessment and Diagnosis of Dyspraxia

Author Reflection Point!

Dyspraxia in the case of my child emerged slowly, from initial global developmental delay (multiple delayed milestones). My son didn't sit unaided at 9 months old and was making no efforts towards crawling. He was referred to early intervention, and with the support of regular occupational and physio therapy, he eventually was able to sit unaided (at 11 months), began to crawl (more of a bum shuffle) at 13 months and finally mastered walking (aged 19 months). However, once he caught up developmentally, we were signed off from this service.

It wasn't until he was 4 years old that his teacher noticed that he struggled with gross and fine motor skills in school and made the referral for assessment (Mullins, 2022). I had never even heard of dyspraxia and was very grateful to the kind teacher who gently explained to me what this was. Upon reading up on dyspraxia, it described my son perfectly, but I wondered why had I never heard of this condition? And I equally wondered why dyspraxia was not suggested earlier, as a possible cause of global developmental delay?

The *Diagnostic and Statistical Manual* (DSM-5) is used to diagnose dyspraxia/DCD under four specific criteria:

Criterion A: significant and measurable motor difficulties based on age and expected developmental ability skills (Harris, Mickelson, & Zwicker, 2015).
Criterion B: the extent to which the difficulties with motor and coordination, interfere with activities of daily living (Harris et al., 2015). For example: a child who is falling over frequently, has injuries/broken bones

from accidents, a child who is unable to engage in self-care tasks appropriate to their age such as getting dressed, etc.

Criterion C: gathers information on when the coordination difficulties first became apparent and what the early development of the child looked like (e.g. pre-term birth, birth weight, sitting unaided, etc.) (Dyspraxia UK, 2023)

Criterion D: stipulates that motor difficulties experienced cannot be explained by any other cause, condition or disability (Dyspraxia UK, 2023).

Occupational Therapy

Early identification and intervention for children with dyspraxia are vital in improving outcomes and enabling children to develop their motor skills (Gibbs et al., 2007). Occupational therapy is a common therapy provided for children living with dyspraxia (Cleaton, Lorgelly, & Kirby, 2020). Occupational therapists are a key professional relevant to working with dyspraxic children, to enable and empower them to reach their individual goals (Association of Occupational Therapists Ireland, 2023). Occupational therapists assist children with dyspraxia with tasks of daily living which will promote participation, skills development and independence (AOTI, 2023). Occupational therapy supports the child to develop problem-solving skills and break large tasks into smaller, more manageable steps (O'Dea, Coote, & Robinson, 2021). O'Dea et al. (2021) contend that occupational therapists working with children diagnosed with DCD, provide support with motor tasks such as handwriting, using cutlery and cycling. Occupational therapy focuses specifically on role fulfilment for children across different settings where they engage, with a particular emphasis on maximising independence, despite the challenges presented by their dyspraxia (AOTI, 2023).

Case Study 1

Jessica is 7 years old and is three years post dyspraxia diagnosis. Every morning Jessica gets up for school and her Dad brushes her teeth and helps her to get dressed. Jessica struggles with buttons, zips and shoe ties and is unable to dress herself, without substantial support. Jessica's Dad will pack her school bag and double-check that everything she needs is in there, as Jessica frequently misplaces items she needs for school.

In class, Jessica has the support of a classroom assistant for some of her school day. The classroom assistant helps her to write down her homework, prompts her to finish tasks she is falling behind on and reminds Jessica of tasks which have more than one component and what she needs to do next

> *(e.g. read page 12, then answer questions 1–3 on page 13). Jessica needs*
> *help to open her lunch box and pencil case, get her coat on and off, and to*
> *repack her school bag at time to go home.*
>
> Given Jessica's care needs and supports being provided, what would
> you recommend based on your profession/future profession to help
> with developing motor skills?
>
> What type of intervention could contribute to developing Jessica's
> independence?
>
> What practical resources could enable and empower Jessica in her
> daily life?

Impact of Dyspraxia/DCD on the Family

Dyspraxia, like any other disability experienced by a child, impacts each
member of their family and the family as a whole. Because dyspraxia/DCD
influences the child in terms of undertaking everyday tasks, reasoning and
memory, they often require additional practical and emotional support from
parents and potentially siblings. Equally, the additional practical and emotional support provided by parents can result in siblings receiving less attention from parents and feeling left out. The whole family may be further
impacted by the range of family activities/social opportunities accessible to
them, based on the needs and limitations of the child living with dyspraxia.
For example: cycling or swimming as a family may not be possible, as many
dyspraxic children struggle to learn how to ride a bike and master the coordination and planning required for swimming.

The lack of general awareness in society about dyspraxia further influences the whole family of the dyspraxic child. Most people in society have
heard of autism and ADHD, but less so dyspraxia. So when a child is unable
to catch a ball when another child throws it to them, or is 12 years old and
their mother has to tie their shoelaces, this can prompt stares and judgement from other people. It's difficult to know when to explain or whether
to just let people come to their own conclusions. Dyspraxia can present as
an invisible disability, where other people don't see this or identify it, unless
they have an awareness of understanding of this condition.

Yet seeing a child excluded because of their motor function and ability
to keep up with their peers developmentally, can be emotionally devastat-
ing for both parents and siblings. This can manifest in siblings feeling the
need to protect their dyspraxic sibling and even becoming hypervigilant at
school or at social events, to ensure their sibling is not being picked on or
excluded. This protectiveness can extend to parents who may feel they need
to accompany their child, when another child of the same age would not

need accompaniment, for example: at clubs, birthday parties or on field trips with their school.

Some families may be impacted by the frequency of therapy appointments and the additional burden this places on the family in terms of time, work commitments and the financial implications. Therapy appointments further create a need for sourcing childcare for siblings and frequent requests for time off from work for parents.

Author Reflection Point!

Knowledge and insight about dyspraxia and how this impacts the child can enable professionals to tailor supports and interventions uniquely, to meet the child's needs. One fantastic best practice intervention example my child benefitted immensely from was a basketball team specifically for children with dyspraxia. Coaches broke each movement into manageable and specific parts and used repetition and consistency to empower the children to master each skill individually, e.g. bouncing and catching the ball, passing the ball, etc. Only once each skill was mastered individually did the child move on to the next skill and eventually begin assimilating these skills in a more jointed fashion (Mullins, 2022).

This club further presented a space for children who are often considered poor at sports and last picked for the team, to find an environment which was less competitive and tailored to their unique needs (Mullins, 2022). This further contributed to the development of social skills and increased self-esteem. Skills development was reinforced with substantial praise and celebration of each new skill acquired. Children were playing sports and learning coordination skills alongside other children who presented with the same challenges and needs. This meant that the children were less self-conscious and tried things they may not have been confident enough to try in another setting with their neurotypical peers. And every attempt or missed basket, was met with a response of "great try!" or "fantastic effort!" and followed by more specific instruction about what changes would enhance their accuracy for the next shot. This often included modelling from coaches and hand-over instruction, where they would place their hands/arms over the child's and help them to reposition, grasp differently or change their gait or positioning.

Cleaton, Lorgelly, and Kirby (2019), in their UK study, found that one of the aspects of dyspraxia which most negatively affects families of dyspraxic children, is the lack of outside support for their child. Cleaton et al. (2019)

conclude that many families feel like they are left to fend for themselves post diagnosis and that DCD has a negative impact on the overall emotional wellbeing of the family. Caring for a child living with dyspraxia further impacts families in terms of the level of additional personal care needed (Jasmin, Tétreault, Larivière, & Joly, 2018). Jasmin et al. (2018) contend that substantial additional support needs in terms of toileting were required for children with dyspraxia, as reported by parents in their study. Jasmin et al. (2018) further suggest that supporting the dyspraxic child to complete their homework presents additional stress for families.

Jackson and Andipatin (2021) conducted research on the experiences of fathers of children with a dyspraxia diagnosis. The fathers in their study report feeling like their child is not who they expected them to be, and an adjustment needed to occur in their perceptions and expectations (Jackson & Andipatin, 2021). Jackson and Andipatin (2021) conclude that the traditional father-child roles of playing sports together (which fathers had imagined) were not so, and the need to reimagine life with their child because of their disability, caused emotional distress for the fathers.

Case Study 2

Tom is 5 years old and attends kindergarten. Tom falls frequently in the school yard and keeps his hands in his pockets to hide the scratches and cuts from these falls. Tom's teacher has noticed that he struggles with his pencil grip and other fine motor skills such as using scissors and placing pegs on a peg board. Tom's hand-eye coordination is quite poor and he appears less mature than his peers emotionally.

How could the teacher respond initially to Tom's motor issues? How should the teacher approach concerns about Tom with his parents/caregivers? What strategies could be employed in school to support Tom to develop his motor skills?

Dyspraxia in Adulthood

Dyspraxia is a lifelong condition. In adulthood, dyspraxia may impact the individual in terms of accessing and maintaining employment. Colley (2006) suggests that challenges concern the organisation of tasks, remembering information and when undertaking practical tasks, e.g. fine or gross motor activities. Moody (2014) argues that adults with DCD may struggle in employment and educational settings concerning sequencing and timekeeping, which can culminate in feelings of low self-esteem. Yet Kirby, Edwards, and Sugden (2011) argue that very little research to date has focused on the impact of dyspraxia in adulthood, culminating in a poor understanding of what this condition means for those living with it.

Verlinden, De Wijngaert, and Van den Eynde (2023) argue that adults living with dyspraxia who present for support, rarely report problems or issues with motor function, but rather for secondary anxiety or depression. The Dyspraxia Foundation USA (2023) reports that adults living with dyspraxia may have difficulties with perception issues such as spatial awareness and over-/under-sensitivity to temperature and pain. Adults may further struggle with adjusting to new situations and emotionally regarding stress, depression and anxiety (Dyspraxia Foundation USA, 2023).

Tal Saban and Kirby (2018) contend that young adults (15 to 25 years) with dyspraxia can struggle with changing settings and the inability to control their environment. For example: moving from the family home to shared accommodation, with other students on campus. Yet reduced parental support combined with new environments and opportunities to learn and establish themselves, can further be viewed as positive changes for some adults with a diagnosis of DCD (Tal Saban & Kirby, 2018).

A large-scale study which surveyed 1,634 people aged over 16 years, whose use of a screening tool identified them as probable for having dyspraxia, found that many participants reported greater challenges in terms of their motor function in adulthood, compared to childhood (Cleaton, Tal-Saban, Hill, & Kirby, 2021). About 46% of participants considered emerging adults (aged 16–31) reported that friends and family describe them as disorganised and forgetful. Scott-Roberts and Purcell (2018) contend that adults with DCD trip and fall more frequently, which can culminate in anxiety around participation. Verlinden et al. (2023) describe practical challenges which present concerning dyspraxia in adulthood, such as difficulty multi-tasking or undertaking two tasks simultaneously, and difficulty with food preparation.

Author Reflection Point!

Dyspraxia in my experience is the least understood neurodivergent condition, which my children experience. Most people have heard of and understand what it means to live with ADHD or autism, and tend to be more tolerant and actively inclusive as a result. However, I frequently find myself explaining what DCD means and how it impacts my child. This lack of awareness is further evident within the dearth of research on dyspraxia, when compared to ADHD and autism. Hence within this chapter, I found myself using my own practice and personal experiences more frequently, to highlight the reality of dyspraxia for children who live with this disorder.

Self-Assessment

Identify three areas in which dyspraxia/DCD impacts the child in their daily life.
How could dyspraxia/DCD impact a child socially?
Can you describe how dyspraxia/DCD impacts the person in adulthood?

Chapter Summary

This chapter has explored the neurodivergent condition of dyspraxia, also known as DCD, and the extent to which this impacts the child. Dyspraxia affects motor skills, organisation, sequencing, balance and coordination. Tasks requiring multiple steps and coordination of movement can be particularly problematic. This can manifest in difficulties with self-care tasks such as brushing teeth and tying shoes. Learning skills such as cycling and swimming, which require a competent level of planning, coordination and gross motor skills, can further be challenging. This chapter identified the distinct role of occupational therapists, in supporting children with DCD, to develop independence and achieve their goals. DCD is a lifelong condition and can present difficulties with maintaining employment and concerning comorbid mental health conditions, such as anxiety and depression.

Yet notable within this chapter is the lack of research and literature available concerning dyspraxia, when compared to other neurodevelopmental conditions. Such a dearth in research undoubtedly influences awareness and understanding of dyspraxia for practitioners.

References

American Psychiatric Association. (2013). *Diagnostic and statistical manual of mental disorders* (5th ed.). Washington, DC: American Psychiatric Publishing.

Association of Occupational Therapists Ireland. (2023, August 6). *What is occupational therapy?* Retrieved from www.aoti.ie/what-is-ot

Barnett, A.L., & Prunty, M. (2021). Handwriting difficulties in Developmental Coordination Disorder (DCD). *Current Developmental Disorders Reports, 8,* 6–14. https://doi.org/10.1007/s40474-020-00216-8

Blank, R., Barnett, A.L., Cairney, J., Green, D., Kirby, A., Polatajko, H., Rosenblum, S., Smits-Engelmans, B., Sugden, D., Wilson, P., & Vincon, S. (2019). International clinical practice recommendations on the definition, diagnosis, assessment, intervention, and psychosocial aspects of developmental coordination disorder. *Developmental Medicine and Child Neurology, 61,* 242–285. https://doi.org/10.1111/dmcn.14132

Cleaton, M.A.M., Lorgelly, P.K. & Kirby, A. (2019). Developmental coordination disorder: The impact on the family. *Quality of Life Research, 28*, 925–934. https://doi.org/10.1007/s11136-018-2075-1

Cleaton, M.A.M., Lorgelly, P.K., & Kirby, A. (2020). Developmental coordination disorder in UK children aged 6–18 years: Estimating the cost. *British Journal of Occupational Therapy, 83*(1), 29–40. https://doi.org/10.1177/0308022619866642

Cleaton, M.A.M., Tal-Saban, M., Hill, E.L., & Kirby, A. (2021). Gender and age differences in the presentation of at-risk or probable developmental coordination disorder in adults. *Research in Developmental Disabilities, 115*, 104010. https://doi.org/10.1016/j.ridd.2021.104010

Colley, M. (2006). *Living with dyspraxia: A guide for adults with developmental dyspraxia.* London, Philadelphia: Jessica Kingsley Books.

Dyspraxia Foundation. (2015). *Is it a battle of the sexes?* Retrieved from https://dyspraxiafoundation.org.uk/news-archive/dyspraxia-is-battle-sexes/

Dyspraxia Foundation. (2023a, July 31). *What is dyspraxia?* Retrieved from https://dyspraxiafoundation.org.uk/what_is_dyspraxia/dyspraxia-at-a-glance/

Dyspraxia Foundation. (2023b, August 3). *Dyspraxia foundations FAQs.* Retrieved from https://dyspraxiafoundation.org.uk/what_is_dyspraxia/dyspraxia-foundation-faqs/#:~:text=Research%20suggests%20that%3A,a%20diagnosis%20of%20dyspraxia%2FDCD

Dyspraxia Foundation USA. (2023, August 4). *Dyspraxia and adults.* Retrieved from https://dyspraxiausa.org/dyspraxia-and-adults/

Dyspraxia UK. (2023, July 31). *Diagnostic criteria.* Retrieved from www.dyspraxiauk.com/diagnosticcriteria.php

Farmer, M., Echenne, B., & Bentourkia, M. (2016). Study of clinical characteristics in young subjects with Developmental coordination disorder. *Brain and Development, 38*(6), 538–547. https://doi.org/10.1016/j.braindev.2015.12.010

Gibbs, J., Appleton, J., & Appleton R. (2007). Dyspraxia or developmental coordination disorder? Unravelling the enigma. *Archives of Disease in Childhood, 92*(6), 534–539. https://doi.org/10.1136/adc.2005.088054

Harris, S.R., Mickelson, E.C.R., & Zwicker, J.G. (2015). Diagnosis and management of developmental coordination disorder. *The Canadian Medical Association Journal, 187*(9), 659–665. https://doi.org/10.1503/cmaj.140994

Jackson, K., & Andipatin, M. (2021). An exploration of fathers' subjective experiences of parenting a child that presents with dyspraxia. *Current Psychology, 40*, 4863–4874. https://doi.org/10.1007/s12144-019-00433-4

Jasmin, E., Tétreault, S., Larivière, N., & Joly, J. (2018). Participation and needs of children with developmental coordination disorder at home and in the community: Perceptions of children and parents. *Research In Developmental Disabilities, 73*(1), 1–13. https://doi.org/10.1016/j.ridd.2017.12.011

Kirby, A., Edwards, L., & Sugden, D. (2011). Emerging adulthood and developmental co-ordination disorder. *The Journal of Adult Development, 18*, 107–113. https://doi.org/10.1007/s10804-011-9123-1

Lingam, R., Hunt, L., Golding, J., Jongmans, M., & Emond, A. (2009). Prevalence of developmental coordination disorder using the DSM-IV at 7 years of age: A UK population–based study. *Pediatrics, 123*(4), e693–e700. https://doi.org/10.1542/peds.2008-1770.

Meachon, E.J., Melching, H., & Alpers, G.W. (2023). The overlooked disorder: (Un)awareness of developmental coordination disorder across clinical professions.

Advances in Neurodevelopmental Disorders. https://doi.org/10.1007/s41252-023-00334-5

Missiuna, C., & Polatajko, H. (1995). Developmental dyspraxia by any other name: Are they all just clumsy children? *The American Journal of Occupational Therapy*, *49*(7), 619–627. https://doi.org/10.5014/ajot.49.7.619

Moody, S. (2014). Dyslexia, dyspraxia, and ADHD in adults: What you need to know. *British Journal of General Practice*, *64*(622), 252. https://doi.org/10.3399/bjgp14X679859

Mullins, L. (2022). *It takes a village. Navigating the journey of parenting your autistic child*. Dublin: Orpen Press.

National Institute of Neurological Disorders and Stroke. (2023). *Developmental dyspraxia*. Retrieved from www.ninds.nih.gov/health-information/disorders/developmental-dyspraxia

Nowak, A., Gnitecka, J., & Romanowska-Tolloczko, A. (2015). Dyspraxia as a psychomotor disorder of school aged children. *Pedagogika, Psikhologiiã I Medicobiologicheskie Problemy Fizicheskogo Vospitaniiã I Sporta*, *19*(6), 56–59. https://doi.org/10.15561/18189172.2015.0609

O'Dea, Á.E., Coote, S., & Robinson, K. (2021). Occupational therapy practice with children with developmental coordination disorder: An online qualitative vignette survey. *British Journal of Occupational Therapy*, *84*(5), 307–316. https://doi.org/10.1177/0308022620944100

Schoemaker, M.M., & Smits-Engelsman, B.C.M. (2015). Is treating motor problems in DCD Just a matter of practice and more practice? *Current Developmental Disorders Reports*, *2*, 150–156. https://doi.org/10.1007/s40474-015-0045-7

Scott-Roberts, S., & Purcell, C. (2018). Understanding the functional mobility of adults with Developmental Coordination Disorder (DCD) through the international classification of functioning (ICF). *Current Developmental Disorders Reports*, *5*(1), 26–33. https://doi.org/10.1007/s40474-018-0128-3.

Smits-Engelsman, B., Jover, M., Green, D., Ferguson, G., & Wilson, P. (2017). DCD and comorbidity in neurodevelopmental disorder: How to deal with complexity? *Human Movement Science*, *53*, 1–4. https://doi.org/10.1016/j.humov.2017.02.009

Tal Saban, M., & Kirby, A. (2018). Adulthood in developmental coordination disorder (DCD): A review of current literature based on ICF perspective. *Current Developmental Disorders Reports*, *5*, 9–17. https://doi.org/10.1007/s40474-018-0126-5

UNESCO. (2023, August 2). *Living with dyspraxia*. Retrieved from https://mgiep.unesco.org/article/living-with-dyspraxia

Verlinden, S., De Wijngaert, P., &Van den Eynde, J. (2023). Developmental coordination disorder in adults: A case series of a condition that is underdiagnosed by adult psychiatrists. *Psychiatry Research Case Reports*, *2*(2). https://doi.org/10.1016/j.psycr.2023.100148

Zwicker, J.G., Suto, M., Harris, S.R., Vlasakova, N., & Missiuna, C. (2018). Developmental coordination disorder is more than a motor problem: Children describe the impact of daily struggles on their quality of life. *British Journal of Occupational Therapy*, *81*(2), 65–73. https://doi.org/10.1177/0308022617735046

Chapter 4

The ADHD Child and Their Family

Abbreviations

ADHD: Attention Deficit Hyperactivity Disorder
APA: American Psychiatric Association
CDC: Centers for Disease Control and Prevention
DSM: Diagnostic and Statistical Manual of Mental Disorders
NHS: National Health Service
NICE: National Institute for Healthcare Excellence
UK: United Kingdom
US: United States

Introduction

ADHD is classified as a mental health condition and is characterised by inattentiveness, hyperactivity and difficulties with impulse control. But what does this really mean for a child and their family? For some children this may mean they need consistent reminders to stay on task and find it difficult to stay sitting in their seat at school. For other children this could mean they have been removed from mainstream school due to instances of violent outbursts and an inability to control their emotional reactions. Some children living with ADHD may pose a danger to themselves in terms of impulse control and issues surrounding safety and supervision.

This chapter will explore case studies and practice examples in an effort to present the lived reality for children and families, regarding the impact of ADHD on their everyday life. This chapter will examine the different types of ADHD and discuss how ADHD is assessed and diagnosed. The systemic factors which impact children with ADHD and their families will be discussed. Finally, this chapter will consider how ADHD presents in adulthood, in order to contextualise the significance of timely and appropriate intervention and supports.

DOI: 10.4324/9781003455868-4

Learning Outcomes

On completion of Chapter 4, learners should demonstrate an enhanced understanding concerning:

* How ADHD impacts the child in their daily life
* How ADHD is assessed and diagnosed
* The impact of ADHD on the family unit
* The influence of systemic factors in the societal response to ADHD
* How ADHD presents in adulthood

What Is ADHD?

ADHD is a condition which impacts the child in terms of their ability to focus, concentrate and relating to hyperactivity (National Health Service, NHS, 2021). ADHD is a neurodevelopmental disorder (Mahon & Denckla, 2017). ADHD is a lifelong condition and is usually diagnosed in childhood (NHS, 2021). The American Psychiatric Association (APA, 2023) defines ADHD as a mental disorder and suggests that this is the most commonly reported mental disorder among children. ADHD causes significant challenges and disruptions to the child in their home, school and social lives (APA, 2023). The impaired academic achievement associated with ADHD can present long-term negative outcomes for some children into adulthood, including delinquency, unemployment and homelessness (DuPaul & Langberg, 2015; García Murillo, Ramos-Olazagasti, Mannuzza, Castellanos, & Klein, 2016).

Although ADHD has been described for centuries, it has only been identified clearly within the literature for the past 35 years (Mahon & Denckla, 2017). Perhaps most concerning regarding ADHD in childhood is the increased mortality associated with this condition (Dalsgaard, Østergaard, Leckman, Mortensen, & Pedersen, 2015). Dalsgaard et al. (2015) conducted a longitudinal study in Denmark which followed babies from birth to age 32 years. They found that children and adults with ADHD were twice as likely to die when compared to their neurotypical counterparts, and accidents were the leading cause of death for this group (Dalsgaard et al., 2015). ADHD can cause impulsive behaviours, which can manifest in the child taking risks and acting without thinking or planning (NHS, 2021).

Reflection Point!

What do you know about ADHD?
What are some visual external signs of ADHD in children?

Types of ADHD

There are three distinct types of ADHD and an understanding of each can assist practitioners and families in tailoring supports to the child's individual needs. The Centers for Disease Control and Prevention (CDC, 2023) describe these types as shown in Table 4.1.

Table 4.1 Types of ADHD (CDC, 2023)

Type of ADHD	Description
Predominantly Inattentive	Easily distracted, difficulty staying on task/completing tasks
Predominantly Hyperactive/Impulsive	Fidgets, finds it difficult to sit still, impulsive behaviour
Combined Type	A combination of both inattentive and hyperactive types of ADHD

Impact of ADHD on Child's Daily Life

Inattentiveness, hyperactivity and impulsivity impact each child in different ways, while combined type ADHD will present additional daily difficulties. Some common everyday challenges which ADHD can present for children relate to safety, academic pursuits, socially and regarding self-esteem.

Safety

Impulsiveness means that the child may act without thinking and could commence an action or activity without fully thinking it through or considering the outcome or consequence. For example: a child may lash out if another child takes their toy. This may be instinctive and based on how they feel they should react in that moment. The child with ADHD may not have that pause function, between reacting and acting, where logic and reasoning occurs. This pause function enables us to estimate what the outcome of our actions will be, and perhaps not engage in an action that could result in a negative outcome. Some children with ADHD, and in particular the hyperactive/impulsive type, react immediately, without thinking through their actions.

Violent actions and outbursts present safety concerns for everyone the child comes into contact with, e.g. siblings, parents, friends, classmates, school staff or practitioners. The child with ADHD may further self-harm or hurt themselves, presenting safety and supervision concerns for parents and teachers. Such safety concerns can mean that the child requires constant supervision in a one-to-one capacity, e.g. the child cannot be left unattended at any time, cannot be left unsupervised with siblings or classmates, in an effort to keep them safe. In reality, this means that school staff and parents must be supported to provide this one-to-one supervision and must remain hypervigilant at all times. At home this can result in substantial stress for families, parents having to leave employment and siblings receiving less attention. In education settings, if such one-to-one supervision is not available, the child may not have a school place or may be suspended or expelled, due to frequent instances of violence prompting safety concerns.

Impulsivity is an aspect of ADHD which causes particular anxiety for parents/caregivers in terms of safety. Impulsivity can lead to a child running into traffic, absconding from a safe place with adult supervision, climbing/jumping from heights and placing themselves in danger near swimming pools or bodies of water. Statistics on injury and mortality for children with ADHD unfortunately substantiate the fears of parents (İz & Çeri, 2018; Prasad, West, Sayal, & Kendrick, 2018). Children with ADHD have been shown to have higher mortality rates compared to children in the general population (Diallo et al., 2022). The Centers for Disease Control and Prevention (CDC, 2022) report that children with ADHD are more likely to suffer accidents and injuries compared to their typical peers, and further are more likely to be admitted to intensive care units, injure more than one part of their body and be hospitalised for accidental poisoning. Indeed, from meeting with many other families of children with ADHD over the years, all have experienced at least one terrifying situation like this. Their child has left home or school without the knowledge of parents or teachers, has climbed out an upstairs window or climbed to a height, or has narrowly avoided serious injury from a motor vehicle.

Academically

Children with ADHD may struggle to maintain their focus in school or college, despite their best efforts. The child might want to stay present and engaged, but their brain is unable to focus their attention, particularly when they are uninterested or bored by the topic. Inattentiveness further impacts the child in terms of their memory and ability to retain and recall previous learning or information shared with them. They may forget within seconds instructions provided to them or might be unable to carry out tasks with multiple steps, as they can forget the subsequent step while undertaking the previous one. Children with ADHD may struggle particularly with learning/studying for tests or examinations. This can be incredibly frustrating for the child, and they often try extremely hard to maintain their attention, yet can be unable to.

Children living with ADHD are often highly intelligent and perhaps even above average intelligence. However, their academic developments are often hampered by their ADHD symptoms. The child can work extremely diligently and perhaps take twice as long as their neurotypical peers to complete a piece of work. Yet their output may not always match their effort, which can be frustrating and exhausting. It can feel like completing work in a language you are not familiar with, and needing to concentrate and translate consistently to maintain understanding. This is exhausting for children living with ADHD and can culminate in poor self-esteem and feelings of self-doubt.

Socially

Not being invited to the birthday parties of peers, can be particularly distressing for children with ADHD (Mullins, 2022). Speaking out of turn, displaying hyperactivity, having difficulty with waiting in turn, being unintentionally physically rough and challenging behaviour, can dissuade other children from including the child with ADHD. These outward manifestations of ADHD are often not something the child is aware of or can control (without support and guidance), yet other children can be frightened or overwhelmed, which can cause them to avoid interacting with the child with ADHD.

Thompson et al. (2023), in a large-scale longitudinal study on children living with ADHD, found that they are at an increased risk of social isolation. Currie and Szabo (2020) report that children with neurodevelopmental disabilities experience social isolation, in part due to the lack of understanding of their peers. Missing social cues and struggling with reciprocity can make establishing and maintaining friendships more difficult (Leitner, 2014). Social skills for children with ADHD can further be hampered by deficits in their pragmatic language skills (Staikova, Gomes, Tartter, McCabe, & Halperin, 2013). Pragmatic language skills relate to the child's capacity to use language in a social capacity and understand the broader context and meaning embedded within it (Papafragou, 2018).

Challenging behaviour and parental fear of what could or might happen, can further contribute to the social exclusion of children with ADHD. Past behavioural issues or negative experiences at family or social events, can dissuade parents from participating with their child living with ADHD. It can result in a benefits versus potential negative outcomes analysis: although the child may enjoy the social event, if the likelihood of a substantial behavioural issue seems probable (e.g. a physical altercation with another child, an accidental injury, aggressive behaviour etc.), parents may decide not to attend.

Author Reflection Point!

Other children recognise when a child is different and acts out or misbehaves. Unfortunately, sometimes this can encourage children to tease the child with ADHD and/or try to prompt them to act out. Equally, when other children are constantly telling tales/tattling on the neurodivergent child, this can erode their self-esteem and make them feel even more excluded. Consequently, managing other children's behaviour can assist in creating a more supportive environment for a child with ADHD.

Self-Esteem

Children with a diagnosis of ADHD often report lower levels of self-esteem when compared to their neurotypical peers (Harpin, Mazzone, Raynaud, Kahle, & Hodgkins, 2016). When a child is constantly corrected by parents, teachers and professionals, or finds themselves frequently excluded from activities due to safety concerns or challenging behaviour, this can prompt them to become self-critical. Being excluded by their peers due to their ADHD symptoms of impulsivity, hyperactivity or inattentiveness, further contributes to the erosion of the child's self-esteem. Although the child does not always have control over their actions and behaviours, they can begin to feel inadequate, due to their inability to conform in the same ways as their peers. Equally, academic ability and the challenges this presents for the child living with ADHD can further culminate in low self-esteem. It's important to remember that even though the child may be excluded or treated less favourably because of how their ADHD presents, they still cannot control this without specific tailored and appropriate intervention and support.

Figure 4.1 illustrates specific examples of inattentiveness, hyperactivity and impulsiveness as they may present practically, emotionally and behaviourally for children in their everyday lives.

Impulsivity	Hyperactivity	Inattentiveness
Acting without thinking, running out into traffic, inability to stay still, instinctive need to act as soon as a thought comes to mind, interrupting, not waiting turn, blurting out answers, unable to keep themselves safe, needing constant supervision, no understanding of consequences, inability to plan appropriately, reacting aggressively or violently when challenged.	Swinging on chair, rocking, running, spinning, moving too fast, bumping into people, causing unintentional injury to themselves & others, squirming, moving constantly, inability to remain still, fidgeting, repositioning frequently when sitting, speaking out of turn, difficulty waiting/queueing, /hurting other children/adults unintentionally, insomnia/sleep disturbance.	Forgets items they need, forgets time, loses items they need, zooms out, inability to stay focused, trouble maintaining attention on one thing, difficulty recalling information, difficulty completing tasks, starting a new task before completing previous task, difficulty remembering the steps involved in a task or activity.

Figure 4.1 Examples of impulsivity, hyperactivity and inattentiveness

ADHD Assessment and Diagnosis

ADHD is categorised based on three core symptoms or presentations: hyperactivity, inattentiveness and impulsiveness (Lougy, DeRuvo, Rosenthal, & Storey, 2009). ADHD is assessed and diagnosed via use of the DSM-5 criteria (APA, 2023). Difficulties must be present for the child in more than one setting (e.g. at home and in school) for a diagnosis to be concluded upon (National Institute for Healthcare Excellence [NICE], 2019). The NICE (2019) guidelines further state that rating scales can be used in conjunction with the DSM-5, such as the Conner's Scale and the Strengths and Difficulties questionnaire. Yet they caution that a clinical diagnosis must not solely rely on any one method and should be comprehensive and include detailed observation of the child across settings, in order to accurately diagnose ADHD (NICE, 2019). Other diagnostic tools used to create a holistic picture of the child's needs include: the Destructive Behaviour Diagnostic Observation Schedule (DB-DOS), the Test of Variable Attention (TOVA) and the Kiddie Disruptive Behaviour Disorder Schedule (K-DBDS) (Kemper, 2018).

Similar to autism, ADHD is more likely to be diagnosed in boys compared to girls and has been recognised by clinicians as early as 200 years ago (Faraone et al., 2021). ADHD is diagnosed based on clinical observations, detailed questionnaires with parents/caregivers and categorisation within the DSM-5 (Faraone et al., 2021). Yet Faraone et al. (2021) argue that the criteria for diagnoses are quite specific, and the individual must have experienced symptoms of hyperactivity or inattentiveness across settings, since early childhood, and symptoms must be substantial enough to cause impairments to everyday functioning.

Author Reflection Point!

ADHD (hyperactivity type) feels like having 100 tabs open in your brain, all the time! It substantially impacts sleep and creates an inability for the child to sit still. Staying in the same position for extended periods of time can actually cause physical pain and discomfort for children with hyperactivity type ADHD.

Reassessment of Need

Although we understand that ADHD is a lifelong condition and does not need to be re-diagnosed, reassessment of need for children with ADHD is imperative to creating supportive environments, within which they can thrive. The needs of a child at age 4, compared to at ages 8, 12 or 18, are in stark contrast. The settings within which the child interacts will present new challenges and opportunities. Reassessment of need is concerned with establishing at various points in time the child's unique needs across settings and in terms of their personal goals and the needs of their family. Reassessment of need should take place at regular intervals across settings such as school, healthcare settings, community settings or within the context of family support need.

Systemic Factors and ADHD

Societal views and understanding of ADHD, significantly impact children and their families living with this condition. Yet although ADHD is now quite common in children, it remains poorly understood (Richardson et al., 2015). Substantial research has been conducted regarding the causes of ADHD and concludes that it is the result of: genetic, perinatal and gestational factors, premature birth and even exposure to heavy metals (Richardson et al., 2015; Aylward, 2005; American Psychiatric Association, 2023), while the hereditary nature of ADHD is also well established (Kian, Samieefar, & Rezaei, 2022). However, the American Psychiatric Association (2023) contends that there remains no definitive or exclusive identifiable cause for ADHD, from a genetics perspective.

Societal understanding and evidence-based research surrounding ADHD, further influences the availability of resources and supports for children living with ADHD and their families. A notable systemic issue which impacts children with ADHD (or those suspected of having ADHD) and their families, is access to healthcare and educational services. Nasol, Lindly, Chavez, and Zuckerman (2019) conclude that 53% of parents of children with ADHD in the US, report that they were unable to access the medication their child needed, while 50% further report unmet therapy needs for their child (Nasol et al., 2019). Libutzki et al. (2023) argue that medication for ADHD reduces the frequency of accidental injury and consequently is largely deemed the most appropriate and effective first line of treatment, for both children and adults diagnosed with ADHD.

Yet for the general public, the media depiction of ADHD is often the only information they engage with on this topic. The media play a substantial role in communicating information about ADHD to members of the general public (Ponnou & Gonon, 2017). Indeed, such media depictions can contribute to stigma, prejudice and judgement concerning ADHD diagnosis and treatment. An example of such occurred within the UK in 2023. An undercover journalist visited private ADHD assessment clinics, documenting the outcomes (BBC News, 2023). This exposé piece presented a depiction of an individual pretending to have ADHD symptoms, in order to access ADHD medication, via three private providers (BBC News, 2023). The documentary, for someone who had not known about ADHD, would communicate that this condition can be fabricated for those wishing to access stimulant drugs. Criticisms of the documentary came from organisations representing individuals living with ADHD, labelled it sensationalist and argued that it will contribute to the lives of this marginalised group being made even more difficult (ADHD Foundation, 2023). ADHD UK (2023) argue that the documentary has increased the stigma for people with ADHD and discrimination for those who obtained an ADHD diagnosis privately. Yet the ADHD Foundation (2023) surmises that the lack of publicly available assessments in the UK, culminates in patients having no option but to pursue a diagnosis on a private basis.

Stigma based on misconceptions and lack of understanding concerning ADHD, negatively impact children and families. Speerforck et al. (2019) report that for one in four participants in their study on the general perceptions of ADHD, would not recommend someone with ADHD for a job. Stigma is also evident within the classroom, according to a study by Metzger and Hamilton (2021, p. 258). Teachers were found to rate children with ADHD "below grade level" and less likely to report their performance above grade level, regardless of their demonstrated ability on standardised tests (Metzger & Hamilton, 2021).

Negative stereotypes of ADHD further create stigma and discrimination. A boy running around hysterically and climbing all over furniture, represents the typical image people conjure when they think of ADHD. Yet this stereotype is harmful as it fails to take into account the challenges the child faces concerning concentration, impulsivity/safety, socially, academically and regarding self-esteem. Such a stereotype further omits the reality that ADHD also impacts girls and is a lifelong condition.

Case Study 1

Zachary is 6 years old and the eldest of three children. Zachary has been diagnosed with ADHD and presents with substantial difficulties both at home and in school. He has been suspended from school on three separate occasions for hurting other children and frequently absconds from the classroom. At home, Zachary frequently hurts his younger brothers and, most recently, caused a bone fracture to his 2-year-old brother Shane's arm. Zachary's parents Hazel and Yvonne are desperate to help him to control his outbursts and try to resume normal family life. Zachary cannot be left unattended for any duration of time, and his younger brothers' bedroom is locked at night to prevent him from trying to hurt them. Zachary's parents no longer visit family and friends, as this usually resulted in altercations between Zachary and other children. Zachary's school have advised that they will be unable to continue to provide his ed-ucation if this level of aggressive behaviour continues. Hazel and Yvonne are open to any therapies or parenting approaches they can employ to help him, but are vehemently opposed to considering medication.

What are the key issues impacting this family?

How do these issues impact Zachary?

What issue should be prioritised, in responding to this family's needs?

Impact of ADHD on the Family

When supporting a child living with ADHD, it's important to acknowledge and appreciate the impact of the child's condition on their whole family. ADHD impacts parents and siblings emotionally, in addition to influencing their social and employment opportunities.

Siblings

Peasgood et al. (2016), in a large-scale UK study, found that siblings of children living with ADHD, reported lower levels of happiness with their life and family. This study examined data from 476 families of a child with ADHD, and findings indicate increased levels of bullying reported by both siblings and the child with an ADHD diagnosis. According to King, Alexander, and Seabi (2016), siblings report differences in how they are parented, and in particular regarding discipline. Their study concludes that siblings can feel that they receive less parental attention compared to their sibling with ADHD and that parents were most often preoccupied with meet-ing their ADHD sibling's needs (King, Alexander, & Seabi, 2016). This is something I have written about previously, as my only neurotypical child often shared his thoughts on parental attention and being sidelined, as his siblings needs were prioritised (Mullins, 2022). With ADHD in particular, the safety concerns for the ADHD child and their siblings often needs to be prioritised by parents.

Parents

Parents further report the emotional impact of caring for a child with ADHD and suggest that anxiety can be problematic (Shah, Sharma, Chauhan, & Grover, 2021). Shah et al. (2021) suggest that the burden of care associated with parenting a child with ADHD culminates in a constant state of vigilance and anticipating when a complaint about behaviour will emerge. This really resonated with me. The fight-or-flight feeling of being on edge constantly, particularly when interacting with people socially, is something I can attest to. When behavioural outbursts are so frequent, it places an inevitability on an incident of challenging behaviour arising, and consequently the need for the parent to remain hypervigilant at all times. Caring for a child with ADHD has further been found to impact families financially and in terms of employment (Nasol, Lindly, Chavez, & Zuckerman, 2019). Nasol et al. (2019) report that 14% of parents in their sample pertaining to 2,406 children with ADHD in the US have stopped working, due to their child's diagnosis. While the additional level of care and supervision required due to ADHD symptoms, may further reduce the childcare options available for parents who wish to work.

Author Reflection Point!

A particularly challenging aspect of parenting a child with ADHD, is managing the challenging behaviour this can present. Child-to-parent violence is a problem that most parents don't discuss, due to the stigma which surrounds this behaviour. If the parent is experiencing violence from their child, their wellbeing and coping capacity will be significantly negatively impacted by this interaction. Always ask the question if aggressive outbursts and violent behaviours are happening: Is your child hurting you? If the answer is yes, this information will be critical in supporting the child living with ADHD and their family.

Sleep

Sleep disturbance is one of the most challenging elements of neurodivergence, which impacts both children and families. Broken sleep, hours of waking time in the middle of the night, and waking to start the day at 3 or 4 am are common for children with a diagnosis of ADHD. Bondopad-hyay, Diaz-Orueta, and Coogan (2022) surmise that sleep problems are more common for children with ADHD and range from bedtime resistance, to frequent waking and overall shorter sleep duration. Sleep disturbances profoundly influence the child, in terms of their ability to cope with their daily demands. Sleep disturbance negatively impacts behavioural outcomes and contributes to overall worsening of ADHD symptoms (Bondopadhyay et al., 2022). Couple this with a parent or caregiver who is also sleep de-prived, and it can culminate in a distressing environment for each member of the family.

The sleep disturbance of a child with ADHD negatively affects paren-tal mental health (Martin, Papadopoulos, Chellew, Rinehart, & Sciberras, 2019). Martin et al. (2019) contend that sleeplessness associated with chil-dren with ADHD has been shown to impact self-rated parental depression and anxiety. Hence, interventions and therapeutic responses which focus on supporting a good sleep routine for the child, have the potential to posi-tively impact parental mental health and subsequently the wellbeing of the whole family.

Although medication (primarily melatonin) can be used to support sleep for children with ADHD, non-medication alternatives should also be ex-plored (Larsson, Aili, Nygren, Jarbin, & Svedberg, 2021). Larsson et al. (2021) conducted research into the effectiveness of weighted blankets for increasing sleep duration for children with ADHD. This study found that weighted blankets increase sleep duration, sleep onset and sleep continuity (Larsson et al., 2021). Although this study was quite small (consisting of 24 families of children with ADHD), it still emphasises the value in trying practical and available methods of encouraging and supporting sleep (Lars-son et al., 2021).

Sciberras et al. (2020), in their study involving 244 children with ADHD, conducted a pilot study involving an intervention where parents were provided with two sleep consultations with a paediatric clinician. The intervention involved supporting parents to establish a bedtime routine, promote sleep hygiene and manage behaviours associated with sleep dis-turbance (Sciberras et al., 2020). They found a nominal improvement in parental-reported child sleep patterns after 12 months, and suggest that ongoing specialist sleep support may increase positive outcomes (Sciberras et al., 2020).

Parental Marriage and Relationships

Divorce rates are higher for parents of children with ADHD, according to Wymbs et al. (2008). Muñoz-Silva, Lago-Urbano, and Sanchez-Garcia

(2017) report that the behavioural challenges associated with parenting a child with ADHD, impact marital or parental relationships. Yet notable within this study is that perceived social support mediated the effect to which the child's ADHD symptoms and severity, impacted the marital relationship between parents (Muñoz-Silva et al., 2017). They surmise that the impact of parenting a child with ADHD on parental mental health and coping capacity, further impacts the marital relationship (Muñoz-Silva et al., 2017).

Case Study 2

Sarah and Carlos have twins girls aged 7. Millie is neurotypical and Lola has a diagnosis of ADHD and is being assessed for autism. Lola sleeps just two hours per night, and her parents take turns getting out of bed to try to settle her back to sleep. Sarah and Carlos are constantly tired, which can result in them having less patience in their parenting. Lola misses at least one day of school per week due to not having slept the previous night.

Millie is exhausted. She is awake most of the night as she shares a room with Lola. Millie has explained to her parents how difficult this is for her, but they have dismissed her concerns. Millie is falling asleep in class and struggling with her schoolwork. Millie has lost interest in playing with her friends, as Lola constantly interrupts and the other kids don't want to play with her. Millie misses her twice weekly dance classes regularly, as her parents are taking Lola to appointments. Millie feels like her feelings don't count and that her parents barely notice her. She's starting to increasingly resent Lola for taking all of her parents' attention and ruining her chance to play with her friends and go to dance classes.

What would Sarah and Carlos identify as their family's primary need?

What are the key stressors faced by this family, from your perspective?

How could Sarah and Carlos address Millie's needs?

What type of interventions may help to address how Millie is feeling?

Social Impact on the Family

Families can be excluded from social opportunities, due to their child's needs. This includes, yet is not limited to, community events and gatherings, family dinners and celebrations, birthday parties, playdates and even local clubs and groups. Other people may feel unable to understand or cope with the ADHD child's behaviour, and consequently not invite them or their family to social gatherings. Siblings may be impacted socially and not invited to the social opportunities, due to their ADHD sibling's needs.

Even extended family can socially exclude the child with ADHD, their parents and siblings, which is particularly difficult to cope with for families emotionally. Finding out a family party or get-together occurred after the event and not being invited, can be very tough to cope with and further compounds the existing challenges faced by the child and their family.

ADHD in Adulthood

When we think of ADHD, we often think of childhood and hyperactivity. Yet ADHD is so much more than this stereotypical image and impacts the person across the lifespan. People often question how someone could have a diagnosis of ADHD and have a college degree? Or a really good job? The answer is, with a substantial amount of additional time and effort. However, it's equally accurate to discuss that some adults with ADHD will struggle to secure employment, maintain employment and manage general life administration. Considering the steps involved in processes such as applying for a driver's licence, or completing a mortgage application . . . most adults find these tasks tedious and time consuming. Yet an adult with ADHD may find themselves unable to navigate these processes successfully without support. The same three key areas which impact the child with ADHD, continue to impact the adult. They will still experience hyperactivity, inattentiveness and/or impulsivity in their adult life, as illustrated in Figure 4.2.

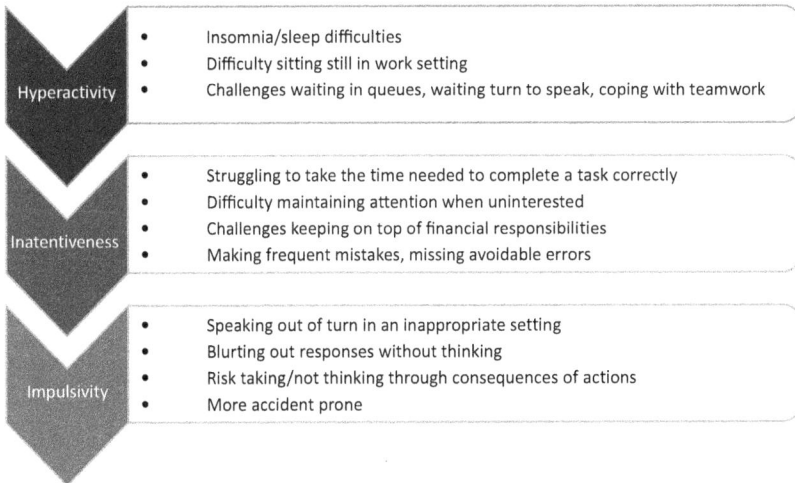

Hyperactivity
- Insomnia/sleep difficulties
- Difficulty sitting still in work setting
- Challenges waiting in queues, waiting turn to speak, coping with teamwork

Inatentiveness
- Struggling to take the time needed to complete a task correctly
- Difficulty maintaining attention when uninterested
- Challenges keeping on top of financial responsibilities
- Making frequent mistakes, missing avoidable errors

Impulsivity
- Speaking out of turn in an inappropriate setting
- Blurting out responses without thinking
- Risk taking/not thinking through consequences of actions
- More accident prone

Figure 4.2 Examples of hyperactivity, impulsiveness and inattentiveness in adulthood

Responsibilities

Yet the impact of hyperactivity, impulsivity and inattentiveness can have much more serious consequences in adult life, compared to childhood. Children are not deemed to have capacity, and consequently their behaviours are not as far-reaching or impactful. Yet when an adult zooms out while driving, this can cause a traffic accident. When they forget something, this can mean a missed flight or an important work meeting. Impulsivity can mean speaking out of turn in situations where this is not considered appropriate, e.g. in the workplace or when communicating in a court or law enforcement setting. Hyperactivity can result in insomnia, which impacts the adult's ability to wake up on time and perform their job or attend their college course.

Accidents

Accidents and injuries are further more likely for adults with ADHD across the lifespan (Libutzki et al., 2023). Brunkhorst-Kanaan et al. (2021) surmise that road traffic collisions are more likely for adults with ADHD as drivers. The hyperactivity, impulsivity and difficulties with inattentiveness, culminate in behaviours which place adults with ADHD more at risk of injury. Libutzki et al. (2023) contend that an ADHD diagnosis is the first step in understanding the increased risk for injuries and accidents, and actively engaging in accident prevention.

Relationships

ADHD has been found to impact intimate relationships in adults, and adults with ADHD are more likely to divorce (Huynh-Hohnbaum & Benowitz, 2022). Bruner, Kuryluk, and Whitton (2015) argue that adults with ADHD may face difficulties with emotional regulation within relationships and demonstrate a poor capacity for engaging in conflict resolution. The spouses of adults living with ADHD report lower levels of intimacy within their relationships and problems with the impulsive and hyperactive behaviours associated with this condition (Ben-Naim, Marom, Krashin, Grifter, & Arad, 2017). Ben-Naim et al. (2017) contend, based on their comparative study with couples diagnosed with ADHD and neurotypical couples, that lower levels of relationship satisfaction are likely for neurotypical partners of adults with ADHD.

Mental Health

Mental health is further relevant to understanding ADHD in adulthood. Adults with ADHD are significantly more likely to experience depression, anxiety, bipolar, substance misuse and personality disorders (Choi, Woo, Wang, Lim, & Bahk, 2022). Bitter et al. (2019) report that ADHD can present for adults receiving psychiatric services, yet may not have previously been assessed or diagnosed. In their multi-centre study undertaken in Hungary and the Czech Republic, they found that half of their sample of 708 adults availing of psychiatric services, met the diagnostic criteria for ADHD (Bitter et al., 2019). While Weibel et al. (2020) contend that the number is much higher and estimate that 89% of adults living with ADHD have a comorbid psychiatric condition. Such research emphasises the importance of practitioner awareness, knowledge and insight concerning ADHD and psychiatric comorbidities. Recognising and responding therapeutically to the comprehensive health and social care needs of adults with ADHD, is fundamental to creating supportive environments and promoting more positive outcomes for this group. Yet even more significant is identifying and diagnosing ADHD as early as possible in childhood and supporting the child and their family to build strategies which empower and enable the child to participate and achieve their goals.

Self-Assessment

Name two symptoms of ADHD which may present in young children.
   What is the most common treatment for ADHD?
   Describe how ADHD impacts the family unit.
   What key learning point will you take away from this chapter and use to inform your practice?

Summary

This chapter has introduced the topic of ADHD and explored the extent to which this disorder impacts the child and their family. ADHD presents challenges regarding inattentiveness, hyperactivity and impulsiveness, resulting in higher rates of accidents, injuries and mortality. ADHD can present as three specific sub-types and can pose significant challenges for children in multiple life domains, from school to home life and within social settings. Comorbidity is particularly high regarding ADHD and psychiatric conditions.

Stigma and a general lack of understanding concerning ADHD at the societal level, further disadvantages children with ADHD and can culminate in social exclusion. The impact on ADHD on the whole family, is pertinent to consider when creating supportive environments for children and their families. ADHD can negatively impact family relationships, social opportunities and, perhaps most notably, regarding sleep disturbance.

Understanding ADHD and how this impacts the child and their family, will empower practitioners to approach their needs from a knowledgeable and informed perspective.

References

ADHD Foundation. (2023, July 28). Response to the panorama "private ADHD clinics exposed". *The Neurodiversity Charity.* Retrieved from www.adhdfoundation. org.uk/2023/05/15/response-to-bbc-panorama-private-adhd-clinics-exposed/

ADHD UK. (2023, July 28). *Our response: Panorama private ADHD clinics exposed.* Retrieved from https://adhduk.co.uk/panorama-adhd-uk-response/

American Psychiatric Association. (2023, July 28). *What is ADHD?* Retrieved from www.psychiatry.org/patients-families/adhd/what-is-adhd

Aylward, G.P. (2005). Neurodevelopmental outcomes of infants born prematurely. *The Journal of Developmental and Behavioral Pediatrics, 26,* 427–440. https://doi.org/10.1097/00004703–200512000–00008

BBC News. (2023, July 28). *I don't have ADHD, but three private clinics say I do* (May 15th). Retrieved from www.bbc.com/news/health-65534449

Ben-Naim, S., Marom, I., Krashin, M., Grifter, B., & Arad, K. (2017). Life with a partner with ADHD: The moderating role of intimacy. *Journal of Child and Family Studies, 26,* 1365–1373. https://doi.org/10.1007/s10826-016-0653-9

Bitter, I., Mohr, P., Balogh, L., Latalova, K., Kakuszi, B., Stopková, P., Zmeškalová-Jelenová, D., Pulay, A., & Czobor, P. (2019). ADHD: A hidden comorbidity in adult psychiatric patients. *ADHD Attention Deficit and Hyperactivity Disorders, 11,* 83–89. https://doi.org/10.1007/s12402-019-00285-9

Bondopadhyay, U., Diaz-Orueta, U., & Coogan, A. (2022). A systematic review of sleep and circadian rhythms in children with attention deficit hyperactivity disorder. *Journal of Attention Disorders, 26*(2), 149–224. https://doi.org/10.1177/10870547209785

Bruner, M.R., Kuryluk, A.D., & Whitton, S.W. (2015). Attention-deficit/hyperactivity disorder symptom levels and romantic relationship quality in college students. *Journal of American College Health, 63*(2), 98–108. https://doi.org/10.1080/07448481.2014.975717

Brunkhorst-Kanaan, N., Libutzki, B., Reif, A., Larsson, H., McNeill, R.V., & Kittel-Schneider, S. (2021). ADHD and accidents over the life span – A systematic review. *Neuroscience & Biobehavioral Reviews, 125,* 582–591. https://doi.org/10.1016/j.neubiorev.2021.02.002

Centers for Disease Control and Prevention. (2023, July 27). *Attention Deficit/ Hyperactivity Disorder (ADHD).* Retrieved from www.cdc.gov/ncbddd/adhd/ facts.html

Centers for Disease Control and Prevention. (2022, July 5). *Other concerns and conditions with ADHD.* Retrieved from www.cdc.gov/ncbddd/adhd/conditions. html

Choi, W.S., Woo, Y.S., Wang, S.M., Lim, H.K., & Bahk, W.M. (2022). The prevalence of psychiatric comorbidities in adult ADHD compared with non-ADHD populations: A systematic literature review. *PLoS One, 17*(11), e0277175. https://doi.org/10.1371/journal.pone.0277175

Currie, G., & Szabo, J. (2020). Social isolation and exclusion: The parents' experience of caring for children with rare neurodevelopmental disorders. *The International Journal of Qualitative Studies on Health and Well-being*, 15. https://doi.org/10.1080/17482631.2020.1725362

Dalsgaard, S., Østergaard, S.D., Leckman, J.F., Mortensen, P.B., & Pedersen, M.G. (2015). Mortality in children, adolescents, and adults with attention deficit hyperactivity disorder: A nationwide cohort study. *Lancet*, 385(9983), 2190. https://doi.org/10.1016/S0140-6736

Diallo, F.B., Pelletier, É., Vasiliadis, H.M., Rochette, L., Vincent, A., Palardy, S., Lunghi, C., Gignac, M., & Lesage, A. (2022). Morbidities and mortality of diagnosed attention deficit hyperactivity disorder (ADHD) over the youth lifespan: A population-based retrospective cohort study. *International Journal of Methods in Psychiatric Research*, 31(1), e1903. https://doi.org/10.1002/mpr.1903

DuPaul, G.J., & Langberg, J.M. (2015). Educational impairments in children with ADHD. In R.A. Barkley (Ed.), *Attention-deficit/hyperactivity disorder: A handbook for diagnosis and treatment* (4th ed., pp. 169–190). New York, NY: Guilford.

Faraone, S., Banaschewski, T., Coghill, D., Zheng, Y., Biederman, J., Bellgrove, M., & Wang, Y. (2021). The world federation of ADHD international consensus statement: 208 Evidence-based conclusions about the disorder. *Neuroscience and Biobehavioral Reviews*, 128, 789–818. https://doi.org/10.1016/j.neubiorev.2021.01.022

García Murillo, L., Ramos-Olazagasti, M.A., Mannuzza, S., Castellanos, F.X., & Klein, R.G. (2016). Childhood Attention-Deficit/Hyperactivity Disorder and homelessness: A 33-year follow-up study. *Journal of the American Academy of Child & Adolescent Psychiatry*, 55(11), 931–936. https://doi.org/10.1016/j.jaac.2016.07.772

Harpin, V., Mazzone, L., Raynaud, J.P., Kahle, J., & Hodgkins, P. (2016). Long-term outcomes of ADHD: A systematic review of self-esteem and social function. *Journal of Attention Disorders*, 20(4), 295–305. https://doi.org/10.1177/1087054713486516

Huynh-Hohnbaum, A.L., & Benowitz, S.M. (2022). Effects of adult ADHD on intimate partnerships. *Journal of Family Social Work*, 25(4–5), 169–184. https://doi.org/10.1080/10522158.2023.2165585

Iz, M., & Çeri, V. (2018). Prevalence of attention deficit hyperactivity disorder symptoms in children who were treated at emergency service due to unintentional injury. *Emergency Medicine International*, 7814910-8. https://doi.org/10.1155/2018/7814910

Kemper, A. (2018). *Attention deficit hyperactivity disorder: Diagnosis and treatment in children and adolescents* (Comparative effectiveness review; Number 203). Rockville (MD): Agency for Healthcare Research and Quality (US).

Kian, N., Samieefar, N., & Rezaei, N. (2022). Prenatal risk factors and genetic causes of ADHD in children. *World Journal of Clinical Pediatrics*, 18, 308–319. https://doi.org/10.1007/s12519-022-00524-6

King, K., Alexander, D., & Seabi, J. (2016). Siblings' perceptions of their ADHD-diagnosed sibling's impact on the family system. *International Journal of Environmental Research and Public Health*, 13(9), 910. https://doi.org/10.3390/ijerph13090910

Larsson, I., Aili, K., Nygren, J., Jarbin, H., & Svedberg, P. (2021). Parents' experiences of weighted blankets' impact on children with attention-deficit/hyperactivity disorder (ADHD) and sleep problems—A qualitative study. *International Journal of Environmental Research and Public Health, 18*(24), 12959. https://doi.org/10.3390/ijerph182412959

Leitner, Y. (2014). The co-occurrence of autism and attention deficit hyperactivity disorder in children: What do we know? *Frontiers in Human Neuroscience, 8,* 1–8. https://doi.org/10.3389/fnhum.2014.00268

Libutzki, B., Neukirch, B., Kittel-Schneider, S., Reif, A., & Hartman, C.A. (2023). Risk of accidents and unintentional injuries in men and women with attention deficit hyperactivity disorder across the adult lifespan. *The Acta Psychiatrica Scandinavica, 147*(2), 145–154. https://doi.org/10.1111/acps.13524

Lougy, R., DeRuvo, S., Rosenthal, D., & Storey, R. (2009). *The school counselor's guide to ADHD: What to know and do to help your students.* Thousand Oaks, CA: Corwin.

Mahon, M.E., & Denckla, M.B. (2017). Attention-deficit/hyperactivity disorder: A historical neuropsychological perspective. *The Journal of the International Neuropsychological Society, 23*(9–10), 916–929. https://doi.org/10.1017/S1355617717000807

Martin, C., Papadopoulos, N., Chellew, T., Rinehart, N., & Sciberras, E. (2019). Associations between parenting stress, parent mental health and child sleep problems for children with ADHD and ASD: Systematic review. *Research in Developmental Disabilities, 93,* 103463. https://doi.org/10.1016/j.ridd.2019.103463

Metzger, A.N., & Hamilton, L.T. (2021). The stigma of ADHD: Teacher ratings of labelled students. *Sociological Perspectives, 64*(2), 258–279. https://doi.org/10.1177/07311214209377

Mullins, L. (2022). *It takes a village: Navigating the journey of parenting your autistic child.* Dublin: Orpen Press.

Muñoz-Silva, A., Lago-Urbano, R., & Sanchez-Garcia, M. (2017). Family impact and parenting styles in families of children with ADHD. *Journal of Child and Family Studies, 26,* 2810–2823. https://doi.org/10.1007/s10826-017-0798-1

Nasol, E., Lindly, O., Chavez, A., & Zuckerman, K. (2019). Unmet need and financial impact disparities for US children with ADHD. *Academic Pediatrics, 19*(3), 315–324. https://doi.org/10.1016/j.acap.2018.09.001

National Institute for Healthcare Excellence. (2019). *Attention deficit hyperactivity disorder: Diagnosis and management.* London: National Institute for Health and Care Excellence (NICE).

NHS. (2021, August 2). *Overview. Attention Deficit Hyperactivity Disorder (ADHD).* Retrieved from www.nhs.uk/conditions/attention-deficit-hyperactivity-disorder-adhd/

Papafragou, A. (2018). Pragmatic development. *Language Learning and Development, 14*(3), 167–169. https://doi.org/10.1080/15475441.2018.1455791

Peasgood, T., Bhardwaj, A., Biggs, K., Brazier, J., Coghill, D., Cooper, C., Daly, D., De Silva, C., Harpin, V., Hodgins, P., Nadkarni, A., Setyawan, J., & Sonuga-Barke, E. (2016). The impact of ADHD on the health and well-being of ADHD children and their siblings. *European Child & Adolescent Psychiatry, 25*(11), 1217–1231. https://doi.org/10.1007/s00787-016-0841-6

Ponnou, S., & Gonon, F. (2017). How French media have portrayed ADHD to the lay public and to social workers. *International Journal of Qualitative Studies on Health and Well-being*, *12*(1). https://doi.org/10.1080/17482631.2017.12 98244

Prasad, V., West, J., Sayal, K., & Kendrick, D. (2018). Injury among children and young people with and without attention-deficit hyperactivity disorder in the community: The risk of fractures, thermal injuries, and poisonings. *Child: Care, Health & Development*, *44*(6), 871–878. https://doi.org/10.1111/cch.12591

Richardson, J.R., Taylor, M.M., Shalat, S.L., Guillot, T.S., III, Caudle, W.M., Hossain, M.M., Mathews, T.A., Jones, S.R., Cory-Slechta, D.A., & Miller, G.W. (2015). Developmental pesticide exposure reproduces features of attention deficit hyperactivity disorder. *The FASEB Journal*, *29*, 1960–1972. https://doi.org/10.1096/fj.14-260901

Sciberras, E., Mulraney, M., Mensah, F., Oberklaid, F., Efron, D., & Hiscock, H. (2020). Sustained impact of a sleep intervention and moderators of treatment outcome for children with ADHD: A randomised controlled trial. *Psychological Medicine*, *50*(2), 210–219. https://doi.org/10.1017/S0033291718004063

Shah, R., Sharma, A., Chauhan, N., & Grover, S. (2021). Parenting experiences of raising a child with Attention-deficit/hyperactivity disorder: A pilot study from India. *Journal of Indian Association for Child and Adolescent Mental Health*, *17*(3), 57–78. https://doi.org/10.1177/097313422021030

Speerforck, S., Stolzenburg, S., Hertel, J., Grabe, H., J., Strauß, M., Carta, M.G., Angermeyer, M.C., & Schomerus, G. (2019). ADHD. Stigma and continuum beliefs: A population survey on public attitudes towards children and adults with attention deficit hyperactivity disorder. *Psychiatry Research*, *282*. https://doi.org/10.1016/j.psychres.2019.112570

Staikova, E., Gomes, H., Tartter, V., McCabe, A., & Halperin, J.M. (2013). Pragmatic deficits and social impairment in children with ADHD. *The Journal of Child Psychology and Psychiatry*, *54*, 1275–1283. https://doi.org/10.1111/jcpp.12082

Thompson, K., Agnew-Blais, J., Allegrini, A., Bryan, B., Danese, A., Odgers, C., & Arseneault, L. (2023). Do children with ADHD symptoms become socially isolated? Longitudinal within-person associations in a nationally-representative cohort. *European Psychiatry*, *66* (S1), S97. https://doi.org/10.1192/j.eurpsy.2023.280

Weibel, S., Menard, O., Ionita, A., Boumendjel, M., Cabelguen, C., Kraemer, C., Micoulaud-Franchi, J.A., Bioulac, S., Perroud, N., Sauvaget, A., Carton, L., Gachet, M., & Lopez, R. (2020). Practical considerations for the evaluation and management of Attention Deficit Hyperactivity Disorder (ADHD) in. adults. *L'Encéphale*, *46*(1), 30–40. https://doi.org/10.1016/j.encep.2019.06.005.

Wymbs, B.T., Pelham, W.E., Jr., Molina, B.S.G., Gnagy, E.M., Wilson, T.K., & Greenhouse, J.B. (2008). Rate and predictors of divorce among parents of youths with ADHD. *Journal of Consulting and Clinical Psychology*, *76*(5), 735–744. https://doi.org/10.1037/a0012719

Chapter 5

Creating Supportive Environments

Abbreviations

ADHD: Attention Deficit Hyperactivity Disorder
APA: American Psychiatric Association
CSDH: The Commission on the Social Determinants of Health
DSM: Diagnostic and Statistical Manual of Mental Disorders
US: United States
WHO: World Health Organisation

Introduction

This chapter will introduce readers to the concept of creating supportive environments, for neurodivergent children and their families. Identified as an action area for health promotion by the World Health Organisation, creating supportive environments relates to a much broader context than just the physical environment or setting within which the child interacts. Supportive environments encapsulate the immediate and systemic multifaceted factors, which culminate to impact the child and their family, in each setting and space, in terms of their capacity to engage and thrive. Mediating the environment to meet the unique needs of the child and their family, is instrumental in promoting inclusion and maximising positive outcomes. Creating supportive environments is concerned with exploring the challenges experienced by the child and their family pertaining to access, participation and opportunities for wellbeing, and altering the environment to reduce such challenges and enhance opportunities. If an environment is not conducive to the needs of their neurodivergent child or their family, change the environment, but never the child or family.

This chapter will begin by exploring health promotion and the emergence of this discipline. The health promotion action area of creating supportive environments will be considered, alongside the social determinants of health and their relevance to practice with neurodivergent children and

DOI: 10.4324/9781003455868-5

their families. This chapter will further develop the idea of creating support-ive environments, concerning its relevance to the lives of neurodivergent children and their families, via practice examples, case studies and reflec-tions. The influence of systemic factors on the family's health and wellbeing will be considered, while strategies of supporting families across settings and sectors in terms of mediating the environment, will be discussed. Finally, this chapter will present specific principles and catalysts which will directly inform practice and empower practitioners in their efforts, towards creating supportive environments for neurodivergent children and their families.

Learning Outcomes

On completion of Chapter 5, learners should demonstrate an enhanced un-derstanding concerning:

- The World Health Organisation action area of creating supportive environments
- The significance of supportive environments for neurodivergent children and families within various settings and spaces
- Tangible and practical strategies of creating supportive environments for neurodivergent children in educational, community and clinical settings
- Approaches to creating supportive environments, based on a socioeco-logical perspective

What Is Health Promotion?

The inherent theme of this book, creating supportive environments, is an action area for health promotion. In order to contextualise what this means, health promotion must first be explored. Health promotion has been de-fined as "the process of enabling people to increase control over, and to improve their health" (WHO, 1986). Viner and Macfarlane (2005) describe health promotion as helping people to make changes which improve their wellbeing. Empowerment is a central concept within the discipline of health promotion and aims to provide people with the information they need and equip them with the skills they require, to take control of their own health and wellbeing (Naidoo & Wills, 2010). Naidoo and Wills (2010) contend that empowerment is concerned with increasing the capacity of individuals and communities, to influence the factors which impact their health.

Health promotion is concerned with supporting children and families to identify their own unique health and wellbeing needs, and empowering them to address these. Upon hearing about health promotion initially, most people think about healthy eating and media campaigns targeting unhealthy behaviours (such as smoking or sedentary lifestyles). Yet health promotion is much broader than this and is concerned with enabling individuals and groups to make decisions for themselves and improve their lives. Ownership is an intrinsic feature of health promotion, within the context of supporting neurodivergent children and families. Health promotion is about supporting families to access the resources they need to improve their family's health and to develop the skills they need to act. Access to information is fundamental within efforts to empower and enable (WHO, 1986). Whether coping with a new diagnosis or responding to new challenges or changes to their child's needs, parents can feel lost and bewildered as they navigate these uncharted territories. Providing access to information (rather than directly providing the information) empowers parents to equip themselves with the knowledge they need to make decisions, concerning the health and wellbeing of their neurodivergent child and family.

Strategies for Health Promotion

The WHO (1986) identified three fundamental strategies for health promotion:

1. *Advocate*: to represent the needs of marginalised individuals and groups, regarding the factors which impact their health (WHO, 1986). Advocacy is not only concerned with being a voice for the voiceless, but also encompasses supporting, empowering and enabling people to find their own voice and have their needs and rights realised. Saan and Wise (2011) suggest that the internet has propelled advocacy capacity, as groups with shared interests can network, mobilise and lobby for change in situ.
2. *Mediate*: collaborate effectively with different disciplines, settings and sectors to enhance access, equity and opportunities for health. The WHO (1986) acknowledge that any single sector alone cannot address the complex and multifaceted dimensions of health. Unique community and cultural considerations, should further be fundamental to informing a variety of settings in health policy, planning, delivery and practice (WHO, 1986).
3. *Enable*: support people to recognise and realise their full health and wellbeing (WHO, 1986). Rather than doing something for someone, enabling them is equipping them with the information, knowledge and skillset they need to do something for themselves. Enablement is largely focused on health literacy and aims to provide education to marginalised groups, which strengthens their position in self-advocacy and working towards having their health needs addressed (Saan & Wise, 2011).

These core strategies for health promotion are the means and methods from which to plan and implement health promotion initiatives and to aim to create supportive environments. Health promotion strategies further equip practitioners and policy makers alike, with a shared understanding of the need to actively promote the power, access and the voice of society's most marginalised communities. Creating supportive environments for neurodivergent children and families can be guided, led and informed by the three fundamental strategies of advocating, mediating and enabling (with and for them) (Saan & Wise, 2011; WHO, 1986; Naidoo & Wills, 2010).

Reflection Point!

Think about your experience in college . . .

What changes could have be implemented to create a more supportive environment for neurodivergent students on your campus? What could be changed in the classroom to create a more supportive environment for neurodivergent students?

Social Determinants of Health

Further relevant to health promotion and consequently the significance of creating supportive environments for neurodivergent children and their families, are the social determinants of health. Marmot and Wilkinson (2006) argue that health exists within a social gradient, with those in higher social classes enjoying greater levels of health and wellbeing. Consistently, people in lower and working-class social backgrounds experience poorer levels of health and wellbeing and greater mortality rates (Marmot & Wilkinson, 2006). Research is now steadfast in asserting that a multitude of social factors, known as social determinants of health, directly impact health and wellbeing (WHO, 2023a; Braveman, Egerter, & Williams, 2011; Navarro, 2009). Social determinants are the non-medical factors which impact health such as education, housing, employment, environment, access to healthcare, community, access to food and sanitation (WHO, 2023a; Braveman et al., 2011). In fact, the WHO (2023a) contend that determinants of health are even more significant to wellbeing and mortality, than lifestyle choices.

This wider understanding and acceptability of the potentially catastrophic impact of the social determinants of health, has been acknowledged by governments in most developed countries and subsequently addressed within policy. For example: the issue of access to medical care in the US and the detrimental impact of such on the health and wellbeing of disadvantaged groups in society, has been addressed within government policies (Donkin, Goldblatt, Allen, Nathanson, & Marmot, 2017). Policy-driven actions such as the Patient Protection and Affordable Care Act (2010) and Healthy

People policy of 2020, acknowledge the substantially negative impact of a tiered access to healthcare on the health, wellbeing and mortality rates of citizens in the US (US Department of Health and Human Services, 2023a, 2023b).

The Commission on the Social Determinants of Health (CSDH, 2008) reports that the economic and societal circumstances which adversely impact people's health, are avoidable. The CSDH (2008) was created by the WHO for the purpose of advising on what specific actions can and should be employed, to increase health equity and close the gap between the haves and the have-nots. Their comprehensive report addresses a broad range of social determinants. The commission proposed that income, education, ethnicity and where people live, should not negatively influence their access to healthcare (CSDH, 2008). Those with the resources to acquire healthcare live, while those without them die from preventable and treatable illnesses (CSDH, 2008). Indeed, the Covid-19 pandemic illustrated such inequity in terms of access to healthcare and mortality. Mortality rates for Covid-19 were four times higher in lower-income countries, when compared to deaths in wealthier nations (Oxfam International, 2022).

The social determinants of health are of fundamental significance to creating supportive environments, for neurodivergent children and their families. Consideration of these non-medical factors which influence this child and their family daily, in every aspect of their lives, should be intrinsic to every conscious effort to create supportive environments. The most effective intervention in the world will not have the desired impact, if a child is suffering because of poverty, is living in an environment which is damaging to their health and wellbeing or if they don't have the tools and resources needed to meet their most basic needs.

Case Study 1

John is a single parent to two children, one of whom, four-year-old Alice, has ADHD. Alice requires consistent attention and care to prevent her from injuring herself or someone else. There have been frequent incidents of Alice unlocking the front door and running into traffic and trying to climb out of upstairs windows. John is unable to work as four childcare facilities to date have been unable to meet Alice's care needs. John is in receipt of social security payments and lives with his ageing parents. John does not have private health insurance since he left his job, and the waiting list for ADHD supports for Alice is three to five years. John is feeling increasingly depressed and overwhelmed. He doesn't sleep well as he feels he needs to be constantly alert should Alice wake during the night.

How are the social determinants of health impacting John? How are the social determinants of health impacting Alice? Consider the unmet needs of this family, compared to a family living in their own home, with steady employment and private health insurance.

Creating Supportive Environments

Creating supportive environments is an action area for health promotion which was initially identified within the first international conference on health promotion, which took place in Ottawa, Canada, in 1986 (WHO, 2023a). The Ottawa Charter for Health Promotion is a guiding cornerstone document, which outlines the key action areas for health promotion (WHO, 2023a). Creating supportive environments describes the irrefutable link between people and their environment and the subsequent impact this has on their health and wellbeing (WHO, 2023b). Work, home, social and community life, and even the society within which people live, impact their health and wellbeing (WHO, 2023b). Health promotion is inherent to creating supportive environments and the underlying aim of empowering people to understand and take control of their own health and wellbeing. Consequently, health promotion should fundamentally inform practice with neurodivergent children and their families, regardless of the setting or sector within which this occurs. Equally as significant to creating supportive environments, is an informed awareness of the social determinants of health and how they have and continue to impact the neurodivergent child and their family.

Author Reflection Point!

A universal component of a supportive environment for neurodivergent children, is one within which the child is included, accepted for who they are and made to feel valued. A supportive environment is one where the child doesn't feel they have to change something about themselves to be accepted. It's an environment which doesn't have prerequisites for entry or norms the child is expected to adhere to. It's a space where the child is just them and that's enough. A supportive environment also affords such acceptance and value to each member of the family, and the values and unique attributes of the family as a whole.

Today at a family birthday party, my son *Alex was given the wifi code and shown a room which was quiet, that he could come to and sit in whenever he wanted. He was shown all around the house, and reassured that he could sit wherever he felt comfortable, but this room was especially for him, if he wanted or needed this space at any time.

This small gesture communicated in a monumental way that:

- Alex's comfort was really important to our family members.
- They acknowledged that the noisy, busy environment might be challenging for Alex and subsequently the rest of our family.
- They gave Alex options, didn't pressure him or make him feel he should do X, Y or Z.

The outcome was that we stayed longer at this event than we ever have. Alex sat in the quiet room for an hour, then sat with us happily for two more hours. He had three helpings of food and even asked for more himself, without prompting. This was unprecedented and a true testament to the positive impact of an environment which feels supportive to a neurodivergent child.

Creating supportive environments is concerned with enhancing the extent to which environments are conducive to the individual's needs. It's about mediating or altering an environment (either physical or social/ societal) to communicate an acknowledgement and acceptance of the neurodivergent child as they present. This means the child does not or their family do not need to change, to fit or conform within the environment. The environment will be such that the child is accepted just as they are, and their unique needs and how they present are valued and catered for. Creating supportive environments for people with mobility issues or wheelchair users often means installing ramps, making buildings and spaces accessible. This same concept is applied to the environments within which neurodivergent children and their families interact. How can we make this more accessible, more inclusive and accepting of the neurodivergent child's needs?

For example: neurodivergent children and their school experiences, vary substantially from one child to the next. An environment which is not conducive to the child's needs, will impede them in their functioning and attainment of their goals (socially, educationally and in terms of coping capacity and executive function). A classroom where teachers change frequently or one where the structure and routine of lessons is inconsistent, would not present a supportive environment for some autistic children. In contrast, a classroom environment with a consistent schedule, consistent staffing and a clear understanding of what to expect communicated consistently to the child, would be considered a much more supportive environment.

Creating supportive environments is as much about attitudes, knowledge and collective understanding, as the physical environments within which people engage. Specific research exploring community-based initiatives during the Covid-19 pandemic, found that targeting hard-to-reach groups such as migrants and older people was effective, via media messages (Fransen, Peralta, Vanelli, Edelenbos, & Calzada Olvera, 2022). Fransen et al. (2022) surmise that upon identifying a vulnerable group, community initiatives garnered financial and practical support via existing and community networks. Imagine if we had such shared understanding, mass media campaigns to promote collective action and a sense of collective urgency, in supporting, engaging and creating supportive environments for neurodivergent children and families?

Yet some neurodivergent children have unique needs, perhaps not experienced by their peers, for example in terms of sensitivity to noise. In an overly noisy classroom, it may be challenging to reduce the overall classroom volume of 22 kindergarten children. Yet supporting the neurodivergent child to use noise-cancelling headphones, could make this environment a more supportive one. Hence, momentous changes are not always necessary to alter an environment to one which is more supportive. However, creating a classroom environment which is inclusive and accepting of the child wearing the noise-cancelling headphones, is a significant demonstration that this is a supportive setting. A practitioner who continually reflects upon the environment and the impact this has on the neurodivergent child and family, can bring about the changes needed to create and maintain an environment which is more conducive to the child's needs.

Reflection Point!

Think about your place of work or future workplace.

What actions could be easily implemented to create more supportive environments, for neurodivergent children and their families within this setting?

What training or knowledge translational activities could be undertaken with the staff team, to create a more supportive environment?

How could your interactions with families be modified to create a more supportive environment?

The Home as a Supportive Environment

Neurodivergent children can struggle to cope across settings such as at home, in school, within public settings and new settings. However, as parents adjust to their child's unique needs, the home environment often becomes one within which the child feels less overwhelmed. Some parents have altered and adapted their home environment to one which is conducive to their child's distinctive needs. This active effort to change the environment relates to not only the physical environment of the home, but also the attitudes, understanding and expectations within the home and the family dynamics.

For example: a supportive environment in the home for a dyspraxic child, is one where their family members are fully aware of the child's condition and how this impacts them. Parents and siblings adjust expectations, break instructions into individual steps, offer practical assistance where needed, have more patience with the child and acknowledge that it may take them more time to complete tasks.

A supportive home environment for an autistic child could be concerned with reducing sensory overload and pressure to engage socially. This may include closing blinds, having adjustable lighting, choices of food which the child likes, quiet areas and clothing, bedding and furnishings which don't cause sensory distress. This supportive environment would not place expectations on the child to engage socially, would support them to have time and space alone and would give the child choice and autonomy regarding engaging with other people outside of the home (when people visit, etc.).

A supportive home environment for a child with ADHD could have sensory equipment to enable the child to move, rock and spin. This supportive home environment would mean that family members' expectations in terms of behaviour are adjusted to meet the child's unique needs, regular breaks are encouraged when doing homework or longer tasks, emotional support and encouragement are offered when completing tasks and times of low or no pressure are maintained. A supportive environment for a child with ADHD may further mean adjusted rules and expectations concerning behaviour, compared to neurotypical siblings or peers (Mullins, 2022).

Creating Supportive Environments in the Clinical/Medical Context

Knowledge and understanding concerning neurodivergence is further relevant to creating and maintaining supportive environments. I can often tell within the first few minutes of interacting with a medical professional, whether or not they have specific training on autism, ADHD or dyspraxia. This awareness and insight, or lack thereof, impacts the remainder of this interaction and every subsequent interaction. It's not possible for a practitioner to create a supportive environment for a child, if they don't have the level of knowledge and understanding needed to begin to assess and comprehend the child's unique needs.

Reflection Point!

If you visit a medical setting/emergency room, what makes this a supportive environment (or not)? What impacts your experience in this setting?

Is it the physical environment, i.e. the waiting room chairs, amount of space, proximity of access to the restroom, charging point, etc.?

Or is your experience weighted more on your interactions with staff? Or how you FEEL when you are being treated?

Or is it staff understanding and insight regarding your condition, which impacts your experience in this setting?

Practitioners actively work to impact the environments within which the neurodivergent child spends their time and modify these spaces, to where the child feels included, valued, accepted, supported and cared for. A supportive environment for a neurodivergent child is one which is tailored to their unique needs, promotes their development, happiness and wellbeing and is conducive to enabling them to reach their goals. The environment should be accepting of the child as they are (and not focused on changing them), should be continually modified as needed to support developing, new and emerging needs and should be focused on encouraging belonging.

A supportive environment for parents/caregivers of a neurodivergent child is one within which parents feel empowered and included in decisions about their child's care and treatment, a space where their family's values and preferences are respected and an environment where the family's unique challenges and strengths are acknowledged. A supportive environment for parents is one which facilitates their child's development, is non-judgemental and where their family feels a sense of belonging and comfort. Supportive environments for parents offer hope during the darkest times and present ideas, solutions and the resources they need to help themselves and their child. Medical settings are more frequently utilised by neurodivergent children and their families, compared to neurotypical children. Clinic and hospital settings are often where children are assessed, diagnosed and treated for issues, illnesses, accidents and therapies associated with their neurodivergence and the challenges presented by this. Consequently, critically considering the extent to which this environment is conducive to the needs of neurodivergent children and their families is pertinent.

Creating Supportive Environments in Education Settings

Within a school/college setting, creating supportive environments should be concerned equally with increasing awareness, challenging stereotypes and fostering a culture of inclusion. By educating the whole school community about neurodivergence, only then can a sense of inclusion and belonging be created and maintained.

On a practical level, a supportive environment in the school/college setting should provide a space for the child to be alone (if they so wish, and never as a consequence or response to challenging behaviour). The sheer size of the education setting, the volume of people and expectations placed on the neurodivergent child, can make school a daunting experience. Creating a quiet space communicates to all children that you value them as individuals and wish to meet their unique needs.

Previous research has identified the impact of the immediate environment on the coping, distress and behaviour of neurodivergent children in the classroom (Conroy, Asmus, Boyd, Ladwig, & Sellers, 2007). Conroy et al. (2007) found that the proximity of adults and group work, versus independent work tasks, directly influences disruptive behaviour in the classroom for autistic children. Although this was a small-scale study of just five autistic children, the observational methodology is an insightful approach from which to gauge the actions of participants (Conroy et al., 2007). Building upon this approach, Reszka, Odom, and Hume (2012) conducted observational research in a preschool with 68 autistic children across 24 classrooms. They argue that the immediate classroom space/environment has a direct influence on the social engagement of autistic children, with engagement increasing in classroom areas such as the book and snack area (Reszka et al., 2012). Reszka et al. (2012) further report that such interactions and social engagement increased in both areas when child-initiated behaviour or activities were occurring, as opposed to the adult-directed interactions.

Author Reflection Point!

The most supportive environments my family have experienced are those which recognise the needs of neurodivergent children and their families, and aim to meet these. A family day at an autism-specific voluntary agency meant that no one stared when a child screamed or threw something, children didn't need to stay in a seat and the culture of understanding was almost tangible in the air. No background, explanation or context was needed, because this culture accepted and celebrated each child and their uniqueness. This example highlights the significance of educating the wider society and actively fostering a culture of acceptance and inclusion.

To truly promote and create supportive environments for neurodivergent children in education settings, we must start with providing education to everyone within that setting. The school ethos is a crucial influential factor in imparting true inclusion and a welcoming space of belonging for neurodivergent children. Some students only know what they've heard in the media about autism, ADHD and dyspraxia, and this may impact how they view and treat neurodivergent people, even if this is subconsciously.

Reflection Point!

Think about general societal understanding of ADHD in the US . . .

How does this understanding or level of awareness impact a child in the school setting? Now compare the societal understanding of ADHD in Nigeria, where research on ADHD is almost non-existent. How might this lack of research and subsequent understanding of ADHD in Nigeria, impact a child living with ADHD within a school setting there? (Chinawa et al., 2014).

A Socioecological Perspective on Creating Supportive Environments

A socioecological model acknowledges and appreciates the impact of the environment on the person and the person on the environment. Bronfenbrenner (1979) contends that to truly understand the needs of a child, the context within which they live, learn, interact and work, must be considered. The Ecological Systems Theory of Human Development recognises the momentous impact of the multiple systems the child interacts within, everyday (Bronfenbrenner, 1979). Bronfenbrenner and Cole (1981) describe ecological systems as like a set of nests, each existing within another, much like a set of Russian dolls. The five systems within Bronfenbrenner's Ecological Systems Theory (1979) are:

Microsystem: this is the immediate level within which the child exists and interacts, usually within the home.

Mesosystem: relates to connections between the micro system of the home and family and the outside world. For example: interactions with schools, medical settings, community support services.

Macrosystem: refers to the wider societal ideas and culture and how these impact the child.

Exosystem: is concerned with broader influences on the child's life and factors which influence them, without direct interaction. Examples might include: parents' jobs, parents' friends and mass media.

Chronosystem: this refers to time and the changes the passage of time present for the child (Bronfenbrenner & Cole, 1981). This could include societal understanding of neurodivergence over time and how this is reflected within policy and awareness.

Ecological systems present practitioners with a lens from which to view the needs of the neurodivergent child and their family. Such a lens can inform practice and help to guide the planning and policy, which can impact the neurodivergent child within each system. For example: the macrosystem can be changed or mediated, with increased understanding and awareness about neurodiversity and how specific conditions or variations of neurotype affects the child. The exosystem may be mediated in terms of employment leave or flexible working conditions for parents, which would enable them to maintain employment, while simultaneously meeting their child's care needs.

Each system the child exists and interacts within, offers opportunities or constraints in terms of child development and wellbeing (Eamon, 2001). Hence, practice which aims to influence or change any one system, to one which is more conducive to the child's unique needs, is a positive intervention for the child and their family. Examples of impacting systems may include:

- A neurodivergent child changing schools to one which is more conducive to their needs.
- Offering parent support and education in an effort to empower them to meet their child's needs within the microsystem.
- Creating public policy which supports the healthcare access needs of neurodivergent children, such as assessment, diagnosis, family support and speech, physio and occupational therapies.

Fundamental Principles of Creating Supportive Environments for Neurodivergent Children and Their Families

In the milieu of the current title, the idea of creating supportive environments is reimagined and fashioned, and applied to the context of practice with neurodivergent children and their families. To contextualise this further, the environment refers to each and every interactional space, which directly or indirectly impacts the child and their family. The environment may be the classroom or clinic setting, or could refer to the communication space online, via post or phone contact, between the practitioner and family. The environment extends to the society and community within which the child and family live, the determinants of health and the individual family dynamics. Supportive environments are not always tangible physical environments, yet will profoundly impact the child and family and subsequently influence their capacity to engage with support services and outcomes for their child. Supportive environments are crafted and maintained via enhancing awareness, understanding and acceptance. How can practitioners change ways of working, alter spaces and amend policies, to decrease barriers and enhance opportunities for children and families? How can access be improved or altered to meet the unique needs of their neurodivergent child and their family?

The six key guiding principles of creating supportive environments for neurodivergent children and families, can assist practitioners in successfully conceptualising this idea and working towards implementing this in practice:

1. *Knowledge and awareness.* Practitioners should have autism, ADHD or dyspraxia-specific training or education, in order to practice effectively with neurodivergent children and their families. Creating supportive environments can only be employed effectively, when the practitioner approaches the child's needs from an informed perspective and based upon the most up-to-date knowledge, research and insights available concerning neurodivergence. Knowledge and awareness is further significant concerning the social determinants of health and the influence of systemic factors, and the extent to which these may be impacting this child and their family.
2. *The power of each interaction.* Every single interaction with the child and their family is fundamental in the process of creating a supportive environment. Whether in writing, electronically, via phone call or in person, each interaction sets the tone for your relationship with this family and subsequent positive outcomes for their child. Each interaction communicates (intentionally or unintentionally) your views, awareness and understanding concerning neurodivergence and shapes the environment within which the child and family interact with you and the service you practice within.
3. *Partnership with parents/caregivers.* This is perhaps the most potent criterion for creating supportive environments for neurodivergent children and families. A strong partnership between practitioners and parents establishes a relationship of trust in which parents feel supported, valued and active participants in their child's journey through education, support and healthcare services. Successful partnerships fuse the insights and expertise of both parents and practitioners, for the purpose of maximising positive outcomes for the neurodivergent child. A supportive environment is one which inherently values the relationship with parents/caregivers and recognises how instrumental this is for the child.
4. *Every neurodivergent child is unique.* No two neurodivergent children will present with the same needs; consequently, there is no standard or one-size-fits-all approach for meeting their needs. The practitioner's role

is underpinned by a determination to establish who this child is and what their distinctive needs, wishes, challenges and hopes are, and devising a practice response which meets these unique attributes. This principle is primarily concerned with meeting the child and their family where they are at.

5. *Supporting parents is supporting children.* Any support provided to parents has the potential to positively impact their children. Practice responses aimed at empowering or assisting parents or improving their health and wellbeing, will enable them to better support their children. Parental awareness, education, access to information and advocacy, increases their capacity to support, enable and empower their neurodivergent child. Investing in parental support and empowerment, lays the foundation for parents to be more confident and informed in their care of their child and family.

6. *Reflective practice.* Creating supportive environments for neurodivergent children and their families, is strongly underpinned by reflective practice. This principle requires practitioners to continually reflect upon and critically review their own practice for effectiveness. Reflective practice evokes the questioning of methods, interactions, appropriateness and continued rationale for practice. Practitioners are prompted to question their own practice consistently, to measure the extent to which this aligns with a creating supportive environments approach and supporting neurodivergent children and families.

Author Reflection Point!

An unsupportive environment for neurodivergent children and families, is one which doesn't attempt to understand or meet their individual needs. As one of my children is dyspraxic (and autistic), we've had quite a few ER visits over the years due to accidents/falls.

One in particular stays with me, for all the wrong reasons. *Lola fell outside and I was concerned she had broken her arm (although she said she was fine). We sat in a waiting room for five hours, a small waiting room with lots of sick children. A doctor walked in and called Lola's name. In the tiny, overcrowded waiting room, she took Lola's hand and tried to straighten her arm. . . . Lola screamed in pain and ran to a corner and began rocking and stimming. I was absolutely horrified. So many things were wrong with this environment.

- The doctor should have introduced themselves and explained why they were there (to both Lola and me as her parent).
- They should have asked Lola's permission to examine her.

- They should have explained exactly what they were going to do.
- They should have done all of this in another room! Space in hospitals globally is notoriously challenging. Yet any space, even a corridor with less people and some additional privacy, would have been more appropriate than a crowded, tiny waiting room, to examine an autistic child with a potential broken bone.

Thankfully after this really horrific experience, after we had x-ray results which confirmed two fractures in Lola's arm, we met the most amazing nurse practitioner, who applied Lola's cast. I was dreading this and thought it would be a disaster (and Lola was on edge and very upset). Yet this medical professional was in a league of their own in terms of how they approached and delivered Lola's care. They gave me a knowing wink as I was trying to coax Lola, and I instantly knew that they knew what they were doing. I stepped back (metaphorically) and they theatrically, yet intentionally captivated Lola completely with their interaction! The nurse practitioner explained exactly what she was about to do and asked Lola before each step, if this was okay. Lola was mesmerised, smiling, even laughing. Before we knew it, the casting was done and Lola was beaming with pride as the nurse heaped praise on her and recapped on their conversation and funny stories.

These are two experiences within the same healthcare setting environment. Yet the environment each professional created within their interaction and understanding of Lola's needs, contrasted entirely. One was a very unsupportive environment where Lola felt overwhelmed, frightened, that she had no control and which left a lasting negative impact. The second was a supportive environment where Lola felt safe, cared for and comfortable. The only difference in these experiences was the attitude, knowledge, expertise and understanding, of the practitioner delivering the care.

Catalysts for Creating Supportive Environments

Creating supportive environments can be an internal process you as a practitioner engage with and a conscious practice effort to generate change. Changing attitudes and enhancing understanding can create supportive environments. The practitioner's knowledge and awareness are instrumental within this process. Three key catalysts within the successful recipe for creating supportive environments for neurodivergent children and their families, are acknowledgement, access and acceptance:

1. *Acknowledgement*: within the setting, sector or metaphorical space, first and foremost, acknowledging the challenges, barriers and unique needs

of neurodivergent child based on their diagnosis/diagnoses, is essential. Only when such acknowledgment exists can actions to create a supportive environment be effective. For example: when an autistic child is visiting the dentist, this can be an extremely traumatic and distressing experience. Dental staff having an understanding of autism, how this impacts the child, how to engage most effectively and using approaches which prompt the least amount of distress for the child, will communicate a supportive environment. It is usually evident very quickly when a practitioner has an understanding of autism or not, and this irrefutably influences the experiences of the child and their family within a setting, service or space.

2. *Access*: practitioners should provide access to all of the information the child and family will need, to navigate the environment and maximise positive outcomes. Access to the tools and resources they need to engage, access to ongoing and continued support and guidance and access to navigation systems are essential. Access should be tailored to the unique needs of the family in terms of literacy, internet access or a preference for face-to-face information sharing.

   • For example: when a neurodivergent child is transitioning from middle school to high school, they (along with their parents) should be furnished with all of the information they need to know about the transition, the setting, the supports, the potential challenges and how these will be addressed, information on where to go when something goes wrong, where the child can seek support during the school day, specific supports and resources for neurodivergent children and information about key points of contact and where additional and further information can be sought (e.g. board of management, area special needs coordination, codes for behaviour, home-school liaison, board of education, specialised services, funding applications, info on the Individual Education Program (IEP), etc.).

3. *Acceptance*: is concerned with valuing, appreciating and welcoming the child and family where they are at and meeting them there. Acceptance within practice is manifested within non-judgemental, open and honest communication and interactions with families. Practitioners should create an environment which welcomes the family's unique attributes and needs, and truly values their background and story as a significant factor, relevant to planning and implementing a practice response to their needs. Acceptance affirms the child's identity and communicates appreciation for who they are and aims to promote a positive sense of self-identity and understanding about themselves. Acceptance is about accommodating the family's distinctive needs,

appreciating the impact of the social determinants of health on the family and valuing the family as they are, when presenting for services.

Practical Considerations for Creating Supporting Environments

Concerning access and engagement with support services, practical issues and considerations can have a particularly profound impact on neurodivergent children and their families. Families often have no input/control over issues such as when and where a therapy session or meeting will occur. Yet in the context of access prior to, during and after the physical meeting with child and families, considering practical implications can culminate in creating and maintaining a truly supportive environment.

Think about enhancing access and creating a supportive environment, in terms of the time of day and day of the week you meet with children and families. A 9 am Monday morning appointment may be challenging for parents who have other children to drop off at school, or indeed as this appointment time would mean their child doesn't take their usual route to school/maintain their morning routine. A mid-week or Friday appointment gives families enough time to adjust to the school week routine and prepare their child for their upcoming appointment. This isn't always feasible in practice, yet where possible, ask families which days and times are most conducive to their needs. If parents are struggling with their own wellbeing or are themselves neurodivergent, the timing of their meeting will be crucial to creating a supportive environment, which both acknowledges and aims to address their needs.

Creating supportive environments in practice with families of neurodivergent children, is further informed by the venue of where you meet, assess and offer support. Is the clinic, hospital or school setting the only place where you can meet with children and families? Could you meet them at their home? Or could you access space in a community setting which is closer to where the family live? Or does this family have a preference about where to meet? Organisational culture may dictate where interactions with families must occur. Yet perhaps no one has suggested meeting a parent and child at the local park before? Or whether or not the child's school could offer a meeting room? Do the parents, caregivers and child prefer meeting in person? Or would an online meeting be more preferential to them? Would the child prefer to communicate via email rather than meet with you in person? And how far away from your workplace does this family live? If it's an hour drive, or multiple buses and trains, perhaps meeting in person every single time is causing more distress than is beneficial for this family. The availability of public transport and the childcare of other children, will further impact the environment for this family, surrounding a meeting with the practitioner.

> **Reflection Point!**
>
> But what about the organisation where you work? What if in-person, face-to-face meetings at the care centre or school is "the way we've always done things" or the status quo? This should never be the reason we keep things the same, especially if this status quo is not as family friendly as possible. If we don't ask, then the answer is always no! Be that change, create the ripples that will create truly supportive environments for neurodivergent children and families, break the mould!

Assessments

Assessments for autism, ADHD and dyspraxia are based on specific criteria as outlined in the DSM-5 (American Psychiatric Association, 2013). Yet are the assessment methodologies conducive to the needs of neurodivergent children and their families? If a parent is expected to attend a two-hour meeting to answer questions about their child's needs and development, but are in fact neurodivergent themselves, this challenge may feel insurmountable. Or if a child is observed in one setting only, which presents just a very brief snapshot of their needs, a comprehensive and holistic summary of their needs may not be gauged. Parents who are struggling financially, or who live one hour away from the assessment venue, may not be in a position to meet in person frequently, or could struggle with getting time off work. Where possible, observe the child in more than one setting, break long parental assessment meetings into shorter meetings, some face to face, some online or over the phone. And ask children and families what their preferences are, what barriers they may face in attending appointments and engaging with the assessment process. Then aim to identify solutions, based on these individual needs and challenges.

Are there grants available from local welfare offices or family services? Is there a budget for exceptional needs available within your organisation? Or does a local charitable organisation have funds available you could support this family to apply for? Would a letter for a parent's employer help them to take time off for assessments? Again, just because this hasn't been done before, that doesn't mean it shouldn't be. Advocating for the exceptional needs of each family who present for support, is actively aiming to influence the culture of both disability support services and the organisational culture within which you are employed. Even unsuccessful advocacy communicates a will to help, support and create equity in access for neurodivergent children and families.

Self-Assessment

What are the social determinants of health?

What is the role of the practitioner in creating supportive environments?

What are the fundamental principles of creating supportive environments for neurodivergent children and their families?

Summary

This chapter has introduced the concept of creating supportive environments and explored the significance of the social determinants of health, to supporting neurodivergent children and their families. This cornerstone chapter will enable the reader to reflect, review and reconsider their practice, in the context of creating more inclusive and accessible spaces for neurodivergent children. The aim of creating supportive environments for neurodivergent children and their families, is to alter and improve the environments within which they live and interact, to be more conducive and accessible to their unique needs. Environments where neurodivergent children and families feel included, valued and comfortable, are spaces which meet their needs and value their diversity. Creating supportive environments is equally concerned with awareness, understanding and influencing the societal environment and systemic factors, which impact the child and their family.

This chapter introduced six key principles for creating supportive environments for neurodivergent children and their families, which can empower practitioners to modify their practice with a conscious focus on creating supportive environments. The catalysts for creating supportive environments for neurodivergent children and families are acknowledgement, access and acceptance. These catalysts further inform practice and prompt practitioners to intentionally critically consider the environment, place or metaphorical space, and how this could be made more supportive.

References

American Psychiatric Association. (2013). *Diagnostic and statistical manual of mental disorders: DSM-5*. Washington, DC: American Psychiatric Association.

Braveman, P., Egerter, E., & Williams, D.R. (2011). The social determinants of health: Coming of age. *Annual Review of Public Health, 32*(1), 381–398. https://doi.org/10.1146/annurev-publhealth-031210-101218

Bronfenbrenner, U. (1979). Contexts of child rearing: Problems and prospects. *American Psychologist, 34*(10), 844–850. https://doi.org/10.1037/0003-066X.34.10.844

Bronfenbrenner, U., & Cole, M. (1981). *The ecology of human development*. London: Harvard University Press.

Chinawa, J.M., Odetunde, O.I., Obu, H.A., Chinawa, A.T., Bakare, M.O., & Ujunwa, F.A. (2014). Attention deficit hyperactivity disorder: A neglected issue in the developing world. *Behavioural Neurology*, 694764. https://doi.org/10.1155/2014/694764

Commission on the Social Determinants of Health. (2008). *Closing the gap in a generation: Health equity through action on the social determinants of health. Final report of the Commission on Social Determinants of Health*. Geneva: World Health Organisation.

Conroy, M.A., Asmus, J.M., Boyd, B.A., Ladwig, C.N., & Sellers, J.A. (2007). Antecedent classroom factors and disruptive behaviors of children with autism spectrum disorders. *Journal of Early Intervention*, 30(1), 19–35. https://doi.org/10.1177/105381510703000103

Donkin, A., Goldblatt, P., Allen, J., & Nathanson, V., & Marmot, M. (2017). Global action on the social determinants of health. *BMJ Glob Health*, 3, e000603. https://doi.org/10.1136/ bmjgh-2017–000603

Eamon, M. (2001). The effects of poverty on children's socioemotional development: An ecological systems analysis. *Social Work (New York)*, 46(3), 256–266. https://doi.org/10.1093/sw/46.3.256

Fransen, J., Peralta, D.O., Vanelli, F., Edelenbos, J., & Calzada Olvera, B. (2022). The emergence of urban community resilience initiatives during the COVID-19 pandemic: An international exploratory study. *The European Journal of Development Research*, 34, 432–454. https://doi.org/10.1057/s41287-020-00348-y

Marmot, M., & Wilkinson, R. (2006). *Social determinants of health* (2nd ed.). Oxford: Oxford University Press.

Mullins, L. (2022). *It takes a Village. Navigating the journey of parenting your autistic child*. Dublin: Orpen Press.

Naidoo, J., & Wills, J. (2010). *Developing practice for public health and health promotion* (3rd ed., Public Health and Health Promotion). St. Louis: Elsevier Health Sciences.

Navarro, V. (2009). What we mean by social determinants of health. *International Journal of Health Services*, 39(3), 423–441. https://doi.org/10.2190/HS.39.3

Oxfam International. (2022, May 25). *Covid 19 death toll four times higher in lower-income countries than rich ones*. Retrieved from www.oxfam.org/en/press-releases/covid-19-death-toll-four-times-higher-lower-income-countries-rich-ones

Reszka, S.S., Odom, S.L., & Hume, K.A. (2012). Ecological features of preschools and the social engagement of children with autism. *Journal of Early Intervention*, 34(1), 40–56. https://doi.org/10.1177/1053815112452596

Saan, H., & Wise, M. (2011). Enable, mediate, advocate. *Health Promotion International*, 26(2), 187–193. https://doi.org/10.1093/heapro/dar069

US Department of Health and Human Services. (2023a, August 9). *About the affordable care act*. Retrieved from www.hhs.gov/healthcare/about-the-aca/index.html

US Department of Health and Human Services. (2023b, August 7). *Healthy people*. Retrieved from https://health.gov/our-work/national-health-initiatives/healthy-people

Viner, R., & Macfarlane, A. (2005). Health promotion. *BMJ, 330*(7490), 527–529. https://doi.org/10.1136/bmj.330.7490.527

World Health Organisation. (1986, May 25). *The Ottawa charter for health promotion.* Retrieved from www.who.int/healthpromotion/conferences/previous/ottawa/en/

World Health Organisation. (2023a, May 21). *Health promotion.* Retrieved from www.who.int/teams/health-promotion/enhanced-well-being/first-global-conference/actions

World Health Organisation. (2023b, May 25). *Social determinants of health.* Retrieved from www.who.int/teams/health-promotion/enhanced-well-being/first-global-conference

Chapter 6

Communication in the Context of Creating Supportive Environments

Abbreviations

AAC: Augmentative and Assistive Communication
ADHD: Attention Deficit Hyperactivity Disorder
APA: American Psychiatric Association
ASHA: American Speech-Language-Hearing Association
ASTDR: Agency for Toxic Substance and Disease Registry
DSM: Diagnostic and Statistical Manual of Mental Disorders
HSE: Health Service Executive
NHS: National Health Service
PLAIN: Plain Language Action and Information Network

Introduction

Successful and appropriate communication with neurodivergent children and their families is a vital prerequisite for successful outcomes, whether in a clinic, education setting, or within a community space. Effective communication directly contributes to creating supportive environments, where children and families have their needs identified clearly and feel a sense of belonging. Using plain language and adopting the preferred means of communication of the neurodivergent child and their family, are key facets of appropriate communication methods, when working with this group. Equally, literacy issues may impede communication for some parents, hence varied, inclusive and open methods of information gathering and sharing, are essential to identify and appropriately meet their needs.

This chapter will explore, using case studies and practice examples, appropriate methods of communicating successfully with neurodivergent children and their parents/caregivers. The unique communication needs of the neurodivergent child will be explored and methods of identifying suitable communication strategies will be examined. Common pitfalls which occur due to ineffective communication will be discussed.

DOI: 10.4324/9781003455868-6

It is important to note from the outset, that a full book in its own right could be wholly dedicated to the topic of communication with neurodivergent children and families. Furthermore, each child and family will present completely uniquely, and their communication needs will be as individual as they are. This chapter will provide an overview of ways to enhance communication with neurodivergent children and their families, with the specific aim of creating supportive environments.

Learning Outcomes

On completion of Chapter 6, learners should demonstrate an enhanced understanding concerning:

- The unique communication needs of neurodivergent children
- The relevance of effective communication and creating supportive environments
- Active listening
- The significance of direct and transparent communication
- Strategies for effective communication with neurodivergent children and their families

Unique Communication Needs of Neurodivergent Children

There is no definitive or prescriptive "how to" regarding communicating with neurodivergent children and their families. Each child, their unique circumstances and their family's values, preferences and wishes, will influence the communication methods and approaches which should be employed. An informed and planned approach to communication can often increase its efficacy and reduce the potential distress for the neurodivergent child and their family. Yet communication should always be choice based for the child and never forced upon them. If a child does not wish to communicate with you, this is their right and should be respected. Ultimately, investing sufficient time to enable the neurodivergent child and their family an opportunity to become more familiar with and comfortable with you, is crucial to identifying the communication methods which are most conducive to their unique needs. The following are some autism, ADHD and dyspraxia-specific methods of enhancing communication, with neurodivergent children and families.

Autism and Communication

Each autistic child (or an autistic parent) will have completely distinctive and individual communication needs. Establishing their communication needs and preferences from the outset, will promote successful communication and subsequently more positive outcomes regarding their goals. Some children may not communicate verbally (although they may or may not communicate verbally in other settings) and may wish to be supported to use Augmentative and Alternative Communication methods (AAC, discussed later in this chapter in more detail).

Some autistic children communicate verbally, but may struggle with social situations, new people and new settings. Some autistic children do not communicate verbally and may be supported to have their voice heard, via their parents/caregivers advocating on their behalf. Yet a child who does not communicate verbally, or who is unable at the time of the interaction to express their thoughts and preferences, should be empowered to have their views heard.

Knowledge and understanding concerning autism and the communication and social challenges unique to autistic children, will enable practitioners to understand the nuances and intricacies of their communication needs. For example: an autistic child teetering on a meltdown or experiencing severe anxiety may not be able to communicate as they would, if they were presenting without these additional challenges/stressors. The capacity of an autistic child to communicate may vary from day to day or even hour to hour, based on the challenges within their environment. The transit to their appointment or the bus to school that morning may have presented acute distress for the child and may impact their capacity to communicate. This distress can be residual and affect the child long after the distressing experience occurred.

Communicating with the child and family prior to meeting to gather relevant recent information which may impact communication, can further aid the effectiveness of communicative efforts. Has the child had a difficult week in school? Or are they unwell? Have they had a few nights of sleeplessness in a row, which is uncharacteristic? Such background information can help the educator/practitioner to predetermine factors which may influence the child's communication capacity at a specific point in time. If the autistic child is having a difficult week or is experiencing distress, it's best to postpone and reschedule their meeting or appointment (if they and their parents are in agreement), in order to reduce the likelihood of creating additional pressure and stress, and maximise the child's capacity to communicate their needs.

Autistic children may struggle to understand and interpret non-verbal cues such as sarcasm or disinterest (National Institute on Deafness and Other Communication Disorders, 2020). Some autistic children may avoid eye contact and feel uncomfortable when communicating with someone looking directly at them. Autism may impact the child's communication concerning their tone and affect, and can mean that the child repeats phrases over and over. Echolalia occurs when the child repeats words or phrases they have heard, at a different time and context, which may not make sense to other people (Neely, Gerow, Rispoli, Lang, & Pullen, 2016). Echolalia can further lead to stigmatisation of autistic children, as other children often do not understand why this is happening. Autistic children may have challenges with turn taking in conversations and understanding what other people are communicating to them. While some autistic children may have verbal language capacity, this could be substantially below that of their peers of the same age (National Institute on Deafness and Other Communication Disorders, 2020).

Practical considerations when communicating with an autistic child and their family should consider the preferences of the child regarding the setting, means of communication and the physical environment, within which the communication occurs. For example: would the child prefer to communicate with or without face-to-face interaction? Could you meet with the child and go for a walk? Would they prefer to turn their chair away and avoid eye contact? Or could you communicate successfully via email, text or by writing a letter? (Mullins, 2022). What appears like a natural or typical communication opportunity, such as meeting face to face, is based on a neurotypical lens. What feels natural or more comfortable for an autistic child, is the most important issue in promoting successful communication and creating a supportive environment for them.

Reflection Point!

Given the hereditary component of neurodivergence, it is likely that some of the parents of neurodivergent children you are communicating with, are themselves neurodivergent, which will shape their own communication needs.

This issue is discussed in more detail within Chapter 10, Parental wellbeing.

Muskat et al. (2015) report that autistic children as patients in a hospital setting, are often vulnerable and a poorly understood group. Muskat et al. (2015) emphasises the significance of identifying the child's unique needs (often via consultation with parents) and recognising the high-stress situation presented within medical settings, for some autistic children. Muskat et al. (2015) recommends training for staff specific to autism and communication and in particular regarding sensory sensitivity, need for sameness and undertaking sufficient information gathering, prior to meeting with the child. Pratt, Baird, and Gringras (2012) concur and report that pre-admission information seeking and collaboration with parents of autistic children, substantially reduces the child's distress upon admission. Such findings accentuate the importance of gathering background information to aid communication with the autistic child and actively aim to create an environment that is conducive to their distinctive communication needs.

ADHD and Communication

Children with ADHD (or a parent with ADHD) may find the volume of information communicated to them overwhelming. They may further find it difficult to identify and retain the most important messages being communicated. Practitioners should approach communication with a child living with ADHD (and/or their parent/s) by first assessing the person's communication needs, based on the specific symptomatology associated with this condition. The best way to establish the most effective methods of enhancing communication based on the person's unique condition-specific communication needs, is to ask them in the first instance. Practitioners can subsequently use their observational skills to identify additional means of engaging the child in communication which meets their needs. Revisiting initial questions as the child becomes more familiar with you and the service, can further contribute to gauging the child's unique communication needs and preferences. The key areas which impact a child/parent living with ADHD concerning communication are as follows:

- Hyperactivity: What could help the child/parent to manage hyperactivity when they are communicating with you? Would an open window or the option to stand up and walk around be helpful? Are there any aids such as wobble cushions, chair bands (for the legs of the chair), rocking chairs or bean bags which could be used to enhance engagement?
- Inattentiveness: What duration of time is the child/parent comfortable with and capable of giving their attention to, for your meeting/interaction? How will the child communicate when they are unable to pay attention or have become disinterested? How could you make the communication more interactive, less boring or more interesting for the child/parent? Could you do a walking meeting? Is a face-to-face meeting necessary or would a phone call or zoom meeting suffice? Or can you meet for a short time and then have a movement break? Does the child need to be present for the whole meeting? Can the meeting/communication proceed without the child present and could they be updated?

Would summaries at the end of the meeting/session help? Or written notes on what was discussed? Would the child/adult prefer this information be emailed to them?

- Impulsivity: the child/parent with ADHD may struggle to wait their turn to speak and may impulsively feel the need to blurt things out. This is often due to worry that they will forget what they wanted to say. Would a meeting agenda help? Would frequent turn taking when communicating enable the child or their parent to feel more in control? What should they do if they feel they impulsively need to say something when someone else is speaking or during an important activity or therapy? Could they write things down as other people are speaking or type questions/thoughts into a laptop or tablet? Practitioners can help the child/parent to plan how they can respond to impulsivity within their communication and further reassure them that it's okay if they need to speak and that you will always listen to them. Ultimately, the child or parent living with ADHD needs to know that you value them, acknowledge their unique communication needs and that you will work *with them*, to establish which communication methods works best for them.

Dyspraxia/DCD and Communication

Dyspraxia impacts the child in terms of planning, sequencing and organisation (Farmer et al., 2016; American Psychiatric Association, 2013). Dyspraxia can impact the child's speech in terms of pronouncing certain words and expressing accurately everything they want to communicate (UNESCO, 2023). The dyspraxic child may have difficulty following long monologues of speech or when provided with too much information at one time. Practitioners should avoid using long sentences with multiple key points. Important pieces of information should be communicated clearly and with emphasis regarding their significance and why. Practitioners should communicate using varied methods (writing, email, pamphlets, pictures, or AAC) as opposed to relying solely on verbal communication.

Taking sufficient time when communicating with a child living with dyspraxia will enhance the effectiveness of this communication. Creating frequent opportunities for the child or parent to ask questions or to think about and plan what they want to say, will help them to feel more comfortable and that you value their views. Facilitating opportunities for asking questions or seeking clarification on information previously communicated, can assist the child in processing the information you are sharing with them. Yet most importantly, practitioners should directly ask the child how they would like to communicate and explore continually what factors empower them to communicate successfully.

Reflection Point!

Close your eyes: imagine you're at a job interview for your dream role. You're nervous, excited and eager to make a good impression. The interview panel of three each introduce themselves and ask you to tell them a little about yourself and why you feel you're right for this role.

Now imagine you try to speak . . . but you are unable to. You will yourself to communicate the thoughts that are at the forefront of your mind . . . yet your mouth, lips, voice and tongue just can't comply. Now imagine how you would feel in this moment? The interview panel allow time for you to respond, yet the silence is now extending to an uncomfortable duration. The interviewer asks you if you are okay? But again . . . you cannot speak. How do you feel? What are the looks on the faces of the interview panel communicating? What should you do?

Selective Mutism

Selective mutism is characterised within the DSM-5 as an inability to speak in certain social situations, which cannot be explained by a language disorder (APA, 2013). Selective mutism occurs when the child does not respond verbally within a situation where they are expected to, yet can communicate verbally in other settings (Muris & Ollendick, 2021). The DSM categorises selective mutism as an anxiety disorder (APA, 2013).

Selective mutism is said to be more common in children who have a diagnosis of autism (Steffenburg, Steffenburg, Gillberg, & Billstedt, 2018; Muris & Ollendick, 2021). Steffenburg et al. (2018) found within their study that selective mutism is more common in girls and that 95% of their sample displayed selective mutism only outside the home. Schwenck et al. (2022) surmise that the trigger for selective mutism is largely associated with a new activity, unfamiliar people or activities or places viewed as stressful by the child. Neurodivergent children may display selective mutism within the context or setting where you are engaging with them (school, clinic, community, hospital setting etc.).

The term *selective mutism* indicates a choice or selection, concerning when to speak or when to remain silent. Yet mutism in some settings often occurs when the child feels anxious, distressed, overwhelmed or paralysed by fear. This is not selective or choice based. This situational or context-based mutism, is a coping strategy and a response to distress. However, the language used can be harmful and can even attribute blame to the child, for their inability to speak or communicate in certain contexts. The term *situational or contextual mutism* is much more appropriate, as it acknowledges that it is not choice based and is instead caused by or manifesting because of the situation or context within which the communication occurs.

Author Reflection Point!

I find myself gathering insights for this book every single day in my interactions with my children and our interactions as a family with the world around us. Every now and then something profound happens which really illuminates the importance of creating supportive environments for neurodivergent children. One of my children has situational/context-based mutism (discussed previously). Their inability to speak is fuelled by anxiety, uncertainty and discomfort. I had been trying for quite some time to support my child to engage more socially in shops and restaurants. However, the more I encouraged and prompted them, the more anxiety fuelled the situation became.

Today, this child said thank you in Spanish to the most flamboyant and hilarious waitress, whose flair just mesmerised her. She also answered a question about what age she was, and wasn't visibly uncomfortable when the waitress was at the table. She has talked non-stop about how amazing this waitress was since we left the restaurant. So this has prompted me to reflect regarding: what was different? What within this environment/context enabled and facilitated my daughter to speak in a setting she has never been able to speak in before? A few things I've noted:

- The restaurant was quiet, just one other family was dining.
- The lady waiting on us was funny and made jokes with each of us.
- The lady tried to engage, but placed no pressure on my daughter (no prompts if she didn't respond, just carried on being comedic).
- The waitress tried different tactics, she told a funny story, then built upon the response (when my daughter laughed, she asked if she thought that was funny? And if she would do X or Y herself?).
- The lady was informal in her approach and this reduced the expectation to communicate.
- She oozed confidence and her flamboyance created a diversion almost, which dissipated the usual formal expectation around interaction and offered a different way to communicate.
- The lady could very well have been neurodivergent herself and emanated a different and unique way of communicating.

*This wonderful lady has no idea how memorable and profound our experience of interacting with her was.

Alternative Methods of Communication

A speech and language therapist or pathologist supports neurodivergent children and families, in identifying methods of communication unique to their needs. The American Speech-Language-Hearing Association (ASHA, 2023) describe a speech pathologist, as a professional who assesses and treats individuals concerning their speech, language, communication and regarding the individual's ability to swallow. Speech and language pathologists support neurodivergent children regarding speech, language and communicating problems, and may work with the child and family to employ alternative methods of communication (ASHA, 2023).

Augmentative and Alternative Communication (AAC) systems can augment (add to and support) or act as an alternative means of communication, for children with varied communication needs (ASHS, 2023). High-tech communication systems include speech-generating devices, or SDGs, which translate the person's wishes or messages electronically to speech (Cook & Polgar, 2015). Such speech-generating devices are advancing in sophistication continually. For example: eye tracking and head movement technology assists users to communicate via computer tracking of their eye and head movements, to indicate their wishes, preferences and thoughts (IntelliGaze, 2023).

Low-tech communication systems are mechanisms of communication which don't require electronics and include community request cards, communication boards, pen and paper, communication books and picture exchange systems (Iacono, Lyon, Johnson, & West, 2013; van de Sandt-Koenderman, 2004). The user may display a card to indicate they wish to make a store purchase or that they need assistance. Or the child may use their communication board to communicate how they are feeling or what activity they would like to do next.

Reflection Point!

If you broke your hip playing sports, would you want a vascular surgeon or a plastic surgeon to operate on you? Or would you insist on an orthopaedic surgeon to perform this surgery?

If a neurodivergent child or young person has not identified a method of communication which works for them and enables them to have their needs met, then a speech and language therapist should be consulted. Speech and language therapists/pathologists possess expert knowledge and expertise, specifically concerning communication.

People with additional communication needs may use different alternative methods of communication in different settings, for example: a child may use a speech-generating device at home, but prefer to use a communication book when socialising (Elsahar, Hu, Bouazza-Maroufm, Kerr, & Mansor, 2019). The preferences and unique communication needs of each child, will inform which method of augmentative and alternative communication they utilise (Unholz-Bowden, Girtler, Shipchandler, Kolb, & McComas, 2023). Unholz-Bowden et al. (2023) surmise that ease of use is a further significant factor in determining the most appropriate method of AAC for the child, which will also encompass parental and family ease of use, as they will interact with the child and use this technology as part of their daily routine. The training and support needs associated with high-tech AAC will further influence the child's and family's ability to access and incorporate this (Unholz-Bowden, 2023). Such practical considerations will be fundamental in identifying an appropriate AAC for the child, which will be successful in meeting their communication needs.

Nilsson et al. (2015) contend that children can feel voiceless concerning decisions about their health. Coyne, Holmstrom, and Soderback (2018) argue that even when parents or professionals are advocating on the child's behalf, their perspective on the child's needs is filtered based on their own interests. Parents often want the best for their child and want to advocate for the most positive possible outcome which enhances wellbeing. However, this may be in contrast to what the child wants for themselves. For example: a parent may be advocating for the use of type-to-voice software for their child to use in school, to assist them in class participation and communicating with their peers. Yet the child may not want to employ this strategy due to feeling uncomfortable, self-conscious or simply because it's not their preference. Consequently, practitioners have a moral and professional obligation to identify a method of communicating which suits this child's needs and preferences, so that they can self-advocate and express their unique preferences.

Active Listening

The concept of active listening may seem like a redundant or previously studied topic for many students and practitioners reading this book. Yet it is quite astonishing how frequently practitioners who work with neurodivergent children and families, do not demonstrate this fundamental skill. The consequence of such within the context of creating supportive environments for neurodivergent children and their families, can be particularly detrimental. Active listening communicates a conscious effort to truly hear what the child or family are telling you and communicate to them that you have received their message. Active listening "is a way of listening and responding to another person, which improves mutual understanding" (Mineyama, Tsutsumi, Takao, Nishiuchi, & Kawakami, 2007, p. 81). Active listening can have a momentous positive impact on building and maintaining partnerships with children and families and subsequently maximising the success of future interventions. Families may be interacting with practitioners after a long period of waiting (often one to two years), perhaps after negative experiences with previous services or providers, or having not been heard or believed, regarding their concerns for the child to date. Hence, active listening is a crucial skill for practitioners to demonstrate in actively working towards creating supportive environments, for neurodivergent children and their families.

Active listening in each interaction and communication with neurodivergent children and families, can be facilitated via the following means:

Providing *feedback* is a key element within active listening and requires the listener to communicate that that they are hearing the messages being conveyed. Methods of feedback include: summarising what the person has said, repeating back what they have communicated, nodding and providing verbal responses which communicate understanding (Tennant, Long, & Toney-Butler, 2023).

Acknowledging and interpreting *non-verbal communication* is a crucial factor in promoting active listening. Reading and responding effectively to the body language of the child or parent, can provide additional insight and context into their needs and what they are trying to communicate. Equally, non-verbal responses from practitioners such as a nod of their head, an open posture facing the person and looking towards the person who is speaking (if they are comfortable with this), communicates your intentional wish to listen (NHS, 2021). Many neurodivergent children (and neurodivergent parents) may live with communication challenges and feel overwhelmed at meetings with professionals. Non-verbal communication may be the only way they can express their feelings and views within this situation. Practitioners should take the time needed to ensure that the child/family have had space and support to express their needs, wishes and preferences, in a format conducive to their needs.

Asking *questions* is further significant when engaging in active listening. Asking questions to clarify, gather more information or to demonstrate your interest, can communicate to the child and family that you have heard what they said and would like to know more (Agency for Toxic Substance and Disease Registry, 2023). Examples of questions could be: you mentioned Laura coped well on Tuesday morning, could you tell me more about this? Or: this sounds so challenging, how did you feel at this time? Such questions further communicate care and a wish to provide support.

Finally, ATSDR (2023) propose that *patience* is a vital prerequisite for effectively demonstrating active listening. It can take time to build rapport with a neurodivergent child and their family. Even after meeting with a neurodivergent child frequently, the initial discomfort at an appointment may prevent them from expressing their wishes. The child needs time to adjust to the setting where the communication is taking place and become comfortable with the practitioner within this setting. This could mean allowing time at the start of a meeting or session for the child to acclimatise and integrate slowly into this new situation.

Author Reflection Point!

After 21 years of parenting neurodivergent children, I'm still learning new things about my children and their communication needs every day. Communication ability, preference and need are never static and change all the time. The context, setting, people and other things happening in the child's life, all impact their ability to communicate at any given time. So re-evaluating and assessing communication methods with neurodivergent children consistently, is essential to maintaining a supportive environment.

Active listening is traditionally provided within a therapeutic setting between the practitioner/professional and the child and their family. Yet in the context of communicating with neurodivergent children and their families, the basic principles can be transferred to meet their unique communication needs. If a child you are supporting is more comfortable communicating through email or text message, or if parents/caregivers prefer to meet via Zoom, you can still exercise active listening via incorporating the points discussed earlier. Eggenberger (2021) contends that listening and more specifically active listening is a learned skill, which requires an active commitment to communicating more effectively. Finally, the NHS (2021) contend that practitioners should not interrupt the person speaking and should also allow space for silences. Silences can feel awkward or uncomfortable, yet they serve as an opportunity for the speaker to process their own emotions and communication efforts, and enable the listener an opportunity to process and digest the information being received.

Case Study 1

Clark is 9 years old, autistic, non-verbal and requires comprehensive care, support and supervision. His mother Ella is a single parent and has little support. Ella has made an appointment to speak to her physician as she is feeling burnout setting in and has had thoughts of self-harm. Ella took three weeks to build the courage to make the appointment and is worried about what the response to her needs might be.

Upon entering the physician's office, Ella notices Dr. Doyle is flustered and furiously typing, while speaking to the receptionist. After the call ends, Dr. Doyle asks Ella what brings her in, while still typing. Ella explains that she is feeling low and that she feels unable to continue providing the level of care that Clark needs. Still looking at her computer screen, Dr. Doyle asks Ella if she is on any medications currently. When Ella replies no, Dr. Doyle types a prescription, prints it and hands it to Ella, explaining that this will help. The doctor's phone rings again, and another doctor knocks and comes in to ask Dr. Doyle for a second opinion on a patient next door. Dr. Doyle apologises and excuses herself. Ella is bewildered and feels like she hasn't had an opportunity to really explain how she feels. When Dr. Doyle returns, she stands over her desk and asks Ella if there is anything else she would like to discuss. Ella replies no and leaves.

What actions or inactions communicated the omission of active listening?

How could active listening have been demonstrated?

What was the impact of poor listening in this situation?

What might the longer-term impacts of this interaction be for Ella and Clark?

Honest and Transparent Communication

Honest and transparent communication with neurodivergent children and their families, is essential within practice aimed at creating supportive environments. Families need to understand the key messages you are sharing with them in order to feel empowered and be in an informed position from which to make decisions. Honest and transparent communication is equally relevant to building partnerships with parents and appreciating the power of each interaction with the child and their family. Honest communication conveys respect and sincerity within the practitioner/family relationship.

Acronyms are frequently used within education, healthcare and social care settings where neurodivergent children and families interact. Standardised testing, diagnoses, names of organisations and regarding legislation, policy, schemes and programs, are often referred to within their abbreviated forms. Abbreviated terms reduce the time and effort required for professionals when communicating with one another. Yet most professionals retain their use of such abbreviations when communicating with families, which presents a barrier to effectively communicating. Some parents will ask for clarification about what the acronym means, yet others will not ask as they are concerned that perhaps this is something they should already know and worry about how they will be viewed if they don't know what the practitioner is referring to. For example: There are multiple application forms a family may need to submit to apply for basic services their child needs in the community, at school and regarding welfare. Forms are often referred to by professionals using acronyms. This can be confusing for families, and in particular if they have more than one form they need to complete.

Ineffective communication results in the child's and family's needs remaining unmet. Consequently, the onus is on the practitioner to ensure they are communicating effectively, based on the unique communication needs of the child and family. Understanding should never be assumed when communicating with neurodivergent children and their families. Although this is your everyday knowledge, this may be completely new information for the family, or they may be feeling confused or overwhelmed at the volume of new information being received. Equally, developments and new programmes, approaches and supports are being introduced all the time. Practitioners should ask if the child/parent is aware of what this is and why you are discussing it with them.

Printing out important information for neurodivergent children and families can assist in enhancing transparent communication and reduce the burden of information retention often required at appointments. Bearing in mind that some parents/caregivers will be neurodivergent (with or without a diagnosis or disclosure of same), the volume of information provided at meetings can be overwhelming. Writing down or printing important information and communicating that you will do this at the start of the meeting, can enable parents to digest more easily the content of the meeting, without consciously trying to remember all of the information. Taking meeting minutes is another method of enhancing communication with neurodivergent families or emailing key points to parents, after the meeting has ended. This is particularly useful when action is required on their part. For example: contact the principal, apply for new services or create a daily diary, etc.

Health Literacy

Health literacy refers to the capacity of an individual to understand and process the knowledge and information needed, to take control of their health (World Health Organisation, 1998). The WHO (1998) contends that health literacy is not simply having the capacity to read pamphlets or make medical appointments, but rather concerned with the person's capacity to access the health information they need and use this effectively.

Health literacy awareness has led to increased calls for utilising plain language, when communicating issues about health and wellness (Stableford & Mettger, 2007). This is the responsibility of both individual practitioners and organisations. Garcia, Hahn, and Jacobs (2010) argue that lower levels of health literacy, culminates in poorer outcomes for patients. Abel and McQueen (2020) surmise that the significance of health literacy became particularly apparent during the Covid-19 pandemic. Much of the health advice provided at that time, was based on the assumption that people would be able to access the information they needed and act accordingly to protect and promote their health. Yet Abel and McQueen argue that the breadth of information available and the sheer volume of sources, presented a unique and unprecedented challenge for public health authorities. The social determinants of health (discussed in Chapter 5) impact health literacy for already disadvantaged and marginalised groups (Sravani, Arpan, Kishore, & Siddappa, 2020). Those with lower levels of education and living in socially deprived low-income areas, suffer greater health problems and had higher mortality rates during the pandemic (Sravani et al., 2020). These low levels of education, in addition to living in poverty, can result in lower levels of health literacy and consequently, reduce the capacity of the individual or family to access the information they need to promote their health.

Plain Language

Closely linked to promoting health literacy, is the use of plain language. The Plain Language Action and Information Network (PLAIN) are a group of federal employees who have worked for more than two decades on incorporating plain language, within government documents (Plainlanguage, 2023). Plainlanguage (2023) define *plain language* as language which is clear, concise and appropriate to the communication needs of the recipient. Plain language communication should be free from jargon or medical terms and use an uncomplicated and clear layout (Health Service Executive, 2023). The HSE (2023) suggest that plain language should be tailored to respect the circumstances of the intended audience such as: disability, age, gender, race, religion, marital status, etc. The Centers for Disease Control and Prevention (CDC, 2023) advise placing written information in order of importance and using headings to enhance clarity. Use short sentences, delete unnecessary words and use pronouns such as you (rather than the patient or family, etc.) (CDC, 2023).

Author Reflection Point!

In my communication with educators and practitioners, there have been frequent occasions where acronyms were used and I had no idea what they meant. Many times I didn't ask what this meant, as I felt there was an assumption I should know, if the practitioner was using this acronym to communicate with me! Equally, using medical terminology or terminology associated with education (which people outside of these sectors would not be familiar with) can further alienate families and cause discomfort and uncertainty.

Communication and Creating Supportive Environments

Communication is a particularly important precursor to creating supportive environments for neurodivergent children and their families, where they feel their wishes and preferences have been heard. Yet communication is so very unique and individual to the child and parents, so consequently a generic approach is never appropriate. Communication which is tailored to the unique communication needs of the neurodivergent child and their family, will increase the likelihood of more positive outcomes.

Effectual communication is an essential component for building and maintaining positive relationships with neurodivergent children and their parents/caregivers. Communication can be considered within the context of the three catalysts for action, in creating supportive environments:

1. *Acknowledgement*: relates to recognising how a specific diagnosis (or suspected diagnosis) may contribute to the communication needs of the child and their family. Acknowledgment is further concerned with the family's journey to date and the extent to which past experiences and barriers may impact their current communication with professionals.
2. *Access*: supporting families to access the information, services and resources they need, to communicate their wishes and preferences accurately. This may involve advocacy, referral and ongoing liaising with other professionals and organisations, to enable the family to access communication supports. Access is further significant in terms of plain language and families being in a position to understand and process the information being shared, based on their individual communication needs.
3. *Acceptance*: is concerned with appreciating and respecting the child and family regarding their communication needs and meeting them where

they are at. Establishing preferred methods of communication and exploring their health literacy, will place practitioners in a more informed position from which to understand and value the child and family's communication needs. Yet the child and family's preferences and comfort in terms of communication, should remain a priority and valued by the practitioner.

Case Study 2

Mirah is a 9-year-old girl with no previous interactions with health/developmental services and with no diagnosis history. Returning to school after summer break, Mirah is now not communicating verbally whatsoever in school. She appears uncomfortable when her teacher or another child communicates with her directly and will squirm in her seat, avoid eye contact and not respond.

Having previously had two close friends, Mirah is now spending all of her time in school alone. Mirah will not queue in the cafeteria for food at lunch time. Her parents report that she is very hungry when she arrives home from school, but aside from this, is her usual self and interacting with her family as before. Although she has always been shy, Mirah's complete aversion to speaking when in school, has caused concern for her parents and teachers.

1. What are your initial thoughts on Mirah's situation?
2. What types of services/referrals might be appropriate to assess and meet Mirah and her family's current needs?
3. How could low-tech communication aides be useful to helping Mirah in school?
4. What other actions could be taken within the school setting to create a more supportive environment, based on Mirah's unique needs?

Self-Assessment

What communication needs do all neurodivergent children have in common?

What does AAC mean?

How does health literacy impact communication with neurodivergent children and their families?

Summary

Effective communication with neurodivergent children and their families, is an essential precursor for creating supportive environments. The communication needs of each child and family will vary considerably and be completely unique. Practitioners have a professional and moral responsibility to empower the child and family to identify what types of communication meet their distinctive needs and to access the resources they need to enable them to communicate. A speech and language pathologist or therapist is a specially trained professional, who should be consulted when supporting a neurodivergent child with communication. Yet practitioners can adopt communication methods aimed at creating supportive environments into their practice, such as actively listening, taking time to build familiarity and communicating in a clear and transparent manner. Communication is an essential building block of a long-term relationship between the practitioner and family. Consequently, the three key catalysts for action when creating supportive environments of acknowledgement, access and acceptance, should inform a practitioner's communication efforts.

References

Abel, T., & McQueen, D. (2020). Critical health literacy and the COVID-19 crisis. *Health Promotion International*, *35*(6), 1612–1613. https://doi.org/10.1093/heapro/daaa040

Agency for Toxic Substance and Disease Registry. (2023, August 1). *A guide to active listening*. Retrieved from www.atsdr.cdc.gov/ceplaybook/docs/active-listening-guide-508.pdf

American Psychiatric Association. (2013). *Diagnostic and statistical manual of mental disorders: DSM-5*. Washington, DC: American Psychiatric Association.

American Speech-Language-Hearing Association. (2023, July 29). *Speech language pathologists*. Retrieved from www.asha.org/students/speech-language-pathologists/#:~:text=Evaluate%20and%20diagnose%20speech%2C%20language, family%2Fcaregivers%20and%20other%20professionals

Centers for Disease Control and Prevention. (2023, August 1). *Plain language materials and resources*. Retrieved from www.cdc.gov/healthliteracy/developmaterials/plainlanguage.html

Cook, A.M., & Polgar, J.M. (2015). *Assistive technologies principles and practices* (4th ed.). New York, NY: Elsevier.

Coyne, I., Holmstrom, I., & Soderback, M. (2018). Centeredness in healthcare: A concept synthesis of family-centered care, person-centered care and child-centered care. *Journal of Pediatric Nursing*, *42*, 45–56. Retrieved from https://doi.org.nuigalway.idm.oclc.org/10.1016/j.pedn.20

Eggenberger, A.L.B. (2021). Active listening skills as predictors of success in community college students. *Community College Journal of Research and Practice*, *45*(5), 324–333. https://doi.org/10.1080/10668926.2019.1706667

Elsahar, Y., Hu, S., Bouazza-Maroufm, K., Kerr, D., & Mansor, A. (2019). Augmentative and alternative communication (AAC) advances: A review of configurations for individuals with a speech disability. *Sensors (Basel)*, *19*(8), 1911. https://doi.org/10.3390/s19081911

Farmer, M., Echenne, B., & Bentourkia, M. (2016). Study of clinical characteristics in young subjects with Developmental coordination disorder. *Brain and Development*, *38*(6), 538–547. https://doi.org/10.1016/j.braindev.2015.12.010

Garcia, S.F., Hahn, E.A., & Jacobs, E.A. (2010). Addressing low literacy and health literacy in clinical oncology practice. *The Journal of Supportive Oncology*, *8*(2), 64–69.

Health Service Executive. (2023, August 1). *Guidelines for communicating clearly using plain English with our patients and service users. A resource to improve the quality and consistency of our communication*. Retrieved from www.hse.ie/eng/about/who/communications/communicatingclearly/guidelines-for-communicating-clearly-using-plain-english.pdf

Iacono, T., Lyon, K., Johnson, H., & West, D. (2013). Experiences of adults with complex communication needs receiving and using low tech AAC: an Australian context. *Disability and Rehabilitation: Assistive Technology*, *8*(5), 392–401. https://doi.org/10.3109/17483107.2013.769122

IntelliGaze. (2023, July 30). *IntelliGaze 11*. Retrieved from www.intelligaze.com/en/home#slide-2

Mineyama, S., Tsutsumi, A., Takao, S., Nishiuchi, K., & Kawakami, N. (2007). Supervisors' attitudes and skills for active listening with regard to working conditions and psychological stress reactions among subordinate workers. *Journal of Occupational Health*, *49*(2), 81–87. Retrieved from https://doi.org.nuigalway.idm.oclc.org/10.1539/joh.49.81

Mullins, L. (2022). *It takes a village. Navigating the journey of parenting your autistic child*. Dublin: Orpen Press.

Muris, P., & Ollendick, T.H. (2021). Selective mutism and its relations to social anxiety disorder and Autism Spectrum Disorder. *Clinical Child and Family Psychology Review*, *24*, 294–325. https://doi.org/10.1007/s10567-020-00342-0

Muskat, B., Burnham Riosa, P., Nicholas, D.B., Roberts, W., Stoddart, K.P., & Zwaigenbaum, L. (2015). Autism comes to the hospital: The experiences of patients with autism spectrum disorder, their parents and health-care providers at two Canadian paediatric hospitals. *Autism*, *19*(4), 482–490. https://doi.org/10.1177/1362361314531341

National Institute on Deafness and Other Communication Disorders. (2020, August 9). *Autism spectrum disorder: Communication problems in children*. Retrieved from www.nidcd.nih.gov/health/autism-spectrum-disorder-communication-problems-children

Neely, L., Gerow, S., Rispoli, M., Lang, R., & Pullen, N. (2016). Treatment of echolalia in individuals with autism spectrum disorder: A systematic review. *Review Journal of Autism and Developmental Disorders*, *3*, 82–91. https://doi.org/10.1007/s40489-015-0067-4

NHS. (2021, August 1). *Active listening* (Online Library of Quality, Service Improvement and Redesign Tools). Retrieved from www.england.nhs.uk/wp-content/uploads/2021/12/qsir-active-listening.pdf

Nilsson, S., Bjorkman, B., Almqvist, A.L., Almqvist, L., Bjork-Willen, P., Donohue, D., Enskär, K., Granlund, M., Huus, K., & Hvit, S. (2015). Children's voices: Differentiating a child perspective from a child's perspective. *Developmental Neurorehabilitation*, *18*(3), 162–168. https://doi.org/10.3109/17518423.2013.801529

Plainlanguage. (2023, August 1). *What is plain language?* Retrieved from www.plainlanguage.gov/about/definitions/

Pratt, K., Baird, G., & Gringras, P. (2012), Ensuring successful admission to hospital for young people with learning difficulties, autism and challenging behaviour: A continuous quality improvement and change management programme. *Child: Care, Health and Development*, *38*, 789–797. https://doi.org/10.1111/j.1365-2214.2011.01335.x

Schwenck, C., Gensthaler, A., Vogel, F., Pffeffermann, A., Laerum, S., & Stahl, J. (2022). Characteristics of person, place, and activity that trigger failure to speak in children with selective mutism. *European Child & Adolescent Psychiatry*, *31*, 1419–1429. https://doi.org/10.1007/s00787-021-01777-8

Sravani, S., Arpan, A., Kishore, C., & Siddappa, N.B. (2020). Impact of social determinants of health on the emerging COVID-19 pandemic in the United States. *Frontiers in Public Health*, *8*. https://doi.org/10.3389/fpubh.2020.00406

Stableford, S., & Mettger, W. (2007). Plain language: A strategic response to the health literacy challenge. *The Journal of Public Health Policy*, *28*, 71–93. https://doi.org/10.1057/palgrave.jphp.3200102

Steffenburg, H., Steffenburg, S., Gillberg, C., & Billstedt, E. (2018). Children with autism spectrum disorders and selective mutism. *Neuropsychiatric Disease and Treatment*, *14*, 1163–1169. https://doi.org/10.2147/NDT.S154966

Tennant, K., Long, A., & Toney-Butler, T., J. (2023). *Active listening*. [Updated 2023 May 1]. In *StatPearls [Internet]*. Treasure Island, FL: StatPearls Publishing. Retrieved August 1, 2023, from www.ncbi.nlm.nih.gov/books/NBK442015/

UNESCO. (2023, August 2). *Living with dyspraxia*. Retrieved from https://mgiep.unesco.org/article/living-with-dyspraxia

Unholz-Bowden, E.K., Girtler, S.N., Shipchandler, A., Kolb, R.L., & McComas, J.J. (2023). Use of augmentative and alternative communication by individuals with Rett Syndrome part 2: High-tech and low-tech modalities. *Journal of Developmental and Physical Disabilities*. https://doi.org/10.1007/s10882-023-09902-

van de Sandt-Koenderman, M.W.M.E. (2004). High-tech AAC and aphasia: Widening horizons? *Aphasiology*, *18*, 245–263. https://doi.org/10.1080/02687030344000571

World Health Organisation. (1998, August 1). *Health promotion glossary*. Retrieved from www.who.int/publications/i/item/WHO-HPR-HEP-98.1

Chapter 7

Making Each Contact Count

Abbreviations

ADHD: Attention Deficit Hyperactivity Disorder
HSE: Health Service Executive

Introduction

Educators, health care workers and social care professionals, aim to support and empower families to meet their child's need for care and support. This is further significant when the child's needs are more substantial, due to their neurodivergence and its impact on their lives. This chapter will explore the fundamental goal of each contact between the professional and family: to leave this family in a better state than they were prior to the contact. Regardless of the type of contact or the initial rationale, each interaction with families should result in a benefit to this family in some way. Primarily, families need hope at a time when they may feel hopeless.

This chapter will present novel practice strategies for each contact, distinctive to the needs of neurodivergent children and their families. Fundamental issues relevant for each interaction with neurodivergent children and families will be discussed, underpinned by the aim of creating supportive environments. This chapter will explore effective ways of engaging parents in positive supportive exchanges of information, with the primary goal of improving outcomes for their neurodivergent child and family. Power dynamics and their relevance to contact opportunities with families, will further be discussed.

Learning Outcomes

On completion of Chapter 7, learners should demonstrate an enhanced understanding concerning:

DOI: 10.4324/9781003455868-7

- The significance of each and every interaction with a neurodivergent child and their family
- Awareness regarding the importance of sufficient preparation and planning prior to each meeting/interaction
- The influence of power dynamics on interactions between parents and professionals
- The role of your interaction with children and parents in the context of creating supportive environments

Key Considerations for Each Contact

Ultimately, what do neurodivergent children and their parents/caregivers need from interactions with professionals? They want to feel like their child matters, that you understand their needs and that you care. They want to feel like you view their child as a person, rather than a case, file or a number. Families need practitioners to make them feel understood, not judged, and that their experiences are valid. You can't always change the family's situation or ensure their child will have access to the supports and resources their child needs. However, you can demonstrate that you hear them, that you understand and that you care.

Interactions with families are often initially shaped and informed by the reputation of your organisation. This includes feedback on services which families have heard from peers who have used this service, information about the organisation in the media, and the policies and ethos of the individual organisation and the sector more broadly. Following are some universal and critical prerequisites to creating supportive environments, in each contact with neurodivergent children and their families.

Initial Contact

Remember that your interaction with the family commences as soon as you make contact with them, whether this is by letter, email or phone. Generic letters which are addressed "dear patient" or "dear parent" are not conducive to creating a supportive environment. Generic contact letters (even letters being sent to hundreds or thousands of families) which don't state the child's name or parents name, yet refer to the child, communicates a generic understanding of their child's and family's needs. It communicates a lack of individuality and can prompt feelings of upset, exasperation and dissatisfaction with the service. Using the parent's and child's name from the outset and continually in your interactions with families, communicates your interest in providing support and that you've taken the time to find out who they are, before making contact with them.

Introduction to Your Role

Assuming what new families know or don't know about why they're attending an appointment, meeting or service, is erroneous. This is particularly true for families who are new to disability support services. Some children and parents may have no idea what your remit is and why they have been asked to attend. This may be their third appointment of the week, and they may be caring for more than one neurodivergent child. Including your role/title within your letter and email signature, is a good method of helping families to familiarise themselves with you and what your remit is concerning helping their family. Assume nothing and start at the beginning, each time you welcome new families into your office, clinic or classroom.

Explaining who you are and what you do, might seem like a very obvious first action when you meet with neurodivergent children and families. Yet it's exceedingly common that professionals meet with families and assume they know the professional's role and what this entails. If I'm attending an appointment at school, I assume I'm meeting with a teacher or principal. Yet it could be the special needs coordinator, the area organiser for special needs coordination, or an educational psychologist or occupational therapist brought in by the school. Equally, neurodivergent children and parents meet with so many professionals on their journey through disability services that clarifying who you are, what your role is and exactly what you do is helpful. Also as important is not to assume that parents/caregivers know generally what the role of a social worker or occupational therapist entails. Although they may have received similar services previously, the organisation of employment and role specifications could mean that a different remit is required, e.g. a child protection and welfare social worker, compared to a disability support social worker, or an occupational therapist within an assessment team, as opposed to a therapy/long-term or family support team.

Preparing for Meeting With Families

Practitioners have an immense responsibility within interactions with families of neurodivergent children. Such interactions can shape and impact all subsequent interactions with you, your organisation and even other healthcare and educational providers. Taking the time to sufficiently prepare prior to meeting with neurodivergent children and families, is a key precondition for creating and maintaining good relationships and creating a supportive environment. Planning for the meeting should involve creating an agenda which includes the key issues to be discussed and a review of developments since the previous meeting. An agenda communicates strong organisational skills and the importance a practitioner places on facilitating a constructive meeting, which will maximise positive outcomes for the child and family.

Reading the child's file prior to meeting with children and families is essential. Attending an appointment with your child and having to explain possibly for the fifth time what brings you there, can be incredibly frustrating for parents and children. When a practitioner has undertaken the necessary preparation and has an overall understanding of the key issues and notable developments to date, this immediately contributes to creating a supportive environment.

Author Reflection Point!

After three years attending a service with one of my children who was really struggling emotionally and regarding challenging behaviour, the most frustrating and redundant question asked was: "what brings you here today?".

This may have been after an hour-long, very challenging car journey, or after being called by the school three times that week because of challenging behaviour. Practitioners should be clear on why they are meeting with children and families and clarify this at the start of the interaction, e.g. "We're meeting to discuss Max's difficulties in school and challenges around managing emotions".

Being Present

Being fully present and engaged facilitates the creation of supportive environments, when meeting with neurodivergent children and families. Ensuring you have sufficient time to meet with families, appears somewhat obvious. Yet when a practitioner is an hour behind schedule and has two other families waiting, the sense of being rushed can impede completely the creation of a supportive environment. Children and families need practitioners to be fully present when they are meeting with them, not watching the clock. Communicating with colleagues, answering the phone or responding to emails, conveys disinterest and acts as a barrier to facilitating an effective interaction.

Being present is also linked to listening intently to the family's experiences. Discussed in more detail within Chapter 6, active listening conveys that you are intentionally paying attention to what the person is saying and are receiving the key messages. Allowing time for the child or parent to answer a question, providing space for the person to share and allowing silence for the child or family to gather their thoughts and process information, are all conducive methods of demonstrating being present and in the moment.

Equally important is consistency in the practitioner delivering the service, where possible. This familiarity and continuity of care is important for neurodivergent children and families and a key prerequisite for positive and supportive therapeutic/professional relationships. Some roles mean that educators change, intake teams may act only for the first six months of service, etc. Clarifying this from the outset is helpful, and a comprehensive handover to the person taking over care of the child and family, can further promote consistency and creating a supportive environment.

Power Dynamics

Power dynamics intrinsically inform and shape every single interaction between professionals and families. Within this professional relationship, it is imperative to acknowledge your own power and privilege, and how such power is influencing your interactions with each neurodivergent child and their family. Families are often dependent on services to meet their child's needs and consequently, can be acutely aware of their lack of power in their contact with practitioners and educators. Power may additionally be impacted by the disadvantage or marginalisation of the child and family, based on ethnicity, income, education or language.

Power dynamics are further dictated by the ethos of the organisation of employment and whether or not co-production is encouraged (Hood, Brent, Abbott, & Sartori, 2019). Hood et al. (2019) argue that some service providers base practice solely on the institutional priorities, leaving little room for the family's wishes or preferences. For example: a children's mental health service could limit service provision to medication provision and school support only, and perhaps not consider providing play therapy or psychology. Or a family support service may be limited in terms of their co-production and have a specific remit to address low-income difficulties and focus on integration within the community. Yet the family may need counselling services or respite care. This organisational remit directly influences the power dynamics between the professional and the parents/caregiver. Essentially, service users are at the mercy of service providers and often have little choice or control over the care, education or therapies they receive (with the exception of those who are in a position to pay for services privately).

Reflection Point!

Imagine you are lying in a hospital bed and feeling extremely unwell. Medical staff are working to find out what your diagnosis is, but you feel terrified. What if they don't find out? What if your condition deteriorates? What if you need to have surgery?

In this situation, you are completely dependent on the professionals tasked with your care. You have little control over the situation you find yourself in. You can't get up and go home. You don't know what's going to happen and you feel tremendously vulnerable. You possess no power over this situation and are entirely reliant on the staff providing your care.

Parents can arrive to meet you feeling desperate, exasperated and aware that they possess little power regarding the services, therapies or supports their child will receive. Your awareness of this within each interaction with families, is a first step in addressing power imbalances. Although you may have little capacity to influence the broader systemic issues which have culminated in this current situation (budget cuts, staffing issues, scope or role, etc.), creating opportunities where families can contribute to decision making is still possible. Although professionals are largely bound by the norms within their profession, pushing these boundaries and creating new ones, is acknowledging the existing power imbalances and committing to address these. Consequently, actively engaging in shared care planning and a partnership approach with parents/caregivers of neurodivergent children, starts the care relationship on a more optimistic note. Parents bring expert insight regarding their child's distinct needs and know and understand their child like no one else. Harnessing this expert insight and further acknowledging the value placed on the parental expertise, is conducive to building strong partnerships with parents and working towards creating a supportive environment.

Acknowledgement as a catalyst for creating supportive environments for neurodivergent children, is significant within the context of power and contact goals. This means actively acknowledging the power you possess as a professional and the lack of power neurodivergent children and families possess, within your interactions with them. This is systemic and ingrained within the organisation, financial resources, government policies and access to healthcare, social care and education. Yet this power exists and is ever present within the room (both literally and metaphorically). Acknowledging this power internally brings it to the fore and places it openly within the space where you interact with families. Power imbalances can only begin to be addressed if they are acknowledged.

The power dynamics within each contact between educators/practitioners and families of neurodivergent children, are significant in the context of choice. Families may not possess the ability to exercise choice concerning the care and education their neurodivergent child receives, again due to broader systemic and resourcing issues. Consequently, identifying areas and issues where the child and family *can* exercise choice, is conducive to acknowledgment of the power dynamics and an active step toward addressing these. Choices can be practical such as the time and day of the meeting/appointment, where they would like to sit and what topics or areas they would like to work on or discuss most. Neurodivergent children in particular appreciate knowing how long the interaction, appointment or piece of work will take, and being able to leave (without judgement or repercussions) when they need to.

Case Study

Dan and Jane received a letter stating that their daughter Abbey's school principal would like to meet with them both. Abbey (aged 6) has a diagnosis of ADHD, but has been coping quite well this semester at school, and no issues have been reported. Dan and Jane have not met the school principal previously.

The homeschool liaison officer and school principal are both in attendance and begin the meeting. The principal opens the meeting by listing the instances of Abbey's challenging behaviour in the previous two weeks and highlights the difficulties each has presented for the staff teacher and other children. The principal then explains that should Abbey's behavioural issues continue, she will be unable to remain on a full timetable, as it's becoming increasingly difficult to meet her needs and keep her and the other children safe. Dan and Jane are quite shocked. They hadn't met either staff member before and weren't sure who they were or what their roles were within the school. Dan and Jane feel blindsided and overwhelmed, as no communication regarding Abbey's behaviour had been raised previously.

What are your initial thoughts on this case?

What should have been done differently?

What could have happened prior to this contact point to create a more supportive environment?

What could have happened during this meeting to create a more supportive environment?

Three Key Contact Issues

Three key contact issues distinctive and relevant to each contact opportunity with neurodivergent children and their families, are fear, hope and impact.

1. *Fear:* many families attending medical, social care, therapy or social work appointments, or those meeting with education staff about their child's neurodivergence (or suspected neurodivergence), feel fear. Some parents may fear they will be judged on their parenting or that their child's behavioural or social issues are their fault. Some parents fear interacting with any professional, perhaps due to negative previous experiences or interactions from their own childhood. This is often evident within social work. Adults who interacted with social workers as children, may fear having their children removed from their care. Getting a call from a teacher or principal to attend a meeting, may invoke fear that their child can't stay in school or fear that they will be blamed for behavioural issues in the classroom. Other parents will feel terrified of what you're going to tell them. For some families, a diagnosis may be associated with really negative stereotyped outcomes, or that their child's life will change completely if they have a diagnosis. Parents might also fear that they will be judged by other family members, for engaging with services or "seeking" a diagnosis. General fear may also present for families where they are afraid of what will happen next, as they don't know what to expect and how this will impact their child and family, after the meeting with you.

   All of these fears are valid. We know that most of these fears may not manifest into reality, but this doesn't detract from their impact on the lives of parents/caregivers. This is particularly the case at the early stages of the child's diagnosis, when families have no idea what to expect and their child and family's future feels uncertain. Acknowledging and responding to some of the fears that parents may present with, is a key part of the professional role in this context. Equally, creating a space where these fears can be discussed, is further conducive to building a good relationship with families and maximising positive outcomes for neurodivergent children. We can only address fear if we name and acknowledge this.

   How can you do this?

   • Leave space: at the end of the meeting, leave enough time to ask parents/carers if there are any worries or fears they would like to discuss, which haven't been addressed or clarified in the meeting to date. This creates an environment where parents know they can express their fears and that you want to listen.
   • Provide information: websites, links, information on parenting groups, etc. The most effective way to reduce fear is to access more information on the issue which is creating the fear. This constructs an environment where families know that you want them to have sufficient information from which to understand their child's needs and that you are responding in a tangible way to their expression of fear/worry.

- Name it: acknowledging and normalising fear helps to ease it. Discussing with parents that families often have fears and worries about their child and what the future holds, will help parents to feel less alone. This creates an environment where the family know you have listened and you hear them.

2. *Hope*: hope is such a small word, but it is more powerful than any negative experience. Hope is a tiny glimmer of light when all you see is darkness in front of you. Hope is a gift that professionals can give to parents, at a time when they need it most. Whether you meet them at the classroom door, in a hospital setting or within a community clinic, if you can't change anything for them, at least give them the gift of hope.

   Hope for families perhaps struggling with a new diagnosis, or grappling with challenging behaviour, or families with no support who are feeling overwhelmed, can make the difference between sinking and swimming. Families need hope for the future, hope that things will get easier and hope that their child will be okay. Sometimes, families need hope regarding practical things which are impacting them, like lack of sleep. Hope that eventually their child may sleep through the night, might fuel an exhausted parent enough to keep going. Families may need hope that their child will continue to develop, at a time when they're not reaching their milestones. Hope for this family might be an intervention example which has helped other families, e.g. physiotherapy to help with developmental milestones or occupational therapy to help with toileting issues. Parents/caregivers could need hope that not every day will be as tough as some days, and hope that they will get through the challenges they currently face. You can't promise an outcome, or perhaps even influence the process (access to services/supports, etc.), but you can instil hope. You can use information to do this, share positive stories of similar families, or make a referral or recommendation which might help. Any of these actions present that little glimmer of hope, that when things feel like they have reached a crisis point, there's a possibility they will improve. All families need to keep going at times of crisis is this possibility, this hopefulness that every day and every week won't feel so difficult, and look to the practitioners they interact with to instil this in them. Offering hope at each opportunity for contact with neurodivergent children and families, is instrumental in building, creating and maintaining supportive environments.

3. *Impact*: the impact of each contact with a neurodivergent child and their family can be immensely powerful. The significance of each interaction, can affect this family long after you leave the office, surgery or school for

the day. In 2016 the Health Service Executive (HSE) in Ireland launched a campaign called "make every contact count", regarding interactions with older people who are at risk of chronic illness (HSE, 2016). The idea is that health and social care professionals have frequent opportunities to make a real impact, on the health and wellbeing of the people who use their services. Although this initiative was targeted towards older people with complex health needs and perhaps experiencing social isolation, it's applicable across sectors and relevant to all marginalised individuals. Practitioners possess the power within each interaction with neurodivergent children and families to "make every contact count" (HSE, 2016).

Equally, the significance of each contact is something we all realised during the lockdowns of Covid-19. Each interaction became more potent and significant. Sometimes, chatting with a shop assistant or the post person felt really profound. For neurodivergent children and families, this potency of each contact and the sense of isolation and marginalisation can be their norm. Each meeting with a professional is a major notable event in their lives. Some may have waited years to meet you, while others may have dreaded this meeting and not slept the night before, with the worry this presented for them. Some parents feel really hopeful that this is the start of the rest of their child's life, towards understanding them and creating an environment where their unique needs are met. Other parents may have spoken to no one other than you about their worries, concerns and hopes for their child. Meeting with families is almost always profound from their perspective. No pressure, right?!

How can you make a positive impact?

- Plan each meeting: identify the key goals of this meeting and how you can achieve these. Allow for sufficient time to have the impact that you hope to have. This could mean planning for the possibility that you or the family may be late, or taking into account the individual needs of the child or parents in relation to making the meeting, e.g. would it be better to meet at the child's school? Would parents feel more comfortable meeting when they can both attend? Ask families what works best for them.
- Read your notes: take time to review your notes on each family and their needs and anything of note from previous meetings. If you need to summarise notes to remember, take the time to do this. If a family is attending a service or school for a while, it can be very frustrating when asked why they are attending. Starting a meeting by summarising the family's needs or previous meetings, can be really helpful in demonstrating that you've planned for this meeting and know the

family's background. For example: "Hi Martina, so we're meeting today to discuss how Sophie is coping in school, since her ADHD diagnosis. You had expressed before that managing behaviour in class was challenging. How have things been since we met last?" This communicates that you are up to speed, present and motivated to keep things moving forward. This is reassuring for families and conveys your competence in understanding the family's unique and individual needs.

- Read the room: all the planning in the world may be irrelevant if you arrive at a meeting with families and they are experiencing a crisis. It's vital to gauge the needs of the family as they present, by actively listening to what they are telling you (verbally and non-verbally). If the family have experienced a particularly difficult week with sleeplessness, or if they've recently experienced a bereavement, this will affect their interactions with you and their ability to really engage. Using a check-in mechanism at the start of the meeting, is an effective way to gauge if any notable events have happened you should be aware of, or if the child or parent's capacity to engage is reduced. For example: asking parents how they are and demonstrating a genuine interest in their answer. Allowing time for silence and probing further as needed. If a child or parent who usually engages well appears withdrawn or if you sense tension perhaps between parents or a stark change in demeanour, take the time to find out what's happening for this family. If parents appear distant or despondent, or their body language communicates despair, take the time to name this and explore it.
- Take-away vibes: often the content of meetings with neurodivergent children and their families are emotional and contain difficult topics to discuss, e.g. challenges, problems, behaviours of concern, etc. Ending the meeting on a hopeful note, presents children and families with a positive finality to your interaction with them. This could mean providing a summary of what you have covered and with tangible actions you, the parents/carers and child will undertake between now and the next time you meet. For example: "I know today was tough, but we've made a lot of progress. I will contact Big Brother Big Sister and make a referral for Josh. You will meet with Josh's teacher once per week, and Josh will have a bath at 7 pm every day, to help him with his bedtime routine". So although the meeting may have discussed behavioural issues in school, persistent insomnia and a Dad who is desperate for respite which isn't available, the family are leaving the meeting with a plan of action for making things better. Again this communicates your consistent engagement and active listening, while finishing this contact opportunity.

Author Reflection Point!

I remember clearly now, even years later, some of the words professionals used when meeting with me and my child. The power dynamics combined with my desperation in some settings, made every single word more potent (both positive and negative). Your words are so powerful and are often all this family will have initially, as they navigate disability services (Mullins, 2022).

The Spectrum of Needs for Each Family

Each neurodivergent child and their family is completely unique, and no two will present with the same needs. Even if two children present with the same diagnosis, each child and their family will interpret and react to this differently, and their needs will be distinctive. Equally, individual family factors and dynamics will influence the needs and coping capacity of the family. Are there other children? Is the parent parenting alone? Do the parent/s have any health issues or are they neurodivergent themselves? The broader family and community supports will further impact how the child and family respond to the needs of the neurodivergent child. A family with a wealth of informal support will not have the same contact needs as a family without any support. The family's culture, values and preferences will further inform their needs within their contact and interactions with professionals. Finally, the wider societal awareness, support and response to the child's disability, will further uniquely impact the contact and interactional needs of the family. The following are three unique case examples of families who you may interact with in a professional capacity. Such examples highlight the diversity of contact needs for neurodivergent children and their families and how these needs can be addressed, using the approaches outlined within this chapter.

Family 1

Sarah is 11 years old and has a dual diagnosis of ADHD and autism. Sarah and her parents are new to your service, and today's meeting is about having Sarah's needs reassessed, to ascertain what types of therapies and supports would most benefit Sarah and her family.

On route to the appointment in the car, Sarah threw a pencil case at her Dad Dan while he was driving and they had a near accident. Sarah's Mom Ella is crying and feels like she can't do this anymore. The day before Sarah punched her younger brother, age 8, in the face, causing a nosebleed. Ella stays at home as each childcare option to date has not worked out, due to Sarah's severe challenging behaviour. Sarah is on a reduced timetable in school, and attends three days per week. As Sarah's behavioural issues are increasing in frequency, Dan has had to leave work to come home and help twice in the previous week. His job have advised that this can't continue.

What do this family need most from their interaction with the practitioner?
How could the practitioner communicate their interest and care?

Family 2

Jack is 6 and has no diagnosis to date. Jack is struggling at school in terms of self-care, and his Mom Karen has to collect him early regularly, as he is unable to toilet himself without support (this leads to accidents in school). Jack's teacher has made the referral for assessment as Jack also struggles with completing tasks requiring fine motor skills such as buttons, zips and holding a pencil. Jack falls quite frequently both in class and in the school yard.
Jack is the eldest of three and Karen is heavily pregnant. Karen doesn't think he needs assessment or intervention and is very resistant to any external input regarding her parenting and private family life. Jack's dad Mark is quieter and expresses some concern regarding his son's development.

What does reading the room tell you about this family's needs?
How might fear be contributing to this family's needs and how these present during this interaction?

Family 3

Matthew is 3 years old and an only child. Matthew has been referred from the community healthcare nurse, at his 3-year developmental check for an autism assessment. Matthew's mom Mary is a single parent and is a stay-at-home mom. She says that Matthew is super smart and understands everything she says, he just doesn't speak. Mary is frustrated that Matthew is only being seen now, as she has had concerns since he was 1 year old. Mary had expressed concerns to her doctor and community nurse at many times in the previous two years, but felt like no one listened. Mary is really worried about the impact of a delay in assessing and diagnosing Matthew. Mary further expresses experiencing insomnia, due to worrying about what will happen to her son if she gets sick or passes away. She has no family and just one or two friends who she doesn't see very often.

How could the practitioner positively impact this contact opportunity?

What take-away feeling would be important to impart for this contact opportunity?

Info Point!

Calling parents/carers by their names is a must! When parents are labelled as Mom and Dad, it can make them feel irrelevant when you meet with them, or that they're on a conveyor belt of families receiving services. Use the parent's name when you first meet them, and ask them what they would like you to call them (i.e. first name, Mrs. Egan, etc.). Make a note of this on their file so you remember the next time you meet them. This creates rapport between you and the family of the child you are supporting, which is an essential ingredient in creating supportive environments and successful outcomes for neurodivergent children.

There or Not There? Should Children Be in the Room

This is an area with which I have extensive personal experience. When a parent is discussing their child's needs, such as extreme challenging behaviour or issues with self-care such as toileting, or about their child's developmental challenges/concerns, the child should NOT be in the room! Some would argue that children should be active participants regarding their care. However, in this context, a child sitting in the room as their parents/caregivers list each aggressive outburst, meltdown or episode of absconding in the previous month, is not conducive to their wellbeing or regarding fostering positive relationships with both the professional providing support or with their parents.

My daughter told me she hated sitting outside the door at appointments, and she remembers this vividly, but when she was younger (>13), I had specifically asked for her not to be in the room while we were discussing the reasons she was no longer allowed to attend dance class or about the hour-long meltdown she had in the car.

These conversations between parents and professionals can be brutal in terms of content. Time is always limited at appointments, and parents often haven't shared this information with anyone else prior to this meeting. Meetings with professionals often present an opportunity for parents to offload and share their worries and experiences. This sharing or reporting of issues and challenges, is part of the parent's journey towards healing after traumatic or upsetting events, and subsequently feeling more capable of parenting after they leave the appointment. Parents are largely eager for professionals supporting their child to be aware of the specific issues and challenges their child is experiencing, in order to elicit the most appropriate response to their child's need. Equally, professionals can't respond effectively, without all of the information about the child and their needs, but children absolutely do not need to hear this.

I often found that the day after my child had a violent outburst or extended meltdown, I was still quite raw as a parent. But when I discussed this with them, it was most often a distant memory. Hence, I consequently stopped doing this. Children bounce back and get on with their day. They don't need to be reminded of their mistakes, a reaction they couldn't control or a situation which was really uncomfortable or upsetting.

So for all of the reasons listed here, if you and the parents/caregivers will be discussing issues which may make a child feel bad, sad, embarrassed, judged, upset or angry, ensure the child is not in the room. Spaces close by should be created to facilitate this, e.g. a second staff member to sit/play with the child in a different room, or a space where the child can play, draw or watch tv, which is visible from where the meeting is occurring.

Reflection Point!

Do you agree that children should not be present when their needs are being discussed? Why?

At what age do you think children/teenagers should be present at every meeting concerning their needs?

In what situations do you think a younger child should be present in the meeting room?

If the meeting between practitioners and parents/caregivers is not concerned with negative behaviours or reporting of issues, then the neurodivergent child should be supported to attend if they so wish. As children get older, they may wish to contribute more to such interactions and express their wishes or preferences. It may be more conducive to the child's needs to meet with educators/practitioners without their parents there, if this makes them feel more comfortable. Having the child present at meetings should be decided on a case-by-case basis and based on careful consideration of the wishes, needs and preferences of each person involved. Reflective questions can assist practitioners in ascertaining whether or not child should be present in the room for discussions about their needs:

- What is the context and rationale for the meeting?
- Does the child want to attend?

- Will the child benefit from participating?
- Is there a likelihood that the child may find the content distressing or embarrassing?
- Could the child attend for part of the meeting? Or meet with the practitioner prior to the meeting starting?

Self-Assessment

What feelings might parents/caregivers be experiencing when attending meetings/appointments with professionals?

Name two key contact issues, relevant to practice with neurodivergent children and families?

What are common errors professionals can make when interacting with neurodivergent children and families?

Summary

Each contact with neurodivergent children and families, regardless of the setting or context, has a profound capacity to impact this child and family. Approaching each interaction with a viewpoint of creating a supporting environment, will enable you to build and maintain a positive relationship with families and maximise positive outcomes for the neurodivergent child. The case studies provided within this chapter emphasise the breadth and diversity of needs children and families present with and the potential impact of each and every interaction with such families. Practitioners may be bound by the limitations of resources available, due to broader societal factors in terms of the resources and services they can provide. Yet offering a glimmer of hope within a supportive environment (particularly for families who are struggling) can be profoundly positively impactful. The potency of each contact with neurodivergent children and their families is substantial; hence acknowledging this and planning accordingly is critical. Practitioners should be acutely aware of the power differentials within each contact with families and recognise the significance of fear, hope and impact.

References

Health Service Executive. (2016). *Making every contact count*. Retrieved from www.hse.ie/eng/about/who/healthwellbeing/making-every-contact-count/about/

Hood, R., Brent, M., Abbott, S., & Sartori, D. (2019). A study of practitioner-service user relationships in social work. *The British Journal of Social Work, 49*(3), 787–805. https://doi.org/10.1093/bjsw/bcy082

Mullins, L. (2022). *It takes a village. Navigating the journey of parenting your autistic child*. Dublin: Orpen Press.

Chapter 8

Managing Conflict With Parents

Abbreviations

ADHD: Attention Deficit Hyperactivity Disorder
IEP: Individualised Education Plan

Introduction

A person can be the calmest, most measured and gentle-natured individual in their everyday life, yet change drastically in their role as a parent and when advocating for their child. Parents may be meeting with professionals after extensive waiting times and delays, in accessing the necessary supports to meet their neurodivergent child's needs. Hence emotions may be high and worry is often palpable. This chapter will explore the emotional presentation of parents when they attend for services and how this may impact their interactions with professionals.

This chapter will examine the employment of validation, reassurance and pre-emptive strategies, to manage conflict between practitioners and parents. Effective methods of establishing and maintaining positive relationships with parents, in an effort to maximise positive outcomes for their child, will further be explored. This chapter will equip practitioners with insight and ideas regarding both preventing and responding to conflict with parents, and collaborating effectively to support their child to reach their goals. Conflict resolution is a key attribute of creating a supportive environment for neurodivergent children and their families, via actively crafting spaces and places where they can participate and belong.

Learning Outcomes

On completion of Chapter 8, learners should demonstrate an enhanced understanding concerning:

- Roger's three core conditions of congruence, empathy and unconditional positive regard

DOI: 10.4324/9781003455868-8

- The importance of remaining non-judgemental
- The impact of previous negative experiences with professionals on neurodivergent children and their parents
- Appropriate methods of conflict resolution and how they can be employed
- The professional and moral responsibility of practitioners to support children and parents, sometimes alongside conflict

Understanding Conflict

In order to be in a position from which to resolve conflict, firstly, practitioners need to fully understand what conflict means and why this occurs. Coser (1957) argues that conflict occurs when individuals or groups have contrasting vested interests and each party expresses their position, via frustration. Jeong (2010) suggests that the pursuit of different objectives or preferences often occurs to the detriment of the other party. For example: a family requests respite care. Yet the practitioner has other families who need this more, based on their assessment. Subsequently, the answer to the request for respite is no. Both parties' goals in this instance appear different, based on the contrasting opinions concerning the response to the expressed need for respite. Yet the objectives in this example are likely the very same: both parties want the best for the child, want the parents to feel supported and want the working relationship to be successful. Conflict can inaccurately indicate that the goals of both parties are opposing, whereas in reality, it may be the process of reaching these goals which are at odds.

There are two distinct types of conflict according to Choi and Sy (2010) and Jehn (1995):

- Task conflict: occurs due to disagreement about the task being undertaken. For example: the approach to supporting a family, the therapeutic response to the neurodivergent child's needs, or disagreements concerning an appropriate educational placement.
- Relationship conflict: occurs when the parties disagree, yet this is not related to the task or goal. An example might be a personality clash or a conflict prompted by contrasting views on issues which are unconnected to the task at hand.

(Choi & Sy, 2010; Jehn, 1995)

Coser (1957) proposes that the strain presented via conflicts, act as a motivating factor for both parties to work towards a resolution. A resolution emerges as a shared vested interest of both parties, as both want to move past the strain and frustration caused by the conflict (Coser, 1957). In this regard, Coser presents conflict as a process which strengthens existing relationships, with parties overcoming their contrasting perspectives in an effort to negotiate successfully and reach agreement (Coser, 1957).

Yet Coser (1957) contends that conflict is not only inevitable but necessary. Conflict is the motivating factor which has seen much-needed change and evolution in society, for example: concerning women's rights and the deinstitutionalisation of disabled people (Coser, 1957). If people didn't disagree and express their disagreement, things would never change or evolve. Conflict can actually clarify the expectations and goals of both parties within the practitioner/parent relationship and lead to greater clarity in terms of goals and wishes thereafter.

Reflection Point!

Imagine a world where no one disagreed . . . where one way, one approach or one movement were the only option. Imagine if no one spoke out, protested or lobbied for change. What would the world look like?

Practice Experiences

Having been on both sides of the therapy table, I can wholeheartedly empathise with the challenges felt by both professionals and families. Both parties can feel overwhelmed and near burnout due to their workload. Both parties can feel frustrated at the limitations of resources and services available. And both parties could be battling with insomnia, personal issues or mental health issues such as depression or anxiety, all while wearing their game face and showing up regardless. All of these factors cumulatively means that disagreement and conflict can and will likely occur, between parents and professionals. Each are coming to the table with their own priorities and rationale for these priorities.

However, the key difference between both parties (parents and professionals) is a pay packet. One party is paid to sit at the table, and the other is there because they are desperate to help their neurodivergent child. Most professionals feel passionate and genuine in their efforts to help neurodivergent children and their families and are vocationally invested in their roles. Yet this is still a role. The professional is paid to be there, bound by a rigid set of organisational protocols and profession-specific set of ethical guidelines. But really, it's a job. At the end of a tough day, you take off your work hat and go home to your own family, the peace of your own home. You look forward to your annual leave, or perhaps make plans regarding moving to a new position or applying for a promotion. All of these characteristics of a job are choice based and present autonomy, yet are steeped within the specific boundaries of your profession.

For parents and families, this is their life. This is their everyday, their 24 hours, 7 days per week, 365 days per year life. When they leave the table, they leave with the same responsibilities and worries they came with. The carer stress and burnout they could be experiencing are often without respite, and for lone parents and parents without family support, this burden of care can feel all consuming.

There are two key approaches to addressing conflict with parents, when aiming to create supportive environments for neurodivergent children and families:

1. *A preventative approach*: these are the actions the practitioner adopts to prevent or reduce the likelihood of conflict occurring in the first place.
2. *A responsive approach*: is concerned with how to respond to conflict should it arise and how you can use this as an opportunity to create a more supportive environment.

A Preventative Approach

A preventative strategic approach to avoiding or reducing the likelihood of conflict with parents is a proactive measure, which communicates professionalism and a commitment to creating a more supportive environment, for the neurodivergent child and their family. The principle of supporting parents to support their children, is closely informed by the communication, relationship and the partnership between the practitioner and the family. This principle, if employed effectively, should underpin each interaction with the child and their family and be explored in more detail as needed, should conflict arise.

Although conflict can and does occur within education, health and social care practice with parents/caregivers of neurodivergent children, there are methods which can be employed to reduce the likelihood of such conflict occurring. Tjosvold and Sun (2002) report that conflict avoidance is more widely employed in China, as the culture and values within this society encourage more harmonious and less aggressive methods of reaching shared goals. They contend that conflict avoidance is motivated by the existing relationship between the parties and the reliance of the parties on one another. Tjosvold and Sun (2002) conducted their research within an organisation, and participants reported on conflict avoidance with their peers, in their work environment (Tjosvold & Sun, 2002). Nonetheless, the findings present a thought--provoking insight regarding conflict avoidance and the motivation of a practitioner to default to this position.

Reflection Point!

Can you think of a time in your practice when you experienced a disa-greement with a client/service user/individual?
What was your internal reaction?
What was your external reaction?
What would you do differently if faced with the same situation again?

Past Negative Experiences

Past negative experiences and interactions with professionals, can greatly influence parents as they interact with new practitioners and services. If families feel they have been mistreated or not listened to in the past, they may expect this same treatment in their interactions with you. Or they may bring a general distrust of educators or practitioners based on previous neg-ative interactions, to their interactions with you. Fundamentally, conflict largely arises between professionals and parents due to the broader systemic factors which negatively impact their child, family and interactions with ser-vices. The amount of time spent waiting for services is a fundamental is-sue which profoundly negatively impacts neurodivergent children and their families. Other broader issues which influence the daily lives and long-term outcomes for families, are the availability of resources and therapies, the availability of staff on multidisciplinary teams and within schools. Such sys-temic factors further impact professionals within their roles. Hence, aware-ness and acknowledgment of such issues and the challenges they present, can help practitioners to remain cognisant of the pressures faced by the families of the neurodivergent children with whom they interact.

It's important to discuss and aim to address these previous past experi-ences at the outset of establishing a new working relationship with parents/caregivers, in an active effort to create a supportive environment and reduce the likelihood of future conflict.

There are some practical steps practitioners can undertake at the start of welcoming a new family into their school/service/clinic, who have had negative experiences with other providers in the past:

- Ask parents if they had a positive or helpful experience with past services they have engaged with, and if not, why their experience was negative.
- Clarify by guiding the parent caregiver to share this experience with-out naming the agency/service/school or the individual practitioners involved.

- Listen to the parent's experiences and provide empathy.
- Refrain from judgement or sharing your opinion, regarding the parent's experience or the practice of other practitioners.
- Explain that you hope providing this space and garnering a greater understanding of the parent's past experiences with other services, may help both of you to move forward with a fresh start and a new approach to supporting their child and family.

Providing this space for parents at the outset, to offload the concerns they've brought with them from previous experiences, enables them to process these. Such a space is aligned with the key catalyst for action of creating supportive environments for neurodivergent children and their families, of acknowledgement. The key goal of raising the issue of past negative experiences, is to acknowledge the impact they have had on the family and hopefully assist them with moving forward. You will not be examining these experiences or deliberating or discussing them in detail, but rather opening a space at the initiation of your contact with this family, where these experiences can be named. Naming such experiences and acknowledging them are fundamental steps in processing and moving forward. At times where I have provided feedback regarding negative experiences in interacting with professionals, often the act of being listened to and having my experiences acknowledged (rather than any specific response or action) was really useful in enabling me to move on from this.

Case Study 1

Orlagh is a 10-year-old student in your class who has a diagnosis of ADHD. Today Orlagh became frustrated during a spelling test and kicked the child next to her, causing injury. You have asked Orlagh's dad Peter to meet with you at school to discuss this incident and how best to respond and move forward. As you begin to explain to Peter what happened, he interrupts and says he is sick of his daughter being picked on for having ADHD and always blamed for anything that happens in the classroom. As you begin to respond, Peter stands up and starts screaming at you that he's had enough of this school, and he will take his daughter out of school and report you to the department of education. You reply that you understand he feels upset, but Peter doesn't let you finish and starts using foul language and moving closer to you as he screams and shouts.
     What's your initial instinct on how to respond?
     How do you think you would respond?
     What else could you do?

Response

In this instance, as soon as Peter raises his voice, this meeting should be ended. Conflict is concerned with a disagreement. However, aggressive behaviour is unacceptable in any context. Using as few words as possible, explain that this conversation is ending as Peter's behaviour is inappropriate, and leave the classroom. Keep your voice calm and low, be clear yet firm. If Peter tries to reengage with you, or follow you as you leave the classroom, ignore any attempts to interact and get to a place where other people are.

Examples of what to say:

- We can't continue this conversation right now; you need to leave.
- It's not appropriate to speak to me like this; this conversation is over now.
- I will call you tomorrow; this meeting can't continue now. Please leave.

Developing a Partnership With Parents/Caregivers

Developing a positive working relationship or partnership with parents is one of the most effective methods of creating supportive environments for neurodivergent children and their families. Consequently, partnerships with parents/caregivers has been identified as a fundamental principle of creating supportive environments. In fact, I would argue that the relationship between the practitioners and parents is a monumental prerequisite for promoting positive outcomes for the child and their family. I may not always agree with the professional supporting my child, yet if we have established a solid partnership from the start of our interactions, then my trust in them means that I can more readily accept our disagreement and usually their alternative suggestion or practice response.

Developing a partnership with parents/caregivers is equally a preventative method and a way of reducing the likelihood of conflict occurring. While a good relationship between practitioners and parents, further contributes to a greater likelihood of the resolution of conflict, if it does occur. This partnership places a positive baseline and context for every future interaction with this family and can make even the most difficult conversation less stressful, overwhelming or combative. For example: Tom is a school teacher who has built and maintained a positive relationship with Keith's parents. Keith is 8 years old and autistic. Tom has established a sense of trust and shared goals with Keith's parents of supporting Keith to be included, engage with his schoolwork and feel safe in school. Although Tom has to have frequent difficult conversations with Keith's parents regarding instances of concern in school and the changing levels of resources available to meet Keith's needs, these difficult conversations and the differences of opinions which stem from them, are addressed and resolved quickly. This is due to the partnership and sense of trust between the teacher and parents and an acknowledgement of shared goals for Keith's wellbeing and education.

Building a successful partnership between practitioners/educators and parents acknowledges the insight and commitment of both parties, in helping the neurodivergent child to reach their full potential and to navigate the challenges they meet on this journey. Parents bring a wealth of in-depth knowledge about their child's unique needs, while practitioners bring their professional expertise, insight and past experiences. Collaborating within this vein amalgamates the expertise of both parents and practitioners, with the aim of comprehensively and holistically supporting the child.

Ways of promoting the building of a positive relationship between practitioners and parents, should commence with discussion and clarification of how the partnership will work. For example: when and where will meetings take place? How will you contact one another? Will you communicate via email or only in person? What will happen if you disagree on how best to support the child? By openly discussing such issues at the outset, a supportive environment of acceptance and sincerity is already being established. Such questions further enable the practitioner to determine the preferences and distinctive needs of the family, in terms of communication and availability to meet.

Parents identify the significance of developing a relationship and working in partnership with practitioners supporting their children, in a research study by Edwards, Brebner, McCormack, and MacDougall (2016). Edwards et al. (2016) report that parents value immensely when they feel involved in their child's therapeutic interventions and have regular and honest communication from their child's therapist. Robert, Leblanc, and Boyer (2014), in their study exploring parent satisfaction with services which support their child with disabilities, suggest that parents having a sense of trust in their practitioner was linked with greater levels of satisfaction with their service provision. Parents who trusted the expertise and decision-making capacity of their child's therapist, expressed feeling more secure in the knowledge that the appropriate therapeutic response for their child is being provided (Robert et al., 2014).

Individualised Education Plans (IEPs) are frequently undertaken based on a partnership approach between educators and parents of children with complex needs (Kurth, Love, & Pirtle, 2020). Kurth et al. (2020) conclude that the relationship between parents and teachers, is closely linked to parents' engagement with the IEP process and their overall satisfaction with the outcomes. Hence, the literature demonstrates that in both healthcare and educational settings, partnerships between educators/practitioners and parents is a considerable factor in determining the family's satisfaction with their child's care (Kurth et al., 2020; Robert et al., 2014; Edwards et al., 2016).

In research concerning the practitioner's experiences, practitioners express that a partnership approach to working with families cultivates and promotes an investment in successful long-term engagement with the family (Rossiter, Fowler, Hopwood, Lee, & Dunston, 2011). Rossiter et al. (2011) contend that a partnership approach to practice with families demonstrates the evolution of traditional hierarchical health services, to one where value is placed on the experiences parents bring to the partnership.

Roger's Three Core Conditions

Carl Rogers was a psychotherapist who wrote extensively on what factors contribute to a successful therapeutic relationship. Rogers (1956) wrote a cornerstone paper which identified core conditions he believed were essential, to promoting positive outcomes from therapeutic interactions between patients and clinicians. Now more than 60 years later, the three core conditions identified by Rogers (1956) are still very relevant to practitioners practicing within the helping professions. Within any setting which aims to create a supportive environment for neurodivergent children and families, adopting Roger's core conditions within practice can help to build and maintain positive relationships with parents and reduce the likelihood of conflict arising. Roger's three core conditions are:

1. *Genuineness*: this refers to the practitioner being themselves as much as is possible within the professional relationship. This means being real, being present and being your authentic self, in your interactions with the person to whom you are providing support.
2. *Empathy*: is concerned with being able to place yourself in the shoes of the person you are providing support to and aiming to view their world from their perspective. Rather than just imagining what their experiences are, you are actively immersing yourself into how the person feels and how they are impacted by their experiences. Empathy is easier to experience as the practitioner/client relationship develops and you become more familiar with the person to whom you are providing support.
3. *Unconditional positive regard*: this condition relates to the practitioner remaining accepting of the person they are supporting, regardless of the experiences they share or whether or not you agree with these. The practitioner maintains this positive regard towards the client/patient/person (Rogers, 1956).

These core conditions are by no means hard-and-fast rules to be rigidly applied when working with parents and families of neurodivergent children.

However, remaining mindful of these three core conditions can help to maintain your focus towards creating and maintaining positive relationships with parents, and indeed contributing to re-establishing these positive relationships, post conflict or disagreement.

A Responsive Approach

A responsive approach to resolving conflicts between practitioners and parents, takes place after a conflict has occurred. A responsive approach enables the practitioner/educator and parent/caregiver to acknowledge and move past a conflict, with the aim of moving forward to support the neurodivergent child.

Resolving Conflict

Furlong (2005) argues that prior to attempting to resolve a conflict, diagnosis of what is causing this is a crucial first step. Just as a doctor wouldn't diagnose you with an illness prior to assessing your symptoms, we shouldn't start trying to resolve a conflict, without full understanding of what the conflict is (Furlong, 2005). Practitioners should reflect with parents and alone, regarding what the disagreement is. How did both parties react? And what else contributed to the conflict occurring?

It's sometimes unrealistic for practitioners and parents, to expect a conflict to be resolved immediately. Walking away from the table and taking time to reflect on the cause of the conflict and to empathise with the perspectives of the other party, often enables more clarity in reaching an agreement. Equally, rather than derail completely the goal for this meeting, it's okay to park the issue causing the conflict temporarily and continue aiming to work towards the meeting objectives. For example: when meeting with a family post assessment to discuss the practice response to their neurodivergent child's needs, if parents disagree with the practitioner's suggestion for applying for a place in an autism-specific classroom, both parties can still discuss and agree the child's other therapy needs and how these will be met. It's okay to acknowledge a disagreement and agree to revisit and discuss this at the end of the meeting or at another time, which enables the discussion of other important issues to continue and progress.

Conflict Negotiation

Fisher and Ury (2011) present four specific principles for negotiation:

1. *Separating people from the problem*: this principle is concerned with both parties discussing the issues, without feeling personally attacked. This may be difficult for parents as the issues are likely very personal for them.

Yet for professionals, differentiating between varying perspectives and personal emotional injury, can enable parties to move past disagreements (Fisher & Ury, 2011). For example: if a parent expresses frustration or anger due to waiting times and says that they are sick of the service, it's useless and has been of no help to their child. A practitioner could perceive this as a message that they are useless, ineffective in their role and have not helped this family sufficiently. However, separating the problem from the person would empower the practitioner to acknowledge the systemic impact of waiting lists, lack of resources and over-worked and under-resourced teams. Recognising this as an external issue which impacts both parties at the table and moving on from this, will enable the practitioner to progress in generating agreement and ultimately a solution for this family.

2. *Focusing on interests rather than positions*: this relates to finding common ground within negotiations and identifying where interests overlap or where parties could meet in the middle (Fisher & Ury, 2011). For example: the parent of a neurodivergent child has decided their child is not returning to school, as this environment is extremely distressing for them. Their position is that they need to protect their child, and currently the school environment is not a protective one. Your position could be that you need to support the parents and child to return to school, as education is a crucial element of child development. But what are your shared interests in this situation? The parent wants their child to be happy, distress free and to feel safe. The practitioner wants all of these same things for the child. So building from these points of agreement, can you facilitate a solution which works for both parties. It may not be based on the original positions of no school or return to school. However, it will be based on the shared interests identified and discussed within the negotiations.

3. *Discussing a variety of options prior to agreement*: this principle refers to the importance of generating multiple broad options, without making a judgement within the initial stages. Rather than debating a win/lose set of options, sufficient time should be dedicated to openly discussing, brainstorming and considering numerous possible solutions. Instead of looking at one or two potential solutions, the practitioner will facilitate a broad range of possible resolutions or outcomes, which can then be discussed further and narrowed down (Fisher & Ury, 2011). For example: a parent who is refusing to engage voluntarily with social work services due to a previous negative experience, yet a child welfare concern has been raised. The obvious options might be to keep trying to have the parent agree to the referral or make a referral without their agreement (only applicable within child protection/welfare concerns). However, what about exploring supports which could be available from the social work

department, which might benefit this family? Or making contact with the social work department to query more generally, what the parent could expect from their referral? Or exploring if the parent could self-refer with the practitioner's support?

4. *Using objective criteria*: Fisher and Ury (2011) contend that using objective criteria provides for both parties to reach a resolution, based on impartial or independent criteria for decision making. This could be evidence in the form of research studies or literature, legislation or professional standards. Both parties must agree to and be open to the use of the criteria to reach a resolution (Fisher & Ury, 2011). For example: parents advocating for play therapy for their child living with ADHD, and professionals having limited resources to provide this. Parents would outline why this is their preferred response to their child's needs, why play therapy specifically? Was this advice from another family, research studies they sourced or another insight the practitioner is unaware of? The practitioner in response and providing objective criteria for their perspective (that play therapy is not the most appropriate response) would share evidence with the parents regarding the most effective method of responding to ADHD (medication). The practitioner may also share the resourcing criteria as evidence, including the guidelines and protocols within the organisation, which dictate the availability of various therapeutic responses.

Case Study 2

You are working as part of a multidisciplinary team and meeting with Laura and Patrick, parents of Marko, aged 6, who was recently diagnosed as autistic. As this is the first meeting, you begin to explain to Patrick and Laura the role of your team and how you will approach Marko's care. When you explain that you will meet with Marko's teachers and observe him in the classroom setting, Laura interjects and says she is not comfortable with this. Laura hasn't discussed Marko's diagnosis with his school and doesn't want you to make contact with his teacher.

What are your initial thoughts?
How would you react?
Could you respond differently?

Context

Why might Laura be apprehensive about sharing her son's diagnosis with school? Could she be afraid that he may need to move schools?

Could her cultural understanding of autism contribute to her fear of the stigma Marko might face? Are there any past experiences which might be contributing to Laura's stance?

Response

1. Acknowledge what Laura has said. Explain that you've listened and heard Laura expressing her wish not to share Marko's diagnosis with his school.
2. Remain non-judgemental. Regardless of your instinctive feelings and professional judgement on this issue, communicate a non-judgemental stance in your response. This means remaining conscious of the words you use and how you are communicating non-verbally. An open posture and maintained eye contact and a reassuring and accepting tone, will all contribute to nurturing your relationship with Marko's parents and building their trust (Rogers, 1956).
3. Ask Laura why she feels reluctant about telling the school Marko is autistic. Probe further (gently) and show you are genuinely interested and open to Laura's response. Also ask Peter if he agrees and why.
4. Take time. This issue doesn't need to be resolved today and can be something to work on as a goal for future interactions. You can agree to pause this conversation for today and discuss other areas of Marko's care which need to be agreed on.
5. Plan for the next meeting, based on the information you have gathered at this first meeting. Look at the evidence base on this issue, engage in reflective practice and critically consider how best to proceed and support Marko, while maintaining a positive working-in-partnership relationship with his parents.

Naming It

Honesty, sincerity and calling a spade a spade, is a candid and direct approach to responding to conflict with parents. What went wrong? What are the main issues? What needs to change to prevent this conflict from rearising? Key to naming it, is acknowledging the responsibility of both parties in contributing to the conflict occurring. Both practitioners and parents may feel as if they have done nothing wrong and have no errors or faults to rectify. Yet upon reflection, there are often ways both parties could have engaged or communicated differently. Acknowledging your role within the conflict is an important part of conflict resolution and in communicating to parents/caregivers that professionals are human and can make mistakes! Parents often genuinely appreciate when professionals acknowledge an error or practice response which could have been more appropriate, and it actually strengthens future relationships. This can be extremely difficult to do as a professional. Yet identifying even one thing you could have done differently and sharing this with parents in an effort to resolve conflict, conveys accountability, professionalism and a sincere commitment to support the child and family. Once both sides have identified their individual actions which may have contributed to the conflict arising, then parents and practitioners can discuss what they can do to prevent similar issues from rearising in the future. This is another active expression of creating a supportive environment and improving outcomes for the child and family. This is outlined in a practice example in the following sections.

Background

Isabel arrives to her scheduled meeting with the practitioner to discuss her daughter Ava, aged 15, who has a diagnosis of ADHD. The practitioner Cody has been working with both Isabel and Ava on managing emotions and reducing violent behaviours. Ava has been trialling a new medication and undergoing behavioural support therapies.

What Happened?

Isabel seems overly quiet at the start of the meeting and is quite abrupt in her responses to the practitioner's questions. Eventually, Isabel declares quite angrily that they are leaving and this service is not helping and in fact, she's never felt so alone. The practitioner is taken aback, as things had been progressing quite well from their perspective. Isabel gets up and leaves, slamming the office door behind her. The practitioner takes the time to reflect on the last few meetings with Isabel, which all seemed fine. But Cody does realise that Isabel has not been in contact between appointments, which she usually would (via phone or email). Double-checking his inbox, Cody finds multiple emails from Isabel in his junk folder, each sounding more desperate than the previous one. Ava has stopped taking her medication and there have been frequent violent outbursts at home, even an occasion where the police were called.

Reflection

Upon reflection, Cody realises that Isabel was experiencing a crisis and had tried unsuccessfully to contact him. Although not intentional, Cody missed these emails, and this resulted in Isabel feeling alone and unsupported.

Cody emails Isabel immediately to apologise and explain what happened. He explains that he will be available later in the week for a meeting, and that he feels sad that Isabel and Ava have been through such a difficult time.

Resolution

When they next meet, Cody holds his hands up and explains honestly that he missed Isabel's emails, as they went into his junk folder. Yet he further acknowledges that this is still his responsibility, and he is genuinely really sorry for not responding. Isabel replies that she appreciates Cody's honesty and that she too is sorry for losing her temper when they last met. Cody then explains that they should discuss what went wrong and what they can both do to reduce the likelihood of something similar happening in the future.

Reflection Point!

If a person you are supporting is shouting at you, behaving aggressively or you feel afraid, do not continue with this interaction. Your safety and wellbeing should remain your key priority. In this instance, remove yourself from this situation. Using as few words as possible, end the interaction and get yourself to a safe environment. For example: Explain that you can't continue with this meeting as it isn't safe, and explain you will make contact at a later date with the person. If this is happening in your office, clinic or classroom, ask the person to leave immediately. If they don't, then leave the room yourself and seek assistance from colleagues.

Power Differentials

Wrong (1997) defines power as the agency to impact the world around you. Power is about the ability of one person or entity to influence, effect or change the circumstances of another person or group of people (Wrong, 1997). I view power as an unseen bargaining chip which weighs heavily on the agenda of both parties, within the practitioner/parent relationship. We don't talk about it, but we both know it's there. Power in this context can profoundly influence each interaction between these parties and begins long before they meet in person.

It's key to acknowledge as a professional from the outset, that power imbalances are intrinsic to practitioner/family relationships. Professionals maintain greater power within their relationships with parents, as they have greater decision-making capacity in terms of resources, access to services, and even appointment times and frequency. Although parents make key decisions about their child's life, for a neurodivergent child, parents often rely on professionals to assist them in meeting their child's needs. Particularly for families accessing services for their child via public systems, parents are completely reliant upon the decisions of professionals in determining major factors which will impact their child's life. For example: school places, further assessments, access to special needs resources in school, access to therapies, family support and even financial entitlements. Each of these substantial areas is wholly dependent on the say-so of professionals, external to this family.

Agusti-Panareda (2004) argues that the less powerful party can resist agreement with the more powerful party, as their suspicions are heightened and they engage in protective behaviour and decision making. While the more powerful party at the negotiation table can inadvertently exert their power, via their enhanced ability to communicate their views, being better equipped to navigate the relevant systems (disability services), or by reducing the decision making afforded to the less powerful party (Qtaishat, 2018). Qtaishat (2018) proposes that each party is distinctly advantaged or disadvantaged at the outset, based on the power they possess within the context of the exchange.

Having awareness of your power as a professional is a key step in overcoming conflict with parents. Imagine a time when you were sick or in the hospital and were dependent on other people to meet even your most basic needs. Imagine having to call someone to ask them to get you a drink or help you to get to the bathroom. In this personal context, you lack power and to some extent are at the mercy of the person who is helping you. This can be what it feels like for parents entering into the maze of disability support services, advocating for their neurodivergent child. They can't access the most basic things their child needs (education, therapies, supports, entitlements) without depending on you to help them. This can feel terrifying for some parents.

The next step after awareness in considering the impact of power dynamics on overcoming conflict with parents in professional practice, is consistent critical reflection on your power and how this is impacting the therapeutic relationship. Reflective practice is identified as a core principle of creating supportive environments for neurodivergent children and families and is concerned with consistently reviewing and questioning your practice. Reflective practice prompts practitioners to critically consider their approach, their interactions, the effectiveness of their practice and the satisfaction of families with whom they engage. Asking yourself questions such as: how is my perceived power impacting this disagreement? How might the parent been perceiving their own power (or lack thereof) regarding the current situation? How could I use my power to support this family? And how could the power within this professional relationship be redistributed? Are there decisions I usually make which could be made by parents or the neurodivergent child? Continually questioning the power imbalance is a key stage of effective conflict resolution, in the context of practice with the parents of neurodivergent children.

Author Reflection Point!

I've often disagreed with professionals who support my children, but I did so in a kind and respectful manner. It's okay for parents to disagree, or question your approach, once they do so respectfully. As a parent who has sat at both sides of the table, I do tend to question, ask for rationale and request additional certainty, in terms of the approach to supporting my children. I'd say without a stretch I'm not the favourite appointment many professionals have in their diary on any given week!

But I also remember that we all share the same goal: supporting my neurodivergent child to reach their goals and live a full and inclusive life. And the professionals who support my children know that I want exactly this too. Building a relationship of partnership with professionals has increased my trust in them and their approach to supporting my child. This takes time to build and maintain, but once established is the greatest asset a neurodivergent child can have: their parent/s and the professionals providing and guiding their care, working really effectively together, to give them the best opportunities possible to succeed and become whoever they want to be.

When to Ask for Additional Support

It can be difficult to call it as a professional and decide that a stalemate or impasse has been reached, concerning conflict with parents. Yet identifying a situation which is unlikely to be resolved and asking for external input to progress the conflict to resolution, is a child-centred approach which should be employed. The longer the conflict continues, the less likely the neurodivergent child is to have their needs met. So if multiple attempts using the skills and processes discussed in this chapter, alongside your clinical expertise and experience to resolve the conflict have been unsuccessful, asking a colleague to assist is the correct approach.

Reflection Point!

Asking for help is a vital skill for practitioners to learn to master. It can feel counterintuitive and even like accepting defeat. However, asking for help is actually illustrating professionalism and a wish to meet the needs of the neurodivergent child, in the most timely manner possible.

A colleague intervening can present a fresh view of the conflict and perhaps a more impartial perspective on how the conflict can be resolved. When you have concluded that your efforts at resolving the conflict have been unsuccessful, speak to the parents about this and inform them that you intend to ask a colleague to assist. It's really important to explain your rationale for this and emphasise that your priority lies with having their child's needs met in the most timely manner possible. Parents will appreciate this honesty and will be equally eager to prioritise meeting their child's needs.

Self-Assessment

Name two reasons why conflict may occur between a professional and parent.

What can the practitioner do to try to prevent or reduce the likelihood of conflict occurring?

How can conflict with parents/caregivers be resolved?

Summary

This chapter has explored the issue of managing conflict with parents, within the context of creating supportive environments for neurodivergent children and families. Notable within this chapter in particular, is the focus on preventing or reducing the likelihood of conflict occurring, as opposed to focusing solely on conflict resolution. A partnership approach to working with parents/caregivers is a key action towards realising the principle of creating a supportive environment for neurodivergent children and families, of supporting parents to support their children.

This chapter explored Roger's three core conditions, in the context of both preventing and responding to conflict with parents. The issue of power was further discussed, as this impacts unreservedly every interaction between the practitioner and the family. This chapter presented ideas and practice-based strategies for reducing and countering conflict between practitioners and parents, within the context of creating supportive environments for neurodivergent children and their families.

References

Agusti-Panareda, J. (2004). Power imbalances in mediation: Questioning some common assumptions. *Dispute Resolution Journal: Of the American Arbitration Association, 59*(2), 24.

Choi, J.N., & Sy, T. (2010). Group-level organizational citizenship behavior: Effects of demographic faultlines and conflict in small work groups. *Journal of Organizational Behavior, 31*, 1032–1054. https://doi.org/10.1002/job.661

Coser, L. (1957). Social conflict and the theory of social change. *The British Journal of Sociology, 8*(3), 197–207.

Edwards, A., Brebner, C., Mccormack, P.F., & Macdougall, C. (2016). "More than blowing bubbles": What parents want from therapists working with children with autism spectrum disorder. *International Journal of Speech-Language Pathology, 1*(5), 493–505. https://doi.org/10.3109/17549507.2015.1112835

Fisher, R., & Ury, W. (2011). *Getting to yes: Negotiating agreement without giving in* (3rd ed.). New York, NY: Penguin Books.

Furlong, G. (2005). *The conflict resolution toolbox models & maps for analyzing, diagnosing, and resolving conflict*. Mississauga: John Wiley & Sons.

Jehn, K. (1995). A multimethod examination of the benefits and detriments of intragroup conflict. *Administrative Science Quarterly, 40*(2), 256–282. https://doi.org/10.2307/2393638

Jeong, H. (2010). *Conflict management and resolution: An introduction*. London and New York: Routledge.

Kurth, J., Love, H., & Pirtle, J. (2020). Parent perspectives of their involvement in IEP development for children with autism. *Focus on Autism and Other Developmental Disabilities, 35*(1), 36–46. https://doi.org/10.1177/10883576198428

Qtaishat, A.K (2018). Power imbalances in mediation. *Asian Social Science, 14*(2). https://doi.org/10.5539/ass.v14n2p75

Robert, M., Leblanc, L., & Boyer, T. (2014). When satisfaction is not directly related to the support services received: Understanding parents' varied experiences with specialised services for children with developmental disabilities. *British Journal of Learning Disabilities, 43*, 168–177. https://doi.org/10.1111/bld.12092

Rogers, C. (1956). The necessary and sufficient conditions of therapeutic personality change. *The Journal of Consulting Psychology, 21*, 95–103.

Rossiter, C., Fowler, C., Hopwood, N., Lee, A., & Dunston, R. (2011). Working in partnership with vulnerable families: The experience of child and family health practitioners. *Australian Journal of Primary Health, 17*(4), 378–383. https://doi.org/10.1071/PY11056

Tjosvold, D., & Sun, H.F. (2002). Understanding conflict avoidance: Relationship, motivations, actions and consequences. *International Journal of Conflict Management, 13*(2), 142–164. https://doi.org/10.1108/eb022872

Wrong, D. (1997). *Power: Its forms, bases, and uses*. New Brunswick: Routledge

Chapter 9

Evidence-Based Practice

Abbreviations

ADHD: Attention Deficit Hyperactivity Disorder
APA: American Psychiatric Association
DCD: Developmental Coordination Disorder

Introduction

We do better . . . because we know better. Evidence-based practice promotes decision making and practice responses which are based on the most up-to-date and reliable evidence available, in combination with the practitioner's perspective and the views and wishes of the neurodivergent child and their family. Consequently, no one-size-fits-all approach is appropriate for supporting neurodivergent children, and each child and family deserve the unique care which accurately reflects their needs. This chapter will examine evidence-based practice and what this means for practitioners working with neurodivergent children and their families. This chapter will equip you with the skills to evaluate and discern appropriate sources of evidence and how to synthesise these with your own experience and insight, alongside the child's and family's hopes and wishes for themselves.

This chapter will commence with an exploration of evidence-based practice and what this means in the context of your work. Tangible methods of promoting and engaging in evidence-based practice will be discussed, via consideration of case studies and practice examples. Finally, the relevance of evidence-based practice within the context of creating supportive environments for neurodivergent children and their families, will be considered.

Learning Outcomes

On completion of this Chapter 9, learners should demonstrate an enhanced understanding concerning:

DOI: 10.4324/9781003455868-9

- Defining evidence-based practice
- Gathering and evaluating evidence
- Evidence-based practice and creating supportive environments

What Is Evidence-Based Practice?

Haynes, Devereaux, and Guyatt (2002) argue that evidence-based practice comprises three key components: research, patient's/client's preferences and clinician expertise. Haynes et al. (2002) caution that evidence-based practice ultimately should be guided by the patient's unique presentation. For example, the literature based on the most recent research data available could indicate that medication is the most effective method of treating ADHD in children. Yet a child with a heart condition, or currently taking another medication, may not benefit from medication, given the increased risks this would present for them. Equally, a family who are firmly committed to supporting their ADHD child without the use of medication, would need their practitioner to use their clinical expertise and a broader consideration of the relevant research, to propose a different response to their child's needs, based on their preferences. Hence, this medley of considering and discerning between sources of evidence, while balancing the complexities involved in decision making concerning people, is the process which is known as using an evidence-based practice approach (Haynes et al., 2002; Allen & Bellamy, 2012). As you may have noted already, the language surrounding evidence-based practice is largely based within the medical field, where this approach emerged. Hence why the term *patient* is more frequently referred to within the literature, and therefore referred to within this chapter.

Reflection Point!

Imagine you are having a pre-surgical consultation for a hip replacement. Your surgeon informs you that they learned the methodology to do this procedure in 1982, and although they know newer methods are available, this method works well.

- What are your initial thoughts?
- Would a 40-year-old approach cause concern . . . even if it's still deemed effective? If so, why?
- Would you proceed with your surgery?

Allen and Bellamy (2012) propose that evidence-based practice is ethical practice, and when delivering human services, evaluating the effectiveness of one's methods is fundamental. Allen and Bellamy (2012, p. 7) define evidence-based practice as "a process for making practice decisions in which practitioners integrate the best research evidence available, with their practice expertise" alongside the client's wishes and preferences.

Evidence-based practice is sometimes misconstrued as being limited to sourcing research and literature from which to inform practice (Fulcher-Rood, Castilla-Earls, & Higginbotham, 2020). Yet evidence-based practice is equally concerned with the unique wishes and preferences of the patient or family, in addition to the expertise of the clinician in discerning the most appropriate course of action (Montori, Brito, & Murad, 2013). Montori et al. (2013) propose that evidence alone is insufficient to inform clinical decision making, and practitioners need to consider as a fundamental starting point, the wishes of the person in receipt of care. Clinician expertise and evidence of this can further be gleaned from peers or other professionals within your network and need not be limited to your own experiences.

Sam, Odom, Tomaszewski, Perkins, and Cox (2021) conducted a very interesting piece of research specifically examining the use of evidence-based practice in an education setting for autistic children. They compared the use of evidence-based practice to "business as usual" or typical practices within 60 elementary schools (Sam et al., 2021). Findings indicate that the employment of evidence-based practice compared to typical practice, resulted in greater educational attainment for autistic children, and Sam et al. (2021) define the difference as significant.

Author Reflection Point!

I approach my children's needs and in fact I parent completely differently now, compared to 10 years ago. Why? Because today we have so much more insight, understanding and sound evidence concerning neurodivergence! We have access to all of this evidence at our fingertips (as opposed to visiting a library and trawling through literature in person), and we have a culture of asking for evidence now. Is this the most effective way? And if so, where's the evidence?

Clinical Expertise

Rycroft-Malone et al. (2004) suggest that knowledge from clinical experience is a key part of the evidence-based practice puzzle and is based upon the practitioner's past experiences and insights. This profession-specific knowledge and understanding enables the practitioner to critique their assumed ways of knowing and discern the most useful and appropriate practice decisions, based on this critique (Rycroft-Malone et al., 2004). For example: a teacher with 20 years of experience will have substantial clinical expertise, based on their extensive practice to date.

Utilising clinical experience within the medley of evidence-based practice, means reflecting on previous practice and valuing clinical judgement and decision making, based upon past practice experience. Practitioners value their unique insight, experience and knowledge pertaining to their profession and, drawing upon this, make informed practice decisions. Yet evidence-based practice does not only advocate for relying on clinical expertise alone and presents a more comprehensive and robust process for informing decision making. Evidence-based practice places significant value on clinical expertise, and also endorses the need for the simultaneous integration of family preferences and research.

Clinical expertise is based on one's past experiences and intuition concerning practice, in addition to previous decision making and subsequent outcomes (Wu, Yang, Liu, & Ye, 2016). Consequently, according to Wu et al. (2016), the duration of experience in the setting or sector enhances clinical expertise and decision-making skills. Yet Wu et al. (2016) further contend that newer practitioners can base clinical decisions on the more up-to-date training qualifications they have received and can commit to actively developing their clinical expertise through practice.

However, errors in clinical decision making based on clinical expertise can and do happen. In medicine, errors based on clinical expertise can potentially be catastrophic and even result in death. Within the context of supporting neurodivergent children and families, errors in clinical expertise relating to decision making could culminate in a wrong diagnosis, a delayed diagnosis, or an ineffective or an inappropriate therapeutic or family support approach to the child's and family's needs. Such errors may culminate in profound distress for the child and their family and contribute to ongoing unmet needs. However, Tsang et al. (2023) reports that practitioners can critically reflect on practice errors and actively aim to learn from these. Such reflection can assist the practitioner to revise their practice based on their previous errors, and use this to inform their clinical expertise going forward.

Author Reflection Point!

As a parent, clinical expertise is something I need to be able to rely on in order to make informed and appropriate decisions, for my neurodivergent children regarding health, social and educational supports. I value immensely the clinical expertise of the educators and practitioners with whom we interact. This confidence has been facilitated largely via creating a partnership approach to care and building familiarity. This enables parents to build trust in the clinical experiences and judgement of practitioners.

Wishes and Preferences of the Child and Family

Practice responses which are based upon the values and preferences of the patient/child/family are more likely to result in positive outcomes (Bastemeijer, Voogt, Van Ewijk, & Hazelzet, 2017). Bastemeijer et al. (2017) propose that patient values – that is, their moral and ethical positioning – are central within health and social care provision. Values can inform practitioners about the issues which are most important to the child and family concerning the care they receive. One family may possess values relating to retaining decision making and autonomy concerning their child's treatment or educational journey, while another family may present with values of cooperation and relationships, or respect. These core values will inform the family's preferences for their child's care or educational plan and each interaction they have with the practitioners.

Ascertaining and respecting the family's preferences concerning their child's needs, contributes to building and maintaining trusting and dependable relationships between parents and professionals. Vingerhoets, Hay-Smith, and Graham (2023) report that the relationship between the practitioner and patient, is a significant factor in determining patient preferences and wishes. Although screening and assessment processes can establish preferences from the outset, reengaging with patients culminates in discovering new insights regarding their preferences and what matters most to them (Vingerhoets et al., 2023). This is certainly my own experience as a recipient parent concerning medical and educational services for my children. At the beginning of interacting with a service, parents often may not have all the information they need to accurately express their preferences for their child's care or education. This may only become apparent to them as they become more familiar with the service and more comfortable with the practitioner or educator.

Den Hertog and Niessen (2019), in their nursing study on incorporating patient preferences into practice, concur that continued communication and revisiting of preferences is necessary, as preferences may change and evolve during the process. For example: a family who initially express a preference to avoid attending parenting courses, or a certain type of therapy for their child, may rethink this as their child's and family's needs evolve during their journey through disability support services. Equally, as the family gather more information and feel more empowered in decision making, they may change their views and preferences. Ultimately, if the child or their family feel that professionals are committed to respecting and facilitating their values and preferences, they are more likely to engage positively.

Reflection Point!

We all make mistakes as practitioners, despite our best efforts and commitment to the individuals and families we educate or provide care to. Think about an error within your previous practice (or an error made by another professional you work with) . . .
  Upon reflecting, what caused this error?
  How was the error rectified or responded to?
  How did the experience inform future practice?

It's important to recognise also that the wishes, needs and preferences of the family may contrast between children, if there are two or more neurodivergent children in the family. Parents use their own past experiences, their own research and their wishes and preferences, to guide their decision making concerning their child's treatment, support needs, etc. For example: parents may wish to trial medication for one of their children, or might be advocating for a school place in an autism-specific school. Whereas with their other child, parents may prefer to avoid medication and maintain their child in mainstream school with supports. This is often based on their unique insight into their child's needs, their experiences of supporting their children to date and the research, evidence and information they have sought and reviewed on the issue at hand.

Case Study 1

The Murphy family are new to the service and are facing a crisis point in managing their child Alex's needs at home. Alex has a recent diagnosis of autism and is regressing in terms of continence/toileting. John and Mary, Alex's parents, communicate that they value privacy and discretion and that this should be considered in all communication with them and interventions for their family. Alex feels embarrassed as he has soiled himself in school and would prefer not to talk about this. Alex's parents express a preference that no intervention or therapy takes place at their home or in school, and they wish Alex to be seen only in clinic appointments, outside of school hours.
  How would this family's values impact the practice response to their needs in terms of dos and don'ts?

What information regarding Alex and his parent's preferences, is important to share with other members of the team (with their permission)?

Why is it pertinent to respect the values and preferences of Alex, Mary and John?

Research

Research concerning neurodivergence and the individual presentations of ADHD, autism and dyspraxia, is being undertaken continually. Should we not consider the emerging evidence, practice would be limited to what we knew about these diagnoses from 20 years ago. Dyspraxia, for example, was also known as clumsy child syndrome (Gubbay, 1975), as symptoms often manifested in children having accidents, falling over and injuring themselves frequently. However, not only is this label insensitive and potentially disrespectful, but it further infers that this problem is the child's responsibility and is a very deficit-based description. Furthermore, understanding of dyspraxia has developed considerably to the extent that it's now understood to further impact the child in terms of their ability to plan and execute sequencing of tasks, which negatively impacts academic endeavours, social and leisure opportunities and independence (American Psychiatric Association, 2013; Dyspraxia/DCD Ireland, 2023).

Dyspraxia is further now known to negatively impact mental health, as well as emotional and social wellbeing across the lifespan (Harrowell, Hollén, Lingam, & Emond, 2017; Engel-Yeger, 2020). Such data emphasises the significance of intervention for children diagnosed with dyspraxia and assists practitioners and educators to create more focused and informed interventions. Should practice be based wholly on the initial evidence base concerning dyspraxia, interventions and subsequent positive outcomes would be substantially limited in scope and perhaps only to fine and gross motor task development.

Reflection Point!

Think of a time when you or a family member presented with unusual or concerning physical symptoms . . . (for qualified medical professionals, think of the early pandemic times when there was little certainty or evidence).

What did you do initially? Did you make an appointment to see your physician immediately or go to the emergency room? Or, did you first try to research your symptoms and find out more about what could be causing them?

The research element of evidence-based practice not only involves identifying research evidence which relates to the area or topic of practice, but also appraising the appropriateness of such research (Fineout-Overholt, Melnyk, Stillwell, & Williamson, 2010). Ellis (2019) contends that having a search strategy is a useful way of time saving when searching for evidence. Clarifying exactly what evidence you are seeking, should begin with a concise question and keywords. The scope of the search can subsequently be expanded or reduced as needed, after the initial search (Ellis, 2019). Fineout-Overholt et al. (2010) propose that appraisal of research should be systematic and begin with identifying the relevant studies based on appropriate search terms, and then documenting these within a table. Include a link to the study and information such as the study location, sample size and method or approach undertaken to gather the data (Fineout-Overholt et al., 2010).

Questions to ask yourself when identifying appropriate research from which to draw upon to inform practice decisions could include but should not be limited to:

- When was this published?
- Is there more recent research on this topic?
- Is it based on primary research or a literature review? (Van Wee & Banister, 2016)
- What do contrasting studies propose?
- What limitations have the author's themselves identified?
- How do the study's conclusions relate to your practice experiences? Are they consistent or contrasting?
- What was the sample size of the study?
- Was it undertaken in one hospital, community or country? Or was it undertaken across different countries?
- What are the strengths and weaknesses of the research?
- What else have the author's published on this topic?
- What makes the researchers qualified to reach the conclusions they have drawn?

Case Study 2

You are working in a clinic setting as part of a multidisciplinary team. Evan, age 14, has been re-referred for services having been previously discharged, as he had three violent outbursts in school in the past month. Evan has diagnoses of dyspraxia and ADHD and has been taking medication for two years. Evan's mother, Kara, is a single parent and advises that Evan's behaviour has changed dramatically over the preceding months and she is frightened of him. Kara explains that Evan has threatened to hurt her. Evan does not want to partake in discussions about his behaviour and turns his chair around so his back is facing you.

From an evidence-based practice perspective:

What would be your research or search question when looking for relevant research concerning the needs of this family?

How would both Evan's and Kara's perspectives and wishes impact your decision making regarding your practice response?

How would your response be informed by your clinical/practice expertise and insight?

Evidence-Based Practice in Practice

A key benefit of engaging in evidence-based practice is the accountability this presents for practitioners. Should a query or complaint arise in the future, practitioners possess a clear process of how they arrived at the decisions and approaches which informed their practice. Furthermore, the evidence gathered and critiqued will be a resource to re-refer to or consider when gathering future evidence for decision making in practice. Hence, documenting the steps undertaken in the evidence-based practice process is important, while retaining research articles and notes on client preferences, wishes and how clinical expertise were utilised to inform decision making, is further good practice and conducive to promoting accountability.

Rather than visiting the library and checking out 27 books on the topic of your practice, evidence-based practice is essentially prompting you to stop and pause, before planning for the needs of a neurodivergent child and their family. Within clinical, community and education settings, tried-and-tested methods and generic responses given the child's needs are often employed. However, evidence-based practice implores you to examine this practice for its effectiveness, consider alternatives and why or why not they could be employed. Evidence-based practice prompts the practitioner to ascertain the wishes and preferences of the unique child and family and then engage in reviewing the literature for new, innovative ideas and emerging methods.

Alqahtani et al. (2022) report that lack of cooperation from other colleagues and professionals, can act as a barrier for implementing evidence-based practice. Whether in a school, medical or community setting, practitioners rarely work in a solitary fashion with neurodivergent children and families and largely practice as part of a team. When one practitioner is committed to incorporating evidence-based practice, yet lacks buy-in from other team members, this can prove challenging (Alqahtani et al., 2022).

Reflection Point!

Within your current or future workplace, what are/might be the key barriers to implementing evidence-based practice? What could you influence or change to remove one of these barriers?

Hamaideh (2017) contends that access for sourcing appropriate research, can act as a challenge when attempting to implement evidence-based practice. Access to online journals and library membership is not commonplace, particularly in human services and state-funded agencies with limited budgets. This may dissuade practitioners from attempting to engage in evidence-based practice, if it's perceived as unattainable. However, targeted action can be taken in an effort to access evidence and facilitate evidence-based practice:

- Seek funding for such access to research databases via advocating upstream, communicating the significance and relevance of access to evidence.
- Query if organisations you collaborate with may have access to a library or online journals and could be willing to share this access.
- Practitioners can create and maintain a database of articles, research studies and literature they have been able to access and pool these resources, increasing access for colleagues and promoting evidence-based practice.
- Practitioners can often access university libraries as alumni, at a reduced rate.
- Staff could create their own clinical expertise evidence, by sharing best practice examples and innovative approaches which were effective and resulted in positive outcomes for neurodivergent children and families.

A further challenge in incorporating evidence-based practice is having insufficient time to undertake gathering and reviewing evidence (Greenwell & Walsh, 2021). However, Greenwell and Walsh (2021) report that training on the topic of evidence-based practice helps staff to overcome perceived barriers and successfully implement evidence-based practice within their practice. Staff can divide and share tasks for sourcing evidence and pool evidence deemed significant to the setting and families in receipt of care.

Lack of research to date on the topic or area of practice may further be problematic, when attempting to source appropriate evidence to utilise to inform practice, when creating supportive environments for neurodivergent children and families. Perhaps research hasn't been undertaken to date on this issue, or it's still within its infancy, with little or no published material. Within this instance, it can be useful to consider evaluating your new or innovative intervention and contributing to the evidence base. For example: trialling a new way of supporting autistic children in the classroom, or exploring the impact of a support group for fathers of children with ADHD. Another way of sourcing evidence and generating new ideas is collaborating with universities and colleges and participating in students' research projects. You can email universities to ascertain if any of their students' research interests/projects align with your practice and goals for sourcing evidence. Or you can specify a distinctive area you would like a student to research, and the university can match you with a student studying this topic.

Reflection Point!

In Ireland, significant changes have occurred within legislation regarding child protection and welfare, as a direct result of a public enquiry. The Roscommon Childcare Case investigated and reported on serious clinical and practice errors, which lead to the sustained abuse of six children.

When a public enquiry occurs and is subsequently reported on, professionals outline their errors, explore what contributed to such errors and identify what should have been done differently. This process teaches and informs the future practice not only of those involved, but also all other practitioners within the profession.

Unfortunately, such detailed enquiries and examination of clinical judgements, often only take place when a significant lapse in care occurs and the damage is catastrophic (e.g. care home deaths of older people during Covid-19, institutional abuse within reformatory schools or maternity deaths).

Google search a public enquiry (or court case) concerning medical, social work or educational negligence in your state. What does the report surmise contributed to the errors? What was the impact of these errors? What recommendations were made concerning future practice?

Evidence-Based Practice and Creating Supportive Environments

Steinbrenner et al. (2020) argue that services for neurodivergent children, must be based on the most effective practices and approaches available and based on robust evidence. Steinbrenner et al. (2020) contend that the volume of research into the effectiveness of interventions for autistic children has experienced exponential growth in the last 10 years and, furthermore, knowledge and terminology have evolved considerably. Incorporating evidence-based practice when supporting neurodivergent children and their families, assists practitioners to reduce complacency and deliver the highest possible level of care, education and support. Utilising evidence-based practice prompts consistent and continued questioning, concerning the appropriateness and usefulness of practice approaches.

Drawing upon the principles of creating supportive environments for neurodivergent children and their families, can facilitate evidence-based practice which is tailored to the uniqueness of the child and their family. The initial and every single interaction with the child and their family should foster an environment of inclusiveness, valuing the child's unique needs, while basing practice decisions and responses on their distinctive goals and hopes for the future. Creating supportive environments is facilitated via the building of partnerships between practitioners and parents, which is further significant in ascertaining accurately the child's individual needs and preferences. Incorporating the principle of reflective practice as a fundamental aspect of your role will consistently actuate the critical questioning of your approach, practice decisions and the efficacy of interactions.

An evidence-based practice approach is conducive to the principle of knowledge and awareness, when creating supportive environments for neurodivergent children and families. Practitioners have a professional and moral obligation to actively engage in knowledge acquisition continually, to maximise positive outcomes. Evidence-based practice recognises the necessity to amalgamate clinical expertise and patient/family preferences alongside research and evidence relating to the needs of the family, highlighting that no single approach is deemed sufficient. Exploring new and emerging evidence concerning neurodivergence, prompts practitioners to consider this new knowledge in the context of their clinical insight and previously acquired knowledge. This process enables a practitioner's awareness to continually evolve and develop in response to newer understandings. This acquisition of new knowledge and understanding communicates professionalism, an aim to reduce complacency in your practice and a commitment to continually critiquing your approach to meeting the needs of the neurodivergent child.

Case Study 3

Amina, age 5, has joined your kindergarten class, and you immediately notice she struggles with communication and does not interact with her peers. Upon speaking with Amina's parents, they advise that she has always been quiet and prefers to spend time alone. Amina's parents explain that Amina was receiving early intervention up to the age of 3 years old due to issues with her speech and language development, but since then, Amina has been receiving no services and does not have a specific diagnosis. Amina's parents express a preference to "wait and see" and feel that Amina's social skills will naturally develop in kindergarten.

Based on an evidence-based practice perspective, how would you approach responding to Amina's needs?

What professional practice experiences would you draw upon?

What sources of research/evidence would you examine?

How would the wishes of Amina's parents contribute to your decision making and subsequent practice response?

Neurodivergent children and families often feel powerless and that they lack autonomy in terms of their healthcare, social care and educational attainment. The availability of services and level of choice afforded to families, can be closely linked to financial resources both of the organisation (school, clinic, service delivery organisation) and the individual family. Equally, families without resources or those facing marginalisation due to race, culture or educational attainment, may feel even more disempowered and dependent on professionals for making decisions which impact them. Evidence-based practice aims to value the voice of each child and family in terms of their wishes about services they engage with and communicate a sense of appreciation and respect for their unique family values. This inclusive and partnership-based approach communicates a supportive environment for families and creates a space where they feel their needs are central to the decision-making processes, regarding care and support for their child.

Self-Assessment

What are the three key components of evidence-based practice?

Name two barriers to incorporating evidence-based practice.

How could implementing evidence-based practice contribute to creating supportive environments, for neurodivergent children and families?

Summary

This chapter has examined evidence-based practice in terms of its relevance to practice, with neurodivergent children and families. Evidence-based practice aims to combine three key elements which maximise positive outcomes for patients/families: research, clinical expertise and the preferences of the child and family. Utilising evidence-based practice contributes to creating and maintaining a supportive environment for neurodivergent children and their families, by enabling a planned, reflective and informed approach to decision making and intervention, which values the individual wishes of the family. Evidence-based practice further enhances positive outcomes via amalgamating analysis of the most recent, effective and innovative research, with practice insights and a continued focus on the unique values and preferences of those in receipt of services, the neurodivergent child and their family.

References

Allen, R., & Bellamy, J. (2012). *Practitioner's guide to using research for evidence-based practice* (2nd ed.). Hoboken, NJ: Wiley.

Alqahtani, J.M., Carsula, R.P., Alharbi, H.A., Alyousef, S.M., Baker, O.G., & Tumala, R.B. (2022). Barriers to implementing evidence-based practice among primary healthcare nurses in Saudi Arabia: A cross-sectional study. *Nursing Reports*, 12(2), 313–323. https://doi.org/10.3390/nursrep12020031

American Psychiatric Association. (2013). *Diagnostic and statistical manual of mental disorders* (5th ed.). American Psychiatric Publishing.

Bastemeijer, C., Voogt, L., Van Ewijk, J., & Hazelzet, J. (2017). What do patient values and preferences mean? A taxonomy based on a systematic review of qualitative papers. *Patient Education and Counseling*, 100(5), 871–881. https://doi.org/10.1016/j.pec.2016.12.019

Den Hertog, R., & Niessen, T. (2019). The role of patient preferences in nursing decision-making in evidence-based practice: Excellent nurses' communication tools. *Journal of Advanced Nursing*, 75(9), 1987–1995. https://doi.org/10.1111/jan.14083

Dyspraxia/DCD Ireland. (2023, July 24). *Adults with dyspraxia/DCD*. Retrieved from www.dyspraxia.ie/Adults-with-Dyspraxia-DCD

Ellis, P. (2019). *Evidence-based practice in nursing* (4th ed.). Thousand Oaks: SAGE Publishing.

Engel-Yeger, B. (2020). The role of poor motor coordination in predicting adults' health related quality of life. *Research In Developmental Disabilities*, 103. https://doi.org/10.1016/j.ridd.2020.103686.

Fineout-Overholt, E., Melnyk, B.M., Stillwell, S.B., & Williamson, K.M. (2010). Evidence-based practice step by step: Critical appraisal of the evidence: Part I. *The American Journal of Nursing*, 110(7), 47–52. https://doi.org/10.1097/01.NAJ.0000383935.22721.9c

Fulcher-Rood, K., Castilla-Earls, A., & Higginbotham, J. (2020). What does evidence-based practice mean to you? A follow-up study examining school-based speech-language pathologists' perspectives on evidence-based practice.

American Journal of Speech-Language Pathology, 29(2), 688–704. https://doi.org/10.1044/2019_AJSLP-19–00171

Greenwell, T., & Walsh, B. (2021). Evidence based practice in speech- language pathology: Where are we now? *American Journal of Speech-Language Pathology, 30*(1), 186–198. https://doi.org/10.1044/2020_AJSLP-20-00194

Gubbay, S.S. (1975). *The clumsy child: A study of developmental apraxic and agnosic ataxia.* Philadelphia: Saunders.

Hamaideh, S. (2017). Sources of knowledge and barriers of implementing evidence-based practice among mental health nurses in Saudi Arabia. *Perspectives in Psychiatric Care, 53*, 190–198. https://doi.org/10.1111/ppc.12156

Harrowell, I., Hollén, L., Lingam, R., & Emond, A. (2017). Mental health outcomes of developmental coordination disorder in late adolescence. *Developmental Medicine & Child Neurology, 59*(9), 973–979. https://doi.org/10.1111/dmcn.13469

Haynes, R., Devereaux, P., & Guyatt, G. (2002). Physicians' and patients' choices in evidence based practice. *BMJ, 324*(7350), 1350. https://doi.org/10.1136/bmj.324.7350.1350

Montori, V.M., Brito, J.P., & Murad, M.H. (2013). The optimal practice of evidence-based medicine: Incorporating patient preferences in practice guidelines. *The Journal of the American Medical Association, 310*(23), 2503–2504. https://doi.org/10.1001/jama.2013.281422

Rycroft-Malone, J., Seers, K., Titchen, A., Harvey, G., Kitson, A., & McCormack, B. (2004). What counts as evidence in evidence-based practice? *Journal of Advanced Nursing, 47*(1), 81–90. https://doi.org/10.1111/j.1365–2648.2004.03068.x

Sam, A.M., Odom, S.L., Tomaszewski, B., Perkins, Y., & Cox, A.W. (2021). Employing evidence based practices for children with autism in elementary schools. *The Journal of Autism and Developmental Disorders, 51*, 2308–2323. https://doi.org/10.1007/s10803-020-04706-x

Steinbrenner, J.R., Hume, K., Odom, S.L., Morin, K.L., Nowell, S.W., Tomaszewski, B., Szendrey, S., McIntyre, N.S., Yücesoy-Özkan, S., & Savage, M.N. (2020). *Evidence-based practices for children, youth, and young adults with Autism.* Chapel Hill: The University of North Carolina at Chapel Hill, Frank Porter Graham Child Development Institute, National Clearinghouse on Autism Evidence and Practice Review Team.

Tsang, M., Martin, L., Blissett, S., Gauthier, S., Ahmed, Z., Muhammed, D., & Sibbald, M. (2023). What do clinicians mean by "good clinical judgment". A qualitative study. *International Medical Education, 2*, 1–10. https://doi.org/10.3390/ime2010001

Van Wee, B., & Banister, D. (2016). How to write a literature review paper? *Transport Reviews, 36*(2), 278–288. https://doi.org/10.1080/01441647.2015.1065456

Vingerhoets, C., Hay-Smith, J., & Graham, F. (2023). Getting to know our patients and what matters: Exploring the elicitation of patient values, preferences, and circumstances in neurological rehabilitation. *Disability and Rehabilitation, 45*(9), 1444–1452. https://doi.org/10.1080/09638288.2022.2063416

Wu, M., Yang, M., Liu, L., & Ye, B. (2016). An investigation of factors influencing nurses' clinical decision-making skills. *Western Journal of Nursing Research, 38*, 974–991. https://doi.org/10.1177/0193945916633458

Chapter 10

Parental Wellbeing

Abbreviations

ADHD: Attention Deficit Hyperactivity Disorder
BMI: Body Mass Index
CDC: Centers for Disease Control and Prevention
ER: Emergency Room
US: United States
WHO: World Health Organisation

Introduction

Caring for a neurodivergent child or children can impact parental wellbeing and parental mental health. Parental wellbeing further influences parenting capacity and creating supportive environments within the home and family life. This chapter will explore the significance of parental wellbeing for parents of neurodivergent children and the relevance of such for creating supportive environments. The role of practitioners will be discussed concerning promoting the wellbeing of parents, as an active practice strategy aimed at creating supportive environments. Effective practice responses to addressing parental wellbeing such as referral pathways, information provision and wellbeing supports, will be considered. Within the context of oftentimes limited resources, any investment in parental wellbeing and coping capacity, is an investment in creating supportive environments for neurodivergent children and their families.

Learning Outcomes

On completion of Chapter 10, learners should demonstrate an enhanced understanding concerning:

- Awareness of the impact of caregiving responsibilities, pertaining to parental mental health and wellbeing

DOI: 10.4324/9781003455868-10

- The relevance of addressing parent/caregiver wellbeing, in the context of creating supportive environments for neurodivergent children
- Awareness of the intergenerational element of neurodivergence
- Approaches to responding to parental wellbeing concerns, including referral pathways

Wellbeing

In order to contextualise parental wellbeing, first we need to examine the concept of wellbeing more generally. Wellbeing can be subjective and based on how each person measures how they feel and the extent to which they feel capable and healthy (World Health Organisation, 2021; Centre for Disease Control, 2018). The WHO (2021) define wellbeing as "the ability of people and societies to contribute to the world with a sense of meaning and purpose". The CDC (2018) describe wellbeing as the individual's self-perception of their life satisfaction and feelings of happiness, as opposed to depression.

Huppert (2009) asserts that wellbeing is associated with feeling a sense of control over your life and feeling a sense of purpose. Wellbeing is closely linked to the WHO's (2023) definition of health, as complete physical, social and mental wellbeing and not solely associated with the absence of disease. Subjective wellbeing is described by Diener et al. (2017) as the individual's appraisal or evaluation of their own state of satisfaction with their life's circumstances. Diener and Chan (2011) contend that subjective wellbeing impacts longevity, hence is a momentous predictive factor in morbidity. People who experience negative subjective wellbeing, lower life satisfaction and negative feelings such as sadness, have shorter life expectancies, whereas people who have a more positive subjective wellbeing, view their life as satisfactory and have feelings of happiness and fulfilment, live for longer (Diener & Chan, 2011). Wellbeing is impacted by the society in which the family lives, their economic circumstances and the availability of resources (WHO, 2021).

Reflection Point!

What activities or actions do you engage in to enhance to your wellbeing?
What factors or life stressors negatively influence your wellbeing?

Parental Wellbeing

Parental wellbeing is defined as the parent's capacity to cope, their satisfaction with their parenting and emotional stability (King, King, Rosenbaum, & Goffin, 1999). King et al. (1999) contend that parental wellbeing is impacted by factors such as child disability, perceived support and psychosocial life stressors, such as child behaviour and the burden of care required. The WHO (2021) define wellbeing as "a positive state" experienced by individuals which is influenced by "social, economic and environmental conditions".

Wellbeing is about perceiving that things are progressing positively in your own life and feeling joy and satisfaction, rather than negative emotions or depression (Centre for Disease Control [CDC], 2018). Hence parental wellbeing is influenced by one's own interpretation of parenting ability and effectiveness and the positive or negative emotions this presents (CDC, 2018; WHO, 2021). From such perspectives wellbeing is subjective and very much based upon how the parent views themselves and their parenting capacity. This is significant to bear in mind when aiming to influence parental wellbeing from a practice perspective. Subjective wellbeing is distinctly unique to each parent and may change from day to day or week to week, based on how they cope with their child's needs, life stressors and the availability of supports.

Ang and Loh (2019) found that, in their study involving parents of autistic children, mothers experienced significantly higher stress levels compared to fathers. Ang and Loh (2019) contend that mothers are more likely to manage their child's behavioural needs and support them with everyday tasks, compared to fathers, which may culminate in their higher self-reported levels of stress. A unique study which compared parental stress levels between parents of children with ADHD and parents of autistic children, found that parents of children with ADHD experienced higher levels of parental stress and depression (Miranda, Tárraga, Fernández, Colomer, & Pastor, 2015). Miranda et al. (2015) report that the behavioural issues which can arise alongside neurodivergence, in addition to perceived role restriction due to such behaviours, contributes to parental stress. Parents in a study conducted by Leitch et al. (2019) report that parental stress pertaining to ADHD, is influenced largely by behavioural outbursts and a sense of losing control, concerning their child's behaviour. Parents in their study contend that a sense of hypervigilance occurs where they are anticipating outbursts, and they must consistently monitor their child's behaviour and interactions (Leitch et al., 2019).

Author Reflection Point!

Parental hypervigilance can culminate in persistent anxiety. I remember jumping at the slightest sound and being unable to relax in anticipation of something happening with my child regarding challenging behaviour. Previous incidents of my child hurting other children (or their siblings), absconding and placing themselves in danger, prompted my constant need for vigilance. Yet this profoundly negatively impacted my parental wellbeing and also my capacity to socialise at family gatherings.

Parental wellbeing is a fundamental prerequisite for the ability to adequately cope with the ever-changing needs, of caring for a neurodivergent child. If a parent feels well mentally, emotionally and physically, they will be more competent and capable of meeting their child's needs on a daily basis and cope with the challenges associated with caring for a neurodivergent child. This is particularly relevant for parents who are responding to challenging behaviour and find themselves being subjected to physical violence and/or aggressive outbursts on a regular basis.

Case Study 1

Rachel is a single parent to 8-year-old twin boys, both with diagnoses of ADHD. The twins are very active and engage in play fighting frequently, which often results in serious fighting and subsequent injuries. Both twins have presented at the emergency room (ER) on multiple occasions in the previous two years, with broken bones, minor head injuries and lacerations, due to their physical fighting. A referral to child protective services was made at their last ER visit, where one of the boys required 15 stitches to his head after hitting it on a doorframe, when fighting with his brother.

Upon meeting with the social worker, Rachel expresses a wish to place her boys into foster care. Rachel says she is feeling depressed, overwhelmed and unable to continue parenting her sons without any family support. Rachel discloses feeling on constant high alert in anticipating her boys fighting and hurting one another, which causes severe anxiety.

What are the initial parental wellbeing concerns in this case?

What factors could be impacting Rachel's wellbeing?

How could Rachel's wellbeing be influencing her parenting?

Caregiving for Neurodivergent Children and Parental Mental Health

Research supports the notion that parental wellbeing is directly impacted by caring responsibilities (Samadi, McConkey & Bunting, 2014; Shivers & Resor, 2020; Gunderson & Barrett, 2017). Gunderson and Barrett (2017) argue that there is a direct link between the number of hours of emotional support provided to children and parental self-rated mental health. Their research surmises that the additional emotional support some mothers provide, results from sacrificing their own wellbeing needs (Gunderson & Barrett, 2017). In an Iranian study involving both fathers and mothers, Samadi et al. (2014) found that mothers reported poorer wellbeing compared to fathers, regarding caring for their disabled child.

Samadi et al. (2014) argue that care relating to autism in particular, resulted in higher parental stress levels and poorer wellbeing, in comparison to caring for a child living with an intellectual disability. An Australian study found that the severity of the child's clinical health needs, culminated in poorer parental wellbeing (Mori, Downs, Wong, Heyworth, & Leonard, 2018). Mori et al. (2018) contend that parental education level, working outside of the home and having other children, manifested in greater levels of self-reported physical and emotional wellbeing for parents.

Shivers and Resor (2020) in the US explored educational attainment and poverty status among parents of children with disabilities, compared to those parenting children without disabilities. They found that mothers (but not fathers) of disabled children reported greater levels of poverty, while both mothers and fathers reported lower levels of educational attainment, compared to their counterparts parenting non-disabled children. Both mothers and fathers of disabled children reported lower levels of life satisfaction and overall health, in comparison to their peers parenting children without a disability (Shivers & Resor, 2020). This study is particularly insightful as the research conducted was longitudinal and the sample size consisted of the parents of 4,898 children born between 1998 and 2000, who were followed until the age of 15 years (Shivers & Resor, 2020).

Author Reflection Point!

When I look back on my many appointments with my neurodivergent children over the years, there were times when I was silently screaming: "I'm struggling! I'm not coping as well as I would like to be . . . and I'm terrified of reaching my breaking point!"

Yet I shared only my concerns for my child, the impact of violent behaviour on their siblings, in school and socially. As appointments and interactions with professionals were in response to my child's needs, I felt that my own mental health and wellbeing were perhaps not relevant. When in reality, my mental health and wellbeing were instrumental in impacting my ability to respond to my child's needs and were unequivocally pertinent to my child's appointment and our overall wellbeing as a family.

Parents oftentimes don't share their own wellbeing concerns with professionals, due to fear of judgement and fear that they will be deemed to be incapable in their parenting.

Lanyi, Mannion, Chen, and Leader (2021) found that 91% of parents of autistic children experienced sleep problems. Lanyi et al. (2021) argue that severity and frequency of tantrums and challenging behaviour in their children, resulted in greater self-reported levels of parental anxiety and depression, while repetitive behaviour in children increased parental stress (Lanyi et al., 2021). Seymour, Giallo and Wood (2017) compared the health and wellbeing of fathers of autistic children, with fathers of children with learning disabilities and fathers of children without disabilities. They found that fathers of autistic children were more likely to report psychological distress, global poor health and 79% had a Body Mass Index (BMI) in the obese category.

Jung Lee and Kim (2022) found that ADHD symptoms directly impact the anxiety of mothers, which in turn was found to impact children's ADHD symptoms. Such findings indicate the bidirectional nature of parental stress and the presentation of the neurodivergent child, and subsequently the significance of intervening to alter the process of stress within the family. Paternal wellbeing has also been shown to impact child behaviours (Gulenc, Butler, Sarkadi, & Hiscock, 2018). Gulenc et al. (2018) found that a father's psychological distress, directly relates to children's externalised behaviour problems. UNICEF Innocenti (2020) report that family relationships and appropriate parental support are vital, for promoting child wellbeing.

Support Networks

Support is the single most significant factor, which can positively impact the wellbeing of parents and families of neurodivergent children. Consequently, practitioners and educators working with neurodivergent children and families, have a fundamental role in mobilising supports which culminate in creating supportive environments. Avery, Van Rhijn, and Maich (2021) report that parents of neurodivergent children often prioritise their child's support needs above their own. Most parents within their Canadian study (87%) stated that they have support needs, yet are unaware of how to address these or where to access parental support (Avery et al., 2021). Weiss, Robinson, Riddell, and Flora (2021), in their longitudinal study over a one-year period, found that perceived parental social support, impacted child behaviour positively. This research proposes that perceived social support is substantial enough to reduce parental stress levels and change parenting practices, to the extent that they result in affirmative differences in child behaviour (Weiss et al., 2021).

Kinship Supports

Having a family member who knows the neurodivergent child and understands their unique needs, can assist parents to feel a sense of shared responsibility for parenting and a greater sense of cohesion and solidarity. Kinship support in the form of emotional support and perhaps respite from extended family members, is a key factor in contributing to the coping capacity and wellbeing of parents. Grandparents, aunts and uncles of neurodivergent children, can provide emotional support to parents and practical support in the form of helping with housework or driving siblings to activities. Extended family can help with childcare for neurodivergent children, enabling parents to have a break, or to work while their child is being cared for. Kinship support reduces the isolation and loneliness experienced by some parents of neurodivergent children and increases their capacity to integrate into their community (which may be restricted due to their child's care needs). Kinship support has been instrumental in my coping capacity as a parent and my ability to engage in self-care and actively invest in promoting my own health and wellbeing (Mullins, 2022). Yet many parents of neurodivergent children lack kinship supports.

Research further supports the notion that extended families play an important role in the provision of informal support for parents of neurodivergent children (Goedeke, Shepherd, Landon, & Taylor, 2019; Davis & Gavidia-Payne, 2009; Mbamba, Yeboaa, & Ndemole, 2023). Goedeke et al. (2019) report that familial support is the most common type of support reported by parents of autistic children, and this contributes to a reduction in parental stress. Davis and Gavidia-Payne (2009) report that extended familial support for families of children with disabilities, acts as a notable influence in predicting positive quality of family life. Davis and Gavida-Payne (2023) surmise that support from extended family members directly influences parental satisfaction, family interactions and reducing parental strain. Mbamba et al. (2023) contend that kinship support is particularly significant for promoting the welfare of single parents and their neurodivergent children. Kinship support enables parents to work and subsequently reduce the financial burden they experience. Kindship support regarding childcare enables parents to have respite time away from their children, who may require constant supervision (Mbamba et al., 2023).

Fong et al. (2021) suggest that empowering parents to engage with their existing informal support networks, can be a useful way of supporting parents to enhance their wellbeing. Providing information to parents on the benefits of informal support, can prompt them to reach out to people close to them (Fong et al., 2021). However, it's important to note that many families of neurodivergent children lack kinship supports due to emigration, the stigma associated with neurodivergent conditions and a lack of understanding from family members about their child's condition. Some families of neurodivergent children may have a large network of extended family members living close by, yet still may have no kinship support.

Informal Supports

Families of neurodivergent children who lack kinship support, may benefit from engaging with informal support networks. Peer support in particular, can be instrumental in promoting wellbeing and creating supportive environments for neurodivergent children and families. This informal means of support provides parents with emotional support and a sense of understanding, from other parents of neurodivergent children. Peer support means that support stems from someone with similar experiences, who can truly empathise with the unique challenges parents and families of neurodivergent children experience.

The sheer volume of information available to parents prior to and after their child's diagnosis, can be overwhelming. Informal support from other parents with similar experiences, can assist parents in navigating the sea of information available to them and identify which sources are most relevant/helpful. Informal support can further help parents to process their feelings of stress and to better cope emotionally, with meeting their child's care needs.

Parents may not always recognise when they need peer support and might express instead feeling overwhelmed within their parenting role or unsure what their family's future might look like. Peer support provides a unique avenue for parents to share their concerns and worries without the fear of judgement and is facilitated in a non-professional capacity. Peer support offers a different kind of support and is not a replacement for professional support or therapeutic interventions. It can be a valuable additional mechanism of support for families and can complement professional support provision. For example: a professional most often cannot share parenting tips, recommend a certain type of seamless soft socks, give a much-needed hug or just have a coffee and listen. Equally, practitioners cannot provide their own experiences of different services, e.g. respite care or a soft play area which could be just right. Yet professionals can support parents to source and access peer support and consequently contribute to improving their wellbeing, which in turn will increase the likelihood of positive outcomes for their child.

Reflection Point!

Think about your own wellbeing needs and how and where you access informal supports. Do you have a friend who is a really good listener? Or a co-worker/college peer who will encourage and bolster you after a particularly tough day? What impact do these peers have on your life?

Research further supports the notion that informal supports, play a significant role in building parental resilience (Fong, Gardiner, & Iarocci, 2021). Fong et al. (2021) report that informal support and the companionship associated with this, contributes to wellbeing for parents of autistic children. A well-known and established peer support programme for parents of children with disabilities is Parent 2 Parent USA (P2P, 2023). P2P was created by parents who recognised the need for informal peer support and is now active in 30 states, and facilitates 17,000 matches per year (P2P, 2023). The key goals of P2P are to provide parents with a parent match based on similar characteristics (child's needs/diagnosis) and facilitate emotional support, finding solutions and someone to talk to about the needs of the child and family (Parent to Parent USA, 2023). Research pertaining to the effectiveness of peer support concludes that it greatly benefits parents and results in improved outcomes for children and their families (Bray, Carter, Sanders, Blake, & Keegan, 2017; McLean Pollock, Ming, Chung, & Maslow, 2022; Mills, Vimalakanthan, Sivapalan, Shanmugalingam, & Weiss, 2021). Bray et al. (2017) surmise that parent peer support presents a nurturing mechanism for parents to make sense of their emotions and culminates in a valuable resource for improving parental wellbeing. Recipients of peer support describe this as like finding a guide to assist them in navigating their new reality (Bray et al., 2017).

Mills et al. (2021) researched the feasibility of a peer-delivered group counselling programme, for enhancing parental wellbeing. This study reports significant improvements in terms of parent stress, depression and anxiety Mills et al., 2021). Improvements in these domains were evident even after the first session, which further illustrates the profound potential of such an intervention, in creating supportive environments for neurodivergent children and families (Mills et al., 2021).

UNICEF Innocenti (2020) emphasise the significance of the broader social networks and community factors, on the health and wellbeing of both parents and children. Masi et al. (2021), in their study on neurodivergent children and parents, found that parental wellbeing was negatively impacted by the lack of services and supports available during the Covid-19 pandemic.

Interestingly, Masi et al. (2021) report that almost 20% of the 302 parents who participated in their study, increased their child's medication during this time. Such findings highlight the potency of community interventions, social supports and informal support networks, pertaining to parental wellbeing for parents of neurodivergent children (Masi et al., 2021). The study by Masi et al. (2021) further accentuates the link between parental wellbeing and outcomes for neurodivergent children.

Intergenerational Neurodivergence

A growing body of research demonstrates the hereditary nature of both autism and ADHD (Tick, Bolton, Happé, Rutter, & Rijsdijk, 2016; Thapar & Rutter, 2021; Deng et al., 2015; Larsson, Chang, D'Onofrio, & Lichtenstein, 2014; Brikell, Kuja-Halkola, & Larsson, 2019). Hence, one could safely assume that a proportion of parents presenting with their child for assessment and support regarding ADHD, autism and dyspraxia, are likely themselves neurodivergent. Some parents are coming to this realisation that they too may be neurodivergent, only during or even after their child's assessment journey (Hwang & Heslop, 2023). Other parents may have no idea and may continue to struggle with an undiagnosed or supported condition, which impacts every single aspect of their daily lives.

The process of obtaining an assessment and diagnosis of autism or ADHD for a child is gruelling. For parents, this process involves hours and hours of meetings with professionals and a substantial volume of paperwork. Yet some parents may be engaging with this process and supporting their child, while grappling with their own neurodivergence and the challenges this may present for them. Parental engagement with this process requires a significant amount of communication, concentration and organisation. Practical and emotional resources are further needed during the assessment journey, which will be undertaken alongside parenting a child who has social, emotional and possibly behavioural issues. For parents who may be autistic and/or be living with ADHD, this process can be exhausting, emotionally taxing and particularly challenging on a practical level.

Adult assessments for autism and ADHD are largely obtained privately and consequently at a substantial financial cost (Zener, 2019; Russell et al., 2022). Financial constraints significantly limit access to assessment and diagnosis, for many parents of neurodivergent children. Caregiving responsibilities, lack of access to childcare and fear of judgement and stereotyping, may further dissuade parents from seeking an assessment for themselves. Hence, the likelihood of practitioners engaging with neurodivergent parents of neurodivergent children who are undiagnosed, is probable.

Hwang and Heslop (2023) contend that autistic parents often feel misunderstood by professionals and judged on their parenting, based on neurotypical standards. Autistic parents further report that negative stereotyping by professionals, adversely impacted their interactions when accessing supports for their children (Hwang & Heslop, 2023). Autistic parents may experience less parenting satisfaction and greater parenting difficulties, when they live with a greater number of autistic traits (Dissanayake, Richdale, Kolivas, & Pamment, 2020). Hence, being aware of a parent's neurodivergence or indeed supporting them to explore this, will enable practitioners to appropriately meet their wellbeing needs and, subsequently, contribute to creating a more supportive environment for their child and family.

The neurodivergent status of parents will further influence their level of difficulty with managing appointments, communicating with practitioners (discussed in Chapter 6) and coping with the multiple demands of the assessment process for their child. Awareness and understanding concerning the possibility of parental neurodivergence, will place practitioners in a more open and informed position from which to support parents within this process.

Author Reflection Point!

I remember completing the very detailed ADHD questionnaires when my first child was 5 years old and thinking . . . this sounds a lot like me. I find it hard to sit still, lose and forget things and struggle to stay on task. Yet I was focused on helping my daughter; these services were for her, and I didn't have any information regarding how to access an assessment for myself or that ADHD is often hereditary. My lack of insight and information meant that it was 15 years later when I eventually pursued an ADHD assessment. Yet undoubtedly having this insight and awareness of my own wellbeing needs at an earlier stage, would have contributed to creating a more supporting environment, in terms of my interactions with professionals and the support provided/accessed by our family. Equally, the practitioners we engaged with may have altered the environment to meet my needs as a neurodivergent parent or may have suggested resources or supports more specific to my family's needs, based on my diagnosis.

Mobilising Supports for Parental Wellbeing

Supporting parents is supporting children, is a core principle for creating supportive environments for neurodivergent children and their families. This principle recognises the significance of time spent advocating for parents pertaining to their own health and wellbeing, as this unequivocally empowers them in their parenting and enhances their coping capacity. Practitioners can prepare for supporting parents regarding their wellbeing, by being aware of referral pathways and supports available locally and in a position to mobilise such supports. As a teacher, child psychologist or paediatrician, your role may relate specifically to the health, education and wellbeing of the child. Yet having information and resources you can share with parents which can address their wellbeing and mental health needs, will support this family holistically and enhance outcomes for neurodivergent children.

Should practitioners be concerned about the wellbeing of a parent concerning their mental health and suspect the parent may be experiencing mental illness, a referral should be made to their primary care physician at the earliest opportunity. If there is a concern regarding a parent's wish to harm themselves or someone else, the organisational protocols which stipulate exactly how you should respond to such concerns should be enacted. It's important to use clinical insight and training to determine what types of support are most appropriate and when formal rather than informal supports are necessary, to promote parental wellbeing.

Creating and maintaining a database of referral pathways for parents pertaining to mental health and wellbeing, is a useful method of crafting an organisational culture of creating a supportive environment. Insight and information concerning referral pathways for adult assessment for ADHD and autism, are equally significant. Assisting parents to contact their primary care physician or local mental health services, or advocating on their behalf, may be the initial step necessary for exploring potential neurodivergence. Supporting parents to access information regarding how to request private assessment services, is further conducive to reducing barriers and creating supportive environments. Such practice communicates normalising parents prioritising and addressing their own health and wellbeing needs. This may be as simple as providing a printed list of websites or professionals locally and nationally, where the parent could access more information. Practitioners should populate their database of wellbeing resources with information about their nearest peer support and family support services, and be in a position to discuss with parents how such services operate. Practitioners should have contact details for voluntary agencies and support groups for parents locally, and check on a regular basis to ensure such services are still in operation. A printed sheet with the contact information for all of these services is particularly helpful to give parents to take home with them and think about. The volume of information shared during interactions with professionals means that parents can feel overwhelmed and unable to take in the totality of options available to support their wellbeing. Hence, having the list of services/resources printed and handed to them, can help in terms of having a visual reminder and all of the information on one sheet of paper. More information on communicating with neurodivergent children and adults is available in Chapter 6 and can be referred to when creating resources and information for families.

Finally, should you support parents to access wellbeing services, engage in peer support or request assessment services for ADHD or autism, do ascertain the outcome of such supports. This information will continue to enhance your knowledge and awareness concerning these support mechanisms, and enable you in advising and supporting other neurodivergent families effectively.

Case Study

Ben, aged 7, has dual diagnoses of autism and dyspraxia. Ben needs constant support around self-care and toileting. Ben struggles with un-buttoning his school trousers and wiping after a bowel movement. Consequently, Ben avoids using the toilet in school. This has caused Ben to have frequent stomachaches, anxiety and instances of soiling himself.

His parents, Casey and Sharon, explain that they have tried everything to help Ben, but nothing works. Casey breaks down in tears and says he can't imagine how Ben will ever be independent, and Casey feels like he's failing as a parent. Sharon adds that Casey has been feeling increasingly hopeless concerning Ben's care needs, and his mood is quite low.

To what extent is parental wellbeing relevant to this family's needs?

What factors are impacting Casey's wellbeing?

What referral mechanisms or pathways for support may be helpful?

Parental Wellbeing and Creating Supportive Environments

Parental wellbeing is encompassed within the core principle of creating supportive environments for neurodivergent children and their families, of supporting parents is supporting children. By intentionally aiming to improve the wellbeing of parents, practitioners are contributing to the wellbeing of the child. Supporting parents in promoting their wellbeing is conducive to creating a more supportive environment within the home and within the interactions and dynamics of the family. Key to initiating practice interventions to promote parental wellbeing, is providing education and information to parents regarding its significance. Parents of neurodivergent children often prioritise their child's wellbeing over their own and may initially be apprehensive about accepting supports aimed at addressing their wellbeing needs. The practitioner has an active responsibility in empowering parents to value and prioritise their own health and wellbeing needs.

The key catalyst of *access* is particularly pertinent to creating supportive environments for neurodivergent children and families, in the context of parental wellbeing. Enabling parents to access information about their own wellbeing and its significance to their parenting is fundamental. Supporting parents to access services and support for addressing their wellbeing, is a central component in the practice response to meeting the needs of neurodivergent children and their families. Access within this context is about empowering parents to acknowledge the significance of their own wellbeing needs and access services and supports aimed at meeting these unique needs. A key element of access is concerned with information provision. For parents to be in a position to make an informed decision pertaining to their own wellbeing, they need all of the relevant information. Creating accessible information to share with parents and signposting to relevant services and supports, empowers them in addressing their own wellbeing needs and creates a supportive environment.

The key catalyst of *acceptance* further informs practice concerning the issue of intergenerational neurodivergence, regarding parental wellbeing and creating supportive environments. Many parents of neurodivergent children are neurodivergent (whether diagnosed or not). Neurodivergence presents challenges for adults in terms of communication, employment, mental health and social exclusion (discussed in more detail in Chapters 1–4). Supporting parents to explore their neurodivergence will empower them to identify and understand their own needs. Practitioners can create supportive environments for neurodivergent parents via employing practices which promote inclusion and adopting methods of communication conducive to the parent's needs. By providing information concerning assessment and support services and advocating and referring where appropriate, practitioners are communicating acceptance and acknowledging the importance of the parent's wellbeing. This may be the parent's first opportunity to consider and explore their own neurodivergence, hence acceptance is paramount and fundamental to creating a supportive environment.

Self-Assessment

Why is parental wellbeing relevant to creating supportive environments for neurodivergent children?

Why could assessment for autism or ADHD be helpful for some parents?

How can you better equip yourself to respond to parental wellbeing in your practice?

Chapter Summary

Parental wellbeing is a fundamental factor which impacts the families of neurodivergent children. Interventions aimed at enhancing parental wellbeing are intrinsic to creating supportive environments, based on the principle of supporting parents is supporting children. Informal support mechanisms such as peer support and harnessing the support of existing family networks, are instrumental to improving the wellbeing of parents of neurodivergent children. Formal support services such as mental health services, formal family support and community-based services, may further make up the medley of necessary supports for promoting parental wellbeing. The practitioner has a central role in supporting parents to identify and respond to their wellbeing needs, in a conscious effort to contribute to creating supportive environments. Being knowledgeable concerning supports aimed at addressing parental wellbeing is key to supporting parents, particularly regarding neurodivergence. Mobilising such supports via the provision of information and referral, are further key steps in promoting parental wellbeing and subsequently supporting neurodivergent children.

References

Ang, K.Q.P., & Loh, P.R. (2019). Mental health and coping in parents of children with autism spectrum Disorder (ASD) in Singapore: An examination of gender role in caring. *The Journal of Autism and Developmental Disorders, 49*, 2129–2145. https://doi.org/10.1007/s10803-019-03900-w

Avery, K., Van Rhijn, T., & Maich, K. (2021). Understanding the role of formal and informal support resources for parents of children with autism spectrum disorder. *Canadian Journal of Family and Youth, 14*(3), 32–51. https://doi.org/10.29173/cjfy29791

Bray, B., Carter, B., Sanders, C., Blake, L., & Keegan, K. (2017). Parent-to-parent peer support for parents of children with a disability: A mixed method study. *Patient Education and Counseling, 100*(8), 1537–1543. https://doi.org/10.1016/j.pec.2017.03.004

Brikell, I., Kuja-Halkola, R., & Larsson, H. (2019). Heritability of Attention-Deficit Hyperactivity Disorder across the lifespan. *European Neuropsychopharmacology, 29*, S757–S758. https://doi.org/10.1016/j.euroneuro.2017.06.106

Centers for Disease Control and Prevention. (2018, June 6). *Wellbeing concepts.* Retrieved from www.cdc.gov/hrqol/wellbeing.htm

Davis, K., & Gavidia-Payne, S. (2009). The impact of child, family, and professional support characteristics on the quality of life in families of young children with disabilities. *Journal of Intellectual & Developmental Disability, 34*(2), 153–162. https://doi.org/10.1080/13668250902874608

Deng, W., Zou, X., Deng, H., Li, J., Tang, C., Wang, X., & Guo, X. (2015). The relationship among genetic heritability, environmental effects, and autism spectrum disorders. *Journal of Child Neurology, 30*(13), 1794–1799. https://doi.org/10.1177/0883073815580645

Diener, E., & Chan, M. (2011). Happy people live longer: Subjective well-being contributes to health and longevity. *Applied Psychology: Health and Well-Being, 3*, 1–43. https://doi.org/10.1111/j.1758-0854.2010.01045.x

Diener, E., Heintzelman, S.J., Kushlev, K., Tay, L., Wirtz, D., Lutes, L.D., & Oishi, S. (2017). Findings all psychologists should know from the new science on subjective well-being. *Canadian Psychology/Psychologie Canadienne, 58*(2), 87–104. https://doi.org/10.1037/cap0000063

Dissanayake, C., Richdale, A., Kolivas, N., & Pamment, L. (2020). An exploratory study of autism traits and parenting. *The Journal of Autism and Developmental Disorders, 50*, 2593–2606. https://doi/10.1007/s10803-019-03984-4

Fong, V., Gardiner, E., & Iarocci, G. (2021). Satisfaction with informal supports predicts resilience in families of children with autism spectrum disorder. *Autism, 25*(2), 452–463. https://doi.org/10.1177/1362361320962677

Goedeke, S., Shepherd, D., Landon, J., & Taylor, S. (2019). How perceived support relates to child autism symptoms and care-related stress in parents caring for a child with autism. *Research in Autism Spectrum Disorders, 60*, 36–47. https://doi.org/10.1016/j.rasd.2019.01.005

Gulenc, A., Butler, E., Sarkadi, A., & Hiscock, H. (2018). Paternal psychological distress, parenting, and child behaviour: A population based, cross-sectional study. *Child: Care, Health & Development, 44*(6), 892–900. https://doi.org/10.1111/cch.12607

Gunderson, J., & Barrett, A.E. (2017). Emotional cost of emotional support? The association between intensive mothering and psychological well-being in midlife. *Journal of Family Issues, 38*(7), 992–1009. http://dx.doi.org/10.1177/0192513X15579502

Huppert, F.A. (2009). Psychological well-being: Evidence regarding its causes and consequences. *Applied Psychology: Health and Well-Being, 1*(2), 137–64. https://doi.org/10.1111/j.1758-0854.2009.01008.x

Hwang, S.K., & Heslop, P. (2023). Autistic parents' personal experiences of parenting and support: Messages from an online focus group. *The British Journal of Social Work, 53*(1), 76–295. Retrieved from https://doi-org.nuigalway.idm.oclc.org/10.1093/bjsw/bcac133

Jung Lee, Y., & Kim, J, (2022). Effect of maternal anxiety on parenting stress of fathers of children with ADHD. *Journal of Korean Medical Science, 37*(11), 89. https://doi.org/10.3346/jkms.2022.37.e89

King, G., King, S., Rosenbaum, P., & Goffin, R. (1999). Family-centered caregiving and well-being of parents of children with disabilities: Linking process with outcome. *Journal of Pediatric Psychology, 24*, 41–53.

Lanyi, J., Mannion, A., Chen, J., & Leader, G. (2021). Relationship between co-morbid psychopathology in children and adolescents with autism spectrum disorder and parental well-being. *Developmental Neurorehabilitation, 25*(3), 151–161. https://doi.org/10.1080/17518423.2021.1922529

Larsson, H., Chang, Z., D'Onofrio, B., & Lichtenstein, P. (2014). The heritability of clinically diagnosed attention deficit hyperactivity disorder across the lifespan. *Psychological Medicine, 44*(10), 2223–2229. https://doi.org/10.1017/S0033291713002493

Leitch, S., Sciberras, E., Post, B., Gerner, B., Rinehart, N., Nicholson, J.M., & Evans, S. (2019). Experience of stress in parents of children with ADHD: A qualitative study. *International Journal of Qualitative Studies on Health and Well-being*, *14*, 1. https://doi.org/10.1080/17482631.2019.1690091

Masi, A., Mendoza Diaz, A., Tully, L., Azim, S.I., Woolfenden, S., Efron, D., & Eapen, V. (2021). Impact of the COVID-19 pandemic on the well-being of children with neurodevelopmental disabilities and their parents. *Journal of Paediatrics and Child Health*, *57*(5), 631–636. https://doi.org/ 10.1111/jpc.15285.

Mbamba, C.R., Yeboaa, P.A., & Ndemole, I.K. (2023). Autistic children in the care of single mothers: Opportunities and barriers to safeguarding the welfare of special needs children. *Vulnerable Children and Youth Studies*, *18*(1), 46–57. https://doi.org/10.1080/17450128.2022.2080895

McLean Pollock, D., Ming, D., Chung, R.J., & Maslow, G. (2022). Parent-to-parent peer support for children and youth with special health care needs: Preliminary evaluation of a family partner program in a healthcare system. *Journal of Pediatric Nursing*, *66*, 6–14. https://doi.org/10.1016/j.pedn.2022.05.008.

Mills, A.S., Vimalakanthan, K., Sivapalan, S., Shanmugalingam, N., & Weiss, J.A. (2021). Brief report: Preliminary outcomes of a peer counselling program for parents of children with autism in the south Asian community. *The Journal of Autism and Developmental Disorders*, *51*, 334–340. https://doi.org/10.1007/s10803-020-04538-9

Miranda, A., Tárraga, R., Fernández, M.I., Colomer, C., & Pastor, G. (2015). Parenting stress in families of children with autism spectrum disorder and ADHD. *Exceptional Children*, *82*(1), 81–95. https://doi.org/10.1177/00144029155854

Mori, Y., Downs, J., Wong, K., Heyworth, J., & Leonard, H. (2018). Comparing parental well-being and its determinants across three different genetic disorders causing intellectual disability. *The Journal of Autism and Developmental Disorders*, *48*, 1651–1665. https://doi.org/10.1007/s10803-017-3420-x

Mullins, L. (2022). *It takes a village: Navigating the journey of parenting your autistic child*. Dublin: Orpen Press.

Parent to Parent USA. (2023, July 25). *Purpose and mission*. Retrieved from www.p2pusa.org/

Russell, G., Stapley, S., Newlove-Delgado, T., Salmon, A., White, R., Warren, F., Pearson, A., & Ford, T. (2022). Time trends in autism diagnosis over 20 years: A UK population-based cohort study. *The Journal of Child Psychology and Psychiatry*, *63*, 674–682. https://doi.org/10.1111/jcpp.13505

Samadi, S., McConkey, R., & Bunting, B. (2014). Parental wellbeing of Iranian families with children who have developmental disabilities. *Research in Developmental Disabilities*, *35*(7), 1639–1647. https://doi.org/10.1016/j.ridd.2014.04.001

Seymour, M., Giallo, R., & Wood, C.E. (2017). The psychological and physical health of fathers of children with Autism Spectrum Disorder compared to fathers of children with long-term disabilities and fathers of children without disabilities. *Research in Developmental Disabilities*, *69*, 8–17, https://doi.org/10.1016/j.ridd.2017.07.018

Shivers, C., & Resor, J. (2020). Health and life satisfaction among parents of children with physical disabilities. *Journal of Developmental and Physical Disabilities*, *32*(5), 719–733. https://doi.org/10.1007/s10882-019-09716-x

Thapar, A., & Rutter, M. (2021). Genetic advances in autism. *The Journal of Autism and Developmental Disorders*, *51*, 4321–4332. https://doi.org/10.1007/s10803-020-04685-z

Tick, B., Bolton, P., Happé, F., Rutter, M., & Rijsdijk, F. (2016). Heritability of autism spectrum disorders: A meta-analysis of twin studies. *The Journal of Child Psychology and Psychiatry, 57*, 585–595. https://doi.org/10.1111/jcpp.12499

UNICEF Innocenti. (2020). *Worlds of influence: Understanding what shapes child well-being in rich countries* (Innocenti Report Card 16). Innocenti, FL: UNICEF Office of Research.

Weiss, J., Robinson, S., Riddell, R., & Flora, D. (2021). Understanding stability and change in perceived social support in parents of autistic children and adolescents. *Frontiers in Rehabilitation Sciences, 2*, 679974. https://doi.org/10.3389/fresc.2021.679974

World Health Organisation. (2021a, July 18). *Glossary of terms.* Retrieved from www.who.int/publications/i/item/9789240038349

World Health Organisation. (2021b, June 6). *Promoting wellbeing.* Retrieved from www.who.int/activities/promoting-well-being

World Health Organisation. (2023, July 18). *Constitution.* Retrieved from www.who.int/about/governance/constitution

Zener, D. (2019). Journey to diagnosis for women with autism. *Advances in Autism, 5*(1), 2–13. https://doi.org/10.1108/AIA-10-2018-0041

Chapter 11

The Role of Advocacy

Abbreviations

ADHD: Attention Deficit Hyperactivity Disorder
CSDH: Commission on the Social Determinants of Health
HIQA: Health Information and Quality Authority
NICE: National Institute for Health and Care Excellence
WHO: World Health Organisation

Introduction

Advocacy is the act of speaking for or with an individual or group of people, who have been marginalised in some way. Advocacy becomes a central component of life for the family of a neurodivergent child, as parents/caregivers advocate on their child's behalf regarding education, social care, community and healthcare needs. In contrast to the development of a neurotypical child, families of neurodivergent children require and rely upon the support of multiple agencies and professionals to contribute to the development, care and support of their child. A substantial amount of time for parents and professionals is spent seeking, referring and fighting for a broad range of essential supports the neurodivergent child needs, to reach their full potential.

However, issues such as language, literacy and learning disability, mean that some families are unable to advocate for their child, or may not even be aware of where to start. Other families may be marginalised by poverty, ethnicity or the stigma associated with neurodivergence. Consequently, practitioners in education, healthcare and community settings have a key role in advocating for neurodivergent children and their families. Advocacy for neurodivergent children contributes in a planned way to creating supportive environments and culminates in children and their families having access to the resources and services they need to thrive. This chapter will examine what advocacy means and discuss its relevance, within the context of supporting neurodivergent children and their families. Advocacy needs,

DOI: 10.4324/9781003455868-11

challenges and strategies will be explored. Finally, types of advocacy and systemic issues which influence advocacy need, will further be considered.

Learning Outcomes

On completion of Chapter 11, learners should demonstrate an enhanced understanding concerning:

- Advocacy and its relevance to supporting neurodivergent children and their families
- Identifying a need for advocacy
- Referral pathways and services available locally, relevant to the needs of neurodivergent children and their families
- Advocacy in the context of creating supporting environments

What Is Advocacy?

The Health Information and Quality Authority (HIQA, 2023) describe advocacy as a set of actions which enable, empower and support people to have their voices heard and their rights realised. Disability Rights Washington (2008) surmise that advocacy is employed in order to access or increase services, challenge unfair or discriminatory treatment and reduce the barriers faced by individuals and groups in accessing their community and society. Burke, Lee, and Rios (2019) suggest that advocacy is a fundamental part of parenting a child living with disabilities, and parents frequently find themselves advocating for services, supports and entitlements. Advocacy is essentially about supporting, empowering and enabling people to have their rights realised and have access to the services and resources necessary for them to reach their goals (HIQA, 2023; Burke et al., 2019; Disability Rights Washington, 2008).

Reflection Point!

People who are the most marginalised and disadvantaged are often unaware of how marginalised and disadvantaged they are and the extent to which this impacts their lives. If you've always lived in poverty, for example, it can feel acceptable and part of normal life. Families who identify their need for advocacy support and request this are often less marginalised compared to their peers, who perhaps don't have awareness concerning their marginalisation.

Advocacy within health and social care aims to mitigate the impact of health inequalities (Hubinette, Dobson, Scott, & Sherbino, 2017). Hubinette et al. (2017) caution that practitioners must be familiar with health inequalities and how these affect the people they are supporting, to enable them to provide effective advocacy support. When we think about advocacy, we often think about making referrals to other services or speaking on someone else's behalf. Yet advocacy is equally about education, empowerment and the enablement of people who have been disadvantaged, to know their own rights and to be better positioned to advocate and speak for themselves.

For example: if attendance issues are particularly problematic for a neurodivergent child at a school located in a low-income area, exploring the health inequalities faced by the family within the context of the area where they live, can identity marginalisation and perhaps advocacy need. Examining the supports available and challenges presenting for the child and their family, can enable you to ascertain the impact of disability, geographical location and/or poverty on their capacity to attend school. Questions to consider: Does this family have health insurance? Are they paying out of pocket for medical services for their child? Are they a single-parent family? Or a single-income family? Or are one or both parents unable to work due to their child's additional care needs? Are one or both parents living with a disability or chronic health issue? Is the cost of school transport accessible to them? Is there school transport available?

Some families may require more comprehensive support and advocacy concerning accessing welfare/governmental financial supports or grants, understanding entitlements concerning their child's educational needs, information on school transport, childcare schemes or access to information on Medicaid waivers. Families may not be aware of their rights and entitlements or the variety of supports available, which could help their child and family. When the marginalisation and advocacy need is prevalent and similar issues are affecting a group of people, then collective advocacy efforts should be considered. For example, rather than supporting parents to complete welfare or service application forms on a one-to-one basis, having parent classes in the school regularly which discuss rights and entitlements and signposting where and how to apply for services, may be more appropriate to meeting the collective advocacy needs of these families. Parent literacy classes and parent support groups, may further enable parents in their capacity to advocate for themselves.

Advocacy needs will vary significantly from one neurodivergent child and their family to the next (Dhillon, Wilkins, Stewart, & Law, 2016). Dhillon et al. (2016) argue that identification of the problem should be the first step in any advocacy effort, and this should be undertaken in partnership and discussion with the parent/caregiver. Based on the principle of creating supportive environments concerning the uniqueness of each child, advocacy needs will be distinctive to each child and family. Even where two children have the same diagnosis and live in the same area, the whole family's needs and unique characteristics and preferences, will influence their need or preference for advocacy. Some families may be open to and relieved to have advocacy support, while another family may value privacy and discretion, and prefer not to discuss their family's broader needs, or choose to engage with advocacy supports.

Author Reflection Point!

I remember the appointment when my daughter was finally diagnosed with ADHD. This happened after two years of having concerns regarding behavioural and emotional issues, presenting both at home and at school. I left this appointment with a pamphlet explaining what ADHD was . . . that was it!

I didn't receive information about parent supports, rights or entitlements (allowances, tax relief, medical entitlements). I wasn't advised that co-morbidities were highly probable for children with ADHD, or that ADHD was likely hereditary. This important information was sought and accessed by me in small, bite-sized pieces, over a number of subsequent years. I didn't know I needed this information at that time. Yet referral to support organisations, information on self-advocacy or signposting to additional information, would have been so helpful. While the information about co-morbidity would have directly impacted my advocacy efforts for my child in the subsequent years (she was eventually diagnosed as autistic and with Oppositional Defiant Disorder, ODD). Information about peer support for parents would have also been really helpful. I was so unaware of what my child and family needed at that time, that I didn't even realise I was unaware.

Advocacy and Neurodivergent Children and Families

Jansson (2011) argues that marginalisation and fear act as barriers to accessing services, for some healthcare users. A lack of understanding about rights and entitlements, combined with cultural disparity, means that some neurodivergent children and their families will face further disadvantage, even prior to accessing services and supports (Jansson, 2011). Essentially, some families are so marginalised that they don't even realise that they are marginalised, and consequently may not be aware of their need for infor-mation, education and advocacy. Parental wellbeing and intergenerational neurodivergence (which may be undiagnosed) further contribute to the marginalisation of such families and substantiate their advocacy need.

Neurodivergent children and their families often face social exclusion, which persists across the lifespan (Marsack & Perry, 2018). However, re-cent research by Perepa, Wallace, and Guldberg (2023) reports that ethnic minority families – families for whom English is a second language and those from poorer backgrounds – are further disadvantaged in accessing and navigating disability supports services. This study related specifically to autism, yet findings suggest marginalised families are negatively affected by language difficulties and cultural stigma within their communities, which can further act as a barrier to accessing services for their child and family (Perepa et al., 2023).

Author Reflection Point!

I provide informal support quite regularly to other parents and fami-lies, at the beginning of their journey through disability services. One recurrent issue which acts as a major barrier for some families, is liter-acy issues. Most services require extensive paperwork prior to accept-ing a child for assessment or support services. When literacy issues are present, this paperwork can delay access and, in some instances, result in families not seeking support. Remain mindful of literacy issues and don't assume that every family has the skills to complete paperwork (which is often steeped in medical jargon and extensive in terms of the content and depth required). Even parents/caregivers with college degrees, can feel overwhelmed by the volume of paperwork involved in applying for some resources/services/entitlements!

Working in Partnership with Parents/Caregivers

Dhillon et al. (2016) suggest that advocacy often involves working in part-nership, to enable and empower the individual or family, to help themselves. Within this context, rather than making a referral, or contacting another agency or service on their behalf, the practitioner would work alongside the parent/caregiver to support and guide them to make contact with these services and express their needs. Burke, Tovar, and Rios (2022) report that parents advocating for the needs of their child can contribute to developing strong partnerships with education and healthcare providers, which further benefit their child in the long-term.

Working in partnership with parents/caregivers, is identified as a core principle of creating supportive environments for neurodivergent children and their families. Working in partnership with parents concerning advocacy empowers them to identify and communicate their child's and family's needs and places value on their expertise and insight concerning their child. Engaging a partnership approach to advocacy assists parents in building their skills to self-advocate and places them in a more favourable position from which to self-advocate in the future. Equally, partnership in advocacy should be concerned with supporting parents to access the information they need to identify their advocacy needs and make informed decisions. If practitioners do things for parents and families, rather than alongside them, then parents are not provided with the opportunity to cultivate and develop their own skills concerning advocacy.

The National Institute for Health and Care Excellence (NICE, 2022), in their guidelines concerning advocacy, propose working in a face-to-face capacity where possible. Referral pathways and forms should be simple, clear and accessible and available in both hard copy and online (NICE, 2022). The NICE (2022) guidelines further stipulate that advocacy efforts should be person centred and represent the wishes, needs and preferences of the individual and their family, while supporting the family to be as involved as possible. Finally, NICE (2022) suggests reaching clear agreements on advocacy goals and objectives, and revisiting and reassessing these agreements continually, as the situation progresses. The needs of a family in year 1 of their child's diagnosis, will contrast starkly to their needs in year 6 or year 10.

Case Study 1

Jack is 16 years old and has dual diagnoses of dyspraxia and autism. Jack has spoken to you about his wish to do more things alone, without his parents and siblings accompanying him. When you raise this request at your next meeting with his parents, they are horrified at this suggestion and explain that previously when Jack when to the movies with his friends, he was almost beaten up and was very distressed for weeks after this incident. Yet Jack is not dissuaded and is still adamant that he wants to become more independent, especially socially.

What are the advocacy needs within this case study?

What challenges concerning advocacy are presented?

How could advocacy contribute to solutions concerning Jack and his family's wishes and preferences?

Identifying a Need for Advocacy

Identifying a need for advocacy is an inherent skill and one which naturally develops over time as professionals meet with families and advance their awareness about the issues, concerns or disadvantages they face. Understanding and insight concerning the marginalisation of the family, existing supports and key challenges, will inform advocacy need. The familiarity and relationship between the practitioner and the family, will culminate in both parties becoming more comfortable in discussions concerning advocacy need. Yet families may ultimately decide that they do not want advocacy, even if a need for additional supports/services has been identified. This is an individual choice and should be respected. It may take time and relationship building, and the child's and family's unique needs to be established, before parents/caregivers feel in a position from which to explore advocacy and consider accessing the supports they need to pursue this.

It is acceptable to ask parents/caregivers of neurodivergent children and/or the neurodivergent child themselves directly, if they require advocacy support. Explaining what advocacy is, how this is undertaken and where families can access more information on advocacy options, is a key step within the advocacy process. Yet information overload and feeling overwhelmed, particularly at the earlier stages of assessment and diagnosis for their child, can make it difficult for parents to make important decisions during a meeting with professionals. It's often after a meeting or interaction, having had time to think about their child's needs and perhaps after speaking to family members or friends, that parents will make the decision to engage with the advocacy process.

Access to information which will place parents in a more informed position from which to advocate for their child, is fundamental. Considering the social determinants of health and how the child and family may be impacted by their environment, social class, access to services or education levels, can further assist practitioners in ascertaining when advocacy support may be required. Parents may themselves identify challenges faced by their family or specific issues their child is struggling with, which may benefit from advocacy support. Advocacy is often employed or suggested when the needs of the family exceed the supports available by the organisation they are interacting with, or if the practitioner identifies that the information and guidance needed is not their area of expertise. Acknowledging that some issues which arise will be outside of your professional remit, is helpful for families and communicates professional awareness.

Yet it is inherent that practitioners acknowledge and remain mindful of the impact of disadvantage, marginalisation and continued need faced by the families of neurodivergent children. Fear, apprehension and trepidation towards advocacy should be responded to with empathy and compassion.

Previous negative experiences in interacting with services or fear about losing existing services, can dissuade families from advocating for additional services or resources. Parents are often advised to be grateful for any provision of service their child receives and not to rock the boat. Yet if an unmet need exists, or the family are facing continued disadvantage which could be mediated via advocacy efforts, then advocacy should be considered. Families may benefit from reassurance and clarity concerning what advocacy will entail and what the possible outcomes may be. Providing access to information is the first step required in any advocacy effort, and will place families in a more informed position from which to understand their family's needs and the options available to them.

Author Reflection Point!

A notable barrier in accessing services and self-advocacy efforts for neurodivergent children and their families, is the burden of evidence/proof required. This is particularly true for financial resources, and parents often must paint a picture of their child's care needs on their worst day, emphasising explicitly and in great detail their child's deficits and challenges. This is absolutely soul destroying emotionally for any parent/caregiver. Yet many of the families who I provide peer support to are refused the financial allowances they apply for, as they have not sufficiently demonstrated their child's care needs. This is despite submitting a medical certificate stating their child's diagnosis and care needs, completing a 24-page application form, submitting a family daily diary and supplying evidence such as letters from school and other services engaging with the family. Couple this with the emotional and practical challenges of providing care to a neurodivergent child, alongside stress and poor parental wellbeing, and it paints a picture of a system designed for the continued marginalisation of families who are the most marginalised.

Awareness of Referral Pathways and Services Locally

It's important to know when you can't help with a situation or when the advocacy needs of the neurodivergent child and their family, extend beyond the scope of your role. Hence, being aware of formal advocacy services available locally, can enable you to refer the family with confidence to the advocacy service most appropriate to their needs. For example: your state/region may have autism-specific advocacy services, or there may be advocacy agencies who deal explicitly with access to education for children with disabilities.

Furthermore, the unique needs of the child and family may warrant or benefit from the support of peer advocacy services. Peer advocacy consists of people with similar lived experiences, advocating with and for other people experiencing marginalisation. An example could be parent peer support advocacy, where parents attend meetings with their peers to offer accompaniment, information and support. This may be when meeting with health or education professionals, or when trying to access respite, shared care, etc. An example of such peer advocacy is that offered by the Washington Autism Alliance. Washington Autism Alliance (2023) provides family navigators who possess extensive professional and personal experience and support families to access health and social care services, education and to advocate for themselves and their children.

One really useful way of becoming more familiar with locally available services, organisations and supports for neurodivergent children and families, is by engaging in site visits. I found site visits extremely beneficial when training to become a social worker. Identify services linked to the one you are working in, make contact with them and schedule a site visit. You visit the organisation, introduce yourself and your area of work, and find out more about that organisation, what they do and how to make a referral. Examples of site visits I undertook within child protection placements were homeless services, residential care settings for teenagers and community drug support services. This meant that I made contacts and built links within each organisation and knew enough about them, to confidently provide information about each to the families with whom I was working. Site visits would be ideally implemented within organisations at induction, so new staff could build their local networks and grow their advocacy resources for neurodivergent children and families. For staff already in situ, site visits could be adopted to broaden the referral pathways and support options for families using the service. No time spent working towards creating supportive environments for neurodivergent children and families is ever time wasted.

Author Reflection Point!

My capacity to advocate for my children differed substantially from my first neurodivergent child, to my third and fourth. I'm now acutely aware of the profound impact of parental education levels and how these influence my parental advocacy capacity. First time around and being a young mother, lacking a university education, I didn't know what to advocate for. I didn't know the range of possible options available regarding therapies or social skills development, and really took the recommendations of professionals as the only option available. I was disadvantaged educationally, yet was wholly unaware of this disadvantage or how this impacted my advocacy efforts and subsequent outcomes for my child.

*Remember: no one chooses where their starting point is or the advantages or disadvantages they experience. Some families may need you to support them in counteracting this disadvantage and sharing with them the information and guidance they need to best advocate for their child.

Types of Advocacy for Neurodivergent Children and Families

Advocacy examples within practice when supporting neurodivergent children and families, can vary significantly from one case to the next. The family's wishes, values, hopes and needs will guide whether or not they require advocacy support and will inform what type of advocacy is most appropriate. It is important to remember that advocacy must be wanted by the family and cannot or should not be imposed. As professionals we can often identify unmet need, based on our clinical expertise and a genuine wish to help and support the child and family. Yet the family may not wish to or be ready to make substantial changes, or may be fearful of advocacy if they are already marginalised. For example: a family on a very low income with some social security, may be afraid to apply for additional financial supports, due to a fear of losing their existing income. Equally, the fear of losing services is a tangible one experienced by many families of neurodivergent children. If existing services are not sufficient, not appropriate or there are issues of poor practice, families can be hesitant in advocating for change, due to fear of losing their existing service provision. Nonetheless, sharing information with families on the types of advocacy available and how to access these, can be a helpful step on an advocacy journey.

Formal advocacy is advocacy which is provided by a professional (largely in a paid position), who offers specialised advocacy services, focusing on a specific issue or problem. For example, special education advocates can support families in interacting with education services and systems. Such advocates provide information concerning rights and legislation, regarding education for children with complex needs (Goldman, Burke, Casale, Frazier, & Hodapp, 2020). Goldman et al. (2020) report that parents request special education advocates to accompany them to meetings with educational providers, to assist them in managing a change of school for their child, or when a disagreement occurs between parents and educational provider, regarding the child's needs. Goldman et al. (2020) suggest that parents of children with an autism diagnosis, are most likely to request the services of a special education advocate. Many special education advocates review the child's records at the request of parents and assist parents in communicating with their child's school (Goldman et al., 2020).

Self-advocacy is concerned with the individual or family's ability to have their needs communicated effectively and met (Hagan, Rosenzweig, Zorn, van Londen, & Donovan, 2017). In essence, self-advocacy occurs when the neurodivergent child or their parents are in a position to represent their own wishes and campaign to have these wishes realised, within the context of the care/support/services they receive. Hagan et al. (2017) propose that self-advocacy is enabled successfully, when the advocate has access to all of the information necessary to make decisions for themselves and relating to their care. The practitioner role within this context is concerned with enhancing access to information and education, which will empower the child and family in their self-advocacy efforts.

Informal advocacy services are fast becoming more established and utilised, within neurodivergent family networks. Informal advocacy can be provided by other parents with similar experiences. An informal advocate may provide accompaniment to meetings, may assist parents in advocating for themselves via support with writing letters or completing paperwork. Informal advocates can also be family members or friends of the neurodivergent child and family, who help them by speaking on their behalf or by supporting them to speak for themselves (West Virginia University, 2023).

Case Study 2

Maria and Andre, along with their 5-year-old daughter Aliah, have attended for an autism assessment. Maria and Andre explain that they do not want Aliah to be assessed, but her school have said that she will be unable to continue attending unless she is assessed. The school reports that Aliah's challenging behaviour in class is becoming increasingly dangerous to herself, other children and staff members.

Aliah's parents explain that she spends much of her time at home alone and has always preferred her own company. Aliah does have violent outbursts at home, but her parents feel like they manage this well. Maria and Andre explain that they don't want their daughter to be labelled and that, within their culture, autistic people are socially excluded and judged. Yet they fear that if they don't pursue an assessment, Aliah could lose her place in school.

What is the key and most pressing issue for this family?

What might their advocacy needs be?

What could be a first step in advocating for Aliah and her parents?

Advocacy and Creating Supportive Environments

Creating supportive environments is concerned with influencing positively the life of the neurodivergent child and their family across settings, sectors and more generally within society. Due to marginalisation and disadvantage culminating from social determinants of health and disability, some families will need and benefit from advocacy support. The fundamental principles of creating supportive environments for neurodivergent children, which are particularly relevant to advocacy, include knowledge and awareness that every neurodivergent child is unique.

- The practitioner has a responsibility to possess a competent knowledge and awareness concerning the child's diagnosis, the impact of their diagnosis on their daily lives and the lives of their family. Advocacy directly contributes to creating a supportive environment via empowering and enabling families to have their rights realised and receive the services and supports needed for their family to thrive. Further significant is knowledge and awareness of the systemic issues which impact neurodivergent children and families, in addition to supports, resources and services available. Knowledge and insight concerning referral pathways and access to services and supports available locally, contributes to creating a supportive environment for the neurodivergent child and their family. Supporting families to access the information they need to make informed decisions concerning their advocacy need, is further pertinent to creating a supportive environment.
- The recognition and appreciation that every single neurodivergent child is unique, should form the basis of any advocacy effort or subsequent plan. No two autistic, dyspraxic or children with ADHD will present with the same needs. Children with a diagnosis of one neurodivergent condition, are more likely to have a co-occurring neurodivergent condition (whether diagnosed or undiagnosed). Each child will have distinctive wishes and goals, which should further be central to the individual advocacy need and support provided. No assumptions should be made concerning advocacy need, and practitioners should take sufficient time to become familiar with the child and their family, to effectively support them to identify their own advocacy needs and make informed decisions.

Reflection Point!

Information is a fundamental prerequisite for successful advocacy. Sometimes information alone is sufficient to place parents/caregivers in a more informed position from which to advocate for their neurodivergent child. No one professional is expected to have all the information which might possibly be needed, yet having avenues to refer families to, where they can access further information, is a key method of empowering parents and enabling them in their advocacy efforts.

Where could you direct parents/caregivers to so they could access more information about financial entitlements/supports?

What, if any, formal advocacy services are available locally and how do families access these services?

Systemic Issues and Advocacy

Advocacy aimed at creating supportive environments for neurodivergent children and families, must consider and encompass the immediate, but also the broader systemic factors within society, which impact the family in their everyday lives. Ecological systems theory (discussed in more detail in Chapter 5) identifies the impact of societal systems on child development and family function (Bronfenbrenner, 1979). Bronfenbrenner (1979) contends that each child and family exist within a set of immediate and broader systems, each which influence them as they interact with the world around them. The immediate or micro system is concerned with the family and home environment, while the subsequent mesosystem, exosystem, macrosystem and chronosystem, relate to the societal influence of support networks, employment and geographical location, and the culture which shapes this society (Bronfenbrenner, 1979).

Consequently, systemic societal issues which impact neurodivergent children and their families, include the availability and proximity of support networks, having family living close by, employment opportunities/employment conditions of parents, and general societal understandings and reactions to neurodivergence. Burke et al. (2019) contend that such broader systemic issues can contribute to parents experiencing challenges in their advocacy efforts on behalf of their child, sometimes necessitating additional advocacy support. The exosystem which consists of policy, legislation, education and the availability of support services, is particular profound concerning its capacity to influence neurodivergent children and their families (Bronfenbrenner, 1979). Rights, entitlements, financial resources, employment protections and housing, are further momentous concerning such families (e.g. housing subsidies, social security payments, disability benefits, Medicare, etc.) (USAGov, 2023).

For example: a neurodivergent child who does not have a school placement and requires care and supervision around the clock, will be significantly disadvantaged in terms of their educational and academic development, socially, emotionally and regarding inclusion and acceptance. The parents of a child without a school placement will likely have to give up work to provide care for their child, placing them at a further disadvantage financially and in terms of wellbeing. Lack of consistency in employment may influence the family's access to medical insurance and essential therapies for their child. The family's capacity to self-advocate in this instance will be impacted by their access to information, the level of formal and informal support they receive, their education, literacy levels, disability status, ethnicity and parental health. Such an example highlights the cumulative disadvantage and marginalisation presented systemically, regarding neurodivergent children and their families. The most disadvantaged families are even more likely to face additional disadvantage and worsening impact, concerning the social determinants of health.

Advocacy at the macro level is increasingly becoming significant within disability circles, with the primary aim of advancing the agenda of inclusion and access within society. If practitioners and organisations are increasingly advocating for neurodivergent children regarding access to appropriate school places, then this signifies a broader collective issue within that society. Hence, advocating to enact change within policy, legislation and rights is warranted. The Africa Disability Alliance (2015) suggests that advocacy within this context is concerned with organised efforts which aim to question the status quo of existing policies, while consciously lobbying for change which creates equal opportunities for all. This is achieved via collaborations and targeted campaigns between community groups and organisations, with shared goals for inclusion and access (Africa Disability Alliance, 2015). For example: the California Work and Family Coalition is collectively advocating and lobbying for paid leave for parents and a more fair work/life balance. They are actively working together to have their voices heard and change the legislation which governs parental leave (California Work and Family Coalition, 2023).

The collective voices of people who share the same views and come together to instigate change, have the potential to be much more powerful than individual voices, attempting to make things better for themselves and their families. Such efforts directly aim to create supportive environments from the macro level and improve outcomes for children and families from a top-down perspective. This not only improves outcomes for the families immediately impacted, but also builds a legacy of supportive environments for other families and future generations. Hence, documenting all advocacy efforts is essential, so that effective and ineffective methods can be reviewed and revised going forward.

Reflection Point!

Did you know that some families may be entitled to welfare payments to help with internet and phone bills?

Did you know that families can apply for free school meals or child-care/crèche meals? (USAGov, 2023)

Both of these incentives could contribute to mitigating the systemic disadvantage experienced by the families you are supporting. Some families may not be aware of such services and may benefit from you sharing this information with them (including links/info about how to apply). Some families may need you to advocate with them or on their behalf to access such services.

Social Determinants of Health

The social determinants of health are further interlinked with systemic issues and relate to the key non-medical factors, which influence opportunities for health and wellbeing (World Health Organisation, 2023). Issues such as housing, education, employment/unemployment, income and access to health care, fundamentally impact health outcomes (WHO, 2023). In fact, determinants of health are so powerful that they dictate longevity and morbidity. People living in developed countries with a good level of education and income, can live 40 years longer than someone living in poverty in a developing country or a homeless individual (Commission on the Social Determinants of Health, 2008).

Marmot and Allen (2014) argue that wider societal conditions influence health equality and the opportunities of different groups in society, to achieve the highest levels of health. They contend that focus on health behaviours (such as weight loss or smoking cessation) without acknowledging the social and cultural factors at play, limits the potential of success for groups experiencing health inequalities (Marmot & Allen, 2014). Hence, consideration of and focused advocacy targeting the systemic factors which impact the health and wellbeing outcomes for neurodivergent children and families, should be central to advocacy efforts when providing support to such families.

Exploring the family's capacity to engage with therapeutic or behaviour strategies, is a crucial prerequisite for a successful outcome. For example: providing a parent who has literacy issues with a book about sleep hygiene, would likely be ineffective in promoting change to enhance wellbeing. Equally, a dietician plan for a child whose parents can't afford the recommended food, would further be unhelpful. Taking the time to assess and consider the social determinants of health for each child and family, creates a supportive environment which advocates for the most appropriate and attainable response to the family's needs. Advocacy efforts which consider the social determinants of health and the impact of health equity and opportunity on the neurodivergent child and their family, aims to mitigate such factors and create a supportive environment.

Advocating and referring a parent to adult literacy classes, will likely not be listed within your job remit. Yet this could be life changing for this family and their neurodivergent child. Viewing the family's needs holistically and exploring the non-medical factors which impact their environment, enables practitioners and families to more accurately advocate with the aim of making the environment a more supportive one. Supportive environments empower families of neurodivergent children to enhance their opportunities for health and wellbeing and bridge the gap created by systemic disadvantage and marginalisation.

Figure 11.1 illustrates the social determinants of health which impact neurodivergent children and families.

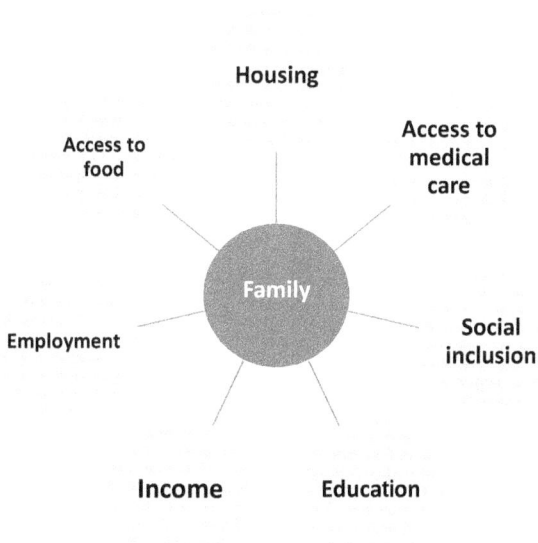

Figure 11.1 Social determinants of health (WHO, 2023)

Case Study 3

Tom is parenting alone and has three neurodivergent children. Tom and his children come from an ethnic minority background. Tom left school at age 13 and is unable to read or write. Tom and his family have been served with an eviction notice from their rented home. Tom has been re-fused financial assistance to help with housing, as he did not submit all of the evidence required with his application. Tom had an aunt who usually assisted him with completing forms/paperwork, yet she has recently passed away. The family have had no electricity in their home for the previous two weeks, as the bill was overdue. Tom is feeling increasingly desperate and is unsure how to advocate for his family's needs and improve their current situation. Tom's interactions with support services to date have been particularly negative, and Tom feels as though his family have been discriminated against due to their ethnicity.

How may systemic factors have contributed to the current situation of Tom's family?

How could such systemic factors influence the engagement of this family with the advocacy process?

What type of advocacy efforts may address these systemic issues both in the short-term and in the long-term?

Self-Assessment

Define what is meant by the term *advocacy*.

Identify two reasons why advocacy is important for neurodivergent children and families.

What can practitioners do to enhance the advocacy they provide?

Summary

This chapter has introduced the topic of advocacy and its relevance in providing support to neurodivergent children and families. Families presenting at school, clinic, hospital and community settings may be marginalised and unaware of their rights, avenues for support or where to get more information. Parents may not even know what questions to ask or where to start. Every interaction with such families is an opportunity to advocate in partnership with parents, with the ultimate goal of creating supportive environments and maximising positive outcomes for neurodivergent children. Practitioner awareness concerning the factors which marginalise neurodivergent children and families, is a vital prerequisite for identifying when families may benefit from advocacy support. Yet advocacy support should not be imparted upon families and should only be provided, when a wish to receive advocacy has been expressed. Nevertheless, empowering families to access information which will enable them to better understand their own needs and the options available to them, and is a key step to opening the door for advocacy efforts.

References

Africa Disability Alliance. (2015, May 21). *Advocacy toolkit for disability main-streaming*. Retrieved from www.cbm.org/fileadmin/user_upload/Publications/Disability_Mainstreaming_Toolkit.pdf

Bronfenbrenner, U. (1979). Contexts of child rearing: Problems and prospects. *American Psychologist, 34*(10), 844–850. https://doi.org/10.1037/0003-066X.34.10.844

Burke, M., Lee, C. E., & Rios, K. (2019). A pilot evaluation of an advocacy programme on knowledge, empowerment, family–school partnership and parent well-being. *Journal of Intellectual Disability Research, 63*, 969–980. https://doi.org/10.1111/jir.12613.

Burke, M., Tovar, J., & Rios, K. (2022). Exploring the advocacy process and its products among parents of children with disabilities. *Exceptionality: The Official Journal of the Division for Research of the Council for Exceptional Children, 30*(3), 187–200. https://doi.org/10.1080/09362835.2021.1968403

California Work and Family Coalition. (2023, May 21). *If you're a worker, parent, caregiver, or all of the above — Your perspective matters, and it should be heard by our lawmakers*. Retrieved from www.workfamilyca.org/advocatewithus

Commission on the Social Determinants of Health (CSDH). (2008). *Closing the gap in a generation: Health equity through action on the social determinants of health*. Geneva: World Health Organisation.

Dhillon, S., Wilkins, S., Stewart, D., & Law, M. (2016). Understanding advocacy in action: A qualitative study. *The British Journal of Occupational Therapy, 79*(6), 345–352. https://doi.org/10.1177/0308022615583

Disability Rights Washington. (2008, May 19). *Advocacy strategies*. Retrieved from www.disabilityrightswa.org/publications/advocacy-strategies/

Goldman, S., Burke, M., Casale, E., Frazier, M., & Hodapp, R. (2020). Families requesting advocates for children with disabilities: The who, what, when, where, why, and how of special education advocacy. *Intellectual and Developmental Disabilities, 58*(2), 158–169. https://doi.org/10.1352/1934-9556-58.2.158

Hagan, T., Rosenzweig, M., Zorn, K., van Londen, J., & Donovan, H. (2017). Perspectives on self-advocacy: Comparing perceived uses, benefits, and drawbacks among survivors and providers. *Oncology Nursing Forum, 44*(1), 52–59. https://doi.org/10.1188/17.ONF.52-59

Health Information and Quality Authority. (2023, May 19). *The fundamentals of advocacy in health and social care*. Retrieved from www.hiqa.ie/sites/default/files/2023-03/The-Fundamentals-of-Advocacy-in-Health-and-Social-Care.pdf

Hubinette, M., Dobson, S., Scott, I., & Sherbino, J. (2017). Health advocacy. *Medical Teacher, 39*(2), 128–135. https://doi.org/10.1080/0142159X.2017.1245853

Jansson, B. (2011). *Improving healthcare through advocacy: A guide for the health and helping professions.* Hoboken, NJ: John Wiley & Sons.

Marmot, M., & Allen, J. (2014). Social determinants of health equity. *American Journal of Public Health, 104,* S517–S519. https://doi.org/10.2105/AJPH.2014.302200

Marsack, C.N., & Perry, T.E. (2018). Aging in place in every community: Social exclusion experiences of parents of adult children with autism spectrum disorder. *Research on Aging, 40*(6), 535–557. https://doi.org/10.1177/0164027517717044

National Institute for Health and Care Excellence. (2022, May 21). Advocacy services for adults with health and social care needs. *NICE Guideline.* Retrieved from www.nice.org.uk/guidance/ng227/resources/advocacy-services-for-adults-with-health-and-social-care-needs-pdf-66143840705989

Perepa, P., Wallace, S., & Guldberg, K. (2023, May 19). *The experiences of marginalised families with autistic children.* University of Birmingham. Retrieved from https://research.birmingham.ac.uk/en/publications/the-experiences-of-marginalised-families-with-autistic-children

USAGov. (2023, August 11). *Government benefits.* Retrieved from www.usa.gov/benefits

Washington Autism Alliance. (2023, May 21). *Advocacy and legal services.* Retrieved from https://washingtonautismalliance.org/

West Virginia University. (2023, July 17). Types of advocacy. *Center for Excellence in Disabilities.* Retrieved from https://cedwvu.org/resources/types-of-advocacy/#:~:text=When%20people%20like%20parents%2C%20friends,for%20a%20group%20of%20individuals

World Health Organisation. (2023, May 21). *Social determinants of health.* Retrieved from www.who.int/health-topics/universal-health-coverage/social-determinants-of-health#tab=tab_1

Chapter 12

Family Support

Abbreviations

ADHD: Attention Deficit Hyperactivity Disorder
FANS: Family Assessment of Needs and Strengths
FSN: Family Support Network
SNAP: Supplemental Nutrition Assistance Program
WHO: World Health Organisation

Introduction

A family support approach to creating supportive environments for neurodivergent children and their families, aims to consider the wellbeing needs of each family member and the impact of such on the whole family. Adopting a family support lens from which to consider practice with neurodivergent children and their families, further appreciates the impact of caregiving responsibilities on the family function and interactions. Theories which inform family support practice, prompt practitioners to critically reflect on the interdependence of family members and how such influence family dynamics, coping capacity and wellbeing. This chapter will explore family support strategies, theory and practice, in terms of their application to supporting neurodivergent children and their families.

This chapter will start by introducing and exploring the concept of family support. The relevance of adopting a family support approach within the context of supporting families living with neurodivergence, will be discussed. This chapter will consider fundamental theories which can inform a family support approach, to supporting neurodivergent children and families. Case studies and practice examples will be utilised throughout this chapter, to illustrate tangibly how family support theory can inform and be applied to practice in a variety of settings. Finally, this chapter will discuss strategies of assessing family support needs, specific to neurodivergent children and their families, and with the core aim of creating supportive environments.

DOI: 10.4324/9781003455868-12

Learning Outcomes

On completion of Chapter 12, learners should demonstrate an enhanced understanding concerning:

- Defining family support
- The rationale for a family support approach to practice with neurodivergent children and families
- Family support theory and how to utilise this to inform and enhance practice
- Assessing the family support needs of neurodivergent children and their families

Family Support

Family support is a style of practice aimed at promoting the health and development of children and their families (Canavan, Dolan, & Pinkerton, 2000). TUSLA (2023) describe family support as focusing on the existing community networks of the family and initiating engagement with these. Family support aims to increase parental coping capacity and consequently improve outcomes for children (TUSLA, 2023). McCurdy and Daro (2001) advocate that family support should be strongly underpinned by theory and should adopt a partnership approach between practitioners and parents/caregivers.

Family support is a method of helping families via the provision of community-based services, with the aim of empowering parents in their role of promoting their child's development (US Department of Health and Human Service, 2023). Family support focuses on "assisting and supporting parents in their role as caregivers" (US Department of Health and Human Service, 2023). Kadiri (2023) argues that family resilience is strongly influenced by the resilience of each individual family member, when the family is caring for a child with a disability. The Community of Practice for Supporting Families of Individuals with Intellectual and Developmental Disabilities (2023) contends that the family unit is fundamental in the care of children and adults living with disabilities and argue that family support for such families, is concerned with strengthening families and enabling them to care for their child at home. Family support specifically tailored to the needs of families of children with developmental disabilities, often comprises a medley of activities including:

- Navigation services regarding disability supports
- Funding to meet their child's and family's unique needs
- Access to information, training and education

- Connecting with peers/other families
- Lifespan care planning for their child

(The Community of Practice for Supporting Families
of Individuals with Intellectual and Developmental Disabilities, 2023;
Family Support Network of North Carolina, 2023)

FSN of North Carolina (2023) argue that the family support needs of children with disabilities are distinctive. Support should be tailored based on the unique stressors associated with caregiving, with the primary goal of increasing parental coping capacity (FSN, 2023). Li and Xu (2022) argue that family support is instrumental in terms of maintaining positive parental mental health and emotional wellbeing.

Reflection Point!

What do you envisage when you hear the term *family support*? In what setting do you think family support traditionally occurs?

Family support focuses a collective effort on promoting the development of a child, relating to their social, emotional and educational wellbeing (Barnados, 2023). Family support engages an assets-based approach to empower and enable families, to counteract adversities they face and equip them with the skills and resilience necessary to cope with changing life circumstances (Barnados, 2023; Biegel, Singer, & Conway, 2012). Strong family relationships have been found to be a substantial precursor for overall family wellbeing (Biegel et al., 2012). Stevenson et al. (2022) argue that positive relationships within families create resilience and enable families to cope and better respond to stressful occurrences.

A family support approach can be leaned upon and used to inform practice from health, social care and education professionals, in an effort to empower families to cope with the challenges presented when raising a neurodivergent child. This approach prompts professionals to consider the holistic needs of the whole family, with the focus remaining on supporting the child to achieve their goals and thrive. Very few professionals will have family support listed within their job description. Yet harnessing the ideas and strategies presented within a family support response, can empower practitioners in their pursuit to make a difference in the lives of neurodivergent children.

Family Support and Neurodivergence

A growing body of evidence supports the notion that employing a family support style of practice, presents distinctive benefits for neurodivergent children and their families (Churchill et al., 2018; Zeng et al., 2020; Mullan, Boyd, & McConkey, 2021). Churchill et al. (2018) conducted longitudinal analysis on the impact of a case management intervention for children with ADHD and their families. This research was based on approaching the family's needs relating to behaviour management, family function and maternal stress, and involved a nurse visiting the home and empowering parents to identify solutions (Churchill et al., 2018). Findings propose that family function can be improved via providing consultation and education to parents, regarding responding to challenging behaviours (Churchill et al., 2018).

Family support has been found to be particularly significant in terms of influencing parental coping capacity and reported stress, in parents of neurodivergent children (Zeng, Hu, Zhao, & Stone-MacDonald, 2020). Zeng et al. (2020) surmise that family support for families of autistic children in China directly impacted parental stress levels. They argue that professionals from educators to medical staff should be provided with education on this significant finding from their study, in an effort to mobilise and engage family support for families of neurodivergent children (Zeng et al., 2020).

Mullan, Boyd, and McConkey (2021) found a home-based family support intervention for families of autistic children, to be particularly effective in improving outcomes for children and families. This intervention aimed to provide parents with emotional support and practical tools to empower them to manage and cope with their child's behaviour (Mullan et al., 2021). Mullan et al. (2021) surmise that post intervention, families reported an increase in their coping capacity, a reduction in their child's challenging behaviours and feeling less parental stress (Mullan et al., 2021).

Case Study 1

Callum is aged 5 and autistic, and has been referred to the disability multidisciplinary team, for ongoing support regarding speech and communication. Callum is pre-verbal, very outgoing and understands everything his parents say to him. Callum is in an autism-specific class and seems to be progressing well. At his first appointment with both parents, Callum hits his 2-year-old brother three times. His parents redirect him, are responsive and act in a protective manner. Yet Callum continually tries to hurt his brother.

What are your thoughts on Callum's needs? What do you think Callum's parent's needs might be? How could you approach these needs after this appointment? What would be the first step?

Rationale for a Family Support Approach to Supporting Neurodivergent Children and Families

Families navigating disability support services, while simultaneously parenting a disabled child, may culminate in increased stress and reduced coping capacity for some parents. Caring for other children, single parenting and/or living in poverty, can further exacerbate the difficulties faced by families of neurodivergent children. Those with a strong support network will be in a position to seek and obtain support in terms of childcare, respite and emotional support. Yet what happens when there are no informal support networks or extended family? Or how do parents cope if they are neurodivergent, are living with a disability or have a mental health issue? The needs and presentation of each family member is impacted consistently by other family members. Hence, adopting a family support approach provides for a more planned yet holistic response to the needs of a family and one which will address their needs comprehensively.

"But that's not my job, I'm a teacher/speech therapist/public health nurse!" This is a very valid initial response, in particular if you are working in an environment where resources are already overstretched and you have a large class/caseload. However, you can still incorporate a family support approach within your existing practice, via consideration of the theoretical framework which informs this approach.

Author Reflection Point!

Some of the most profound and significant support my children and our family have received, has been from professionals wearing different hats. School staff have helped to support one child with anxiety, while our general practitioner has been instrumental in terms of parental emotional support and advocacy. This flexibility in terms of roles and responsibilities of professionals, makes support more accessible and tangible for families who are struggling.

Parents may not directly indicate their need for support, but this may be communicated by their emotion, expressing challenges with parenting or accessing resources, or by perhaps indicating they need someone to talk to. Due to waiting lists and perhaps an inability for some parents to acknowledge that they need support, it's often their child's teacher, public health nurse or physio therapist who may observe a parent asking for help, indirectly. Some parents may not want to ask for help as they are usually interacting with services aimed at addressing their child's needs, as opposed to their own. Equally, there may be no specific service available for parents of neurodivergent children, which offers guidance, information and support. Parents may also fear that asking for help and support might communicate incompetence as a parent, or a lack of knowledge and understanding regarding their child's needs.

Theory and Approaches to Inform Family Support for Neurodivergent Children and Families

Theories and concepts which inform understanding of the factors which influence and affect the families of neurodivergent children, can assist practitioners in the planning and delivery of the family's support needs. Ideas surrounding how families work and interact, in addition to factors which negatively influence their health and wellbeing, and capacity to engage with healthcare and education services, can equip practitioners with a more critical lens from which to comprehensively approach meeting the family's needs. Following are some theories and concepts particularly relevant to holistically evaluating and responding to the family support needs, of neurodivergent children and their families.

Family Systems Theory

Family systems theory was created by Bowen in 1978, yet continues to remain relevant to supporting families today. Family systems theory proposes that each family member is part of the family system, which is a whole system within which the family functions (Allen & Henderson, 2016). Family members are interdependent within this system, and the actions and interactions of one family member impact the other family members and the system as a whole (Allen & Henderson, 2016). Pfeiffer and In-Albon (2017) argue that within the family system, accepted norms and boundaries of behaviour exist, which the family continually reproduces. Such norms of behaviour manifest in rituals which form the reality of the family and their established expectations of themselves and each other (Pfeiffer & In-Albon, 2017). Bowen (1978) proposes that the emotional function of each individual family member influences the family system, while the emotional stability of the family system impacts the individual family members. This manifests within a continued feedback loop, whereby each family member interacts and is impacted emotionally by one another and the overall family emotional stability (Bowen, 1978).

Haefner (2014) contends that based on Bowen's family systems theory, the emotional wellbeing of one family member cannot be separated from that of other family members. This is particularly significant within the context of creating supportive environments for neurodivergent children and their families. Haefner (2014) argues that the application of a family systems approach to supporting families, offers an empowering avenue for each family member to be active in improving their family's wellbeing.

Within the context of family support for neurodivergent children and their families, I have found a family systems approach to be one which is most fitting from which to assess needs and plan supports. Impacting the emotional wellbeing and coping capacity of one family member, influences positively the emotional wellbeing of the other family members and the family as a whole (Mullins, 2022). Support mechanisms which recognise and acknowledge the bidirectional influence of family members on one another and the whole family system, can tailor interventions to break a negative feedback loop and improve the overall function of the family system and consequently positively impact each individual within this system. For example: a parent living with chronic untreated pain will inadvertently negatively impact their spouse, children and family as a whole. Each person in the family will be impacted by the parent's chronic pain, possible low mood associated with this and the emotional toll the parent experiences, because of their prolonged physical discomfort. Pain management for a parent may seem like an issue that is completely irrelevant to creating supportive environments for neurodivergent children and families. Yet consider the impact of a parent living with chronic pain, caring for an autistic child with an additional diagnosis of ADHD or dyspraxia? Would chronic pain impact this parent in their coping capacity and perhaps responding to challenging behaviour or aggressive outbursts? Would chronic pain impact their parent concerning their ability to engage with services, e.g. multiple appointments per week? How could parental chronic pain impact the other children in the home? To what extent would chronic pain influence the parent in their physical and practical support of their child with self-care tasks such as bathing, toileting or dressing? Based on family systems theory, chronic parental pain would most certainly influence emotionally and practically the other members of the family individually and the family as a whole (Bowen, 1978). Supporting the parent to address and manage their chronic pain, could increase their physical and emotional wellbeing and increase their capacity to cope with their child's additional care needs. This enhanced parental emotional wellbeing would impact their spouse and children more positively emotionally and enhance the emotional wellbeing of the whole family system. The parent feeling more capable and well in the parenting and provision of care and support to their neurodivergent child, will have a positive impact on the child and the environment within the home and family life.

Practice supporting families informed by a family systems approach, is further conducive to the principle of creating supportive environments, of working in partnership with parents/caregivers. Parents have an instrumental role in sharing their insight, experience and perspectives concerning their family's needs, history and challenges. Such valuable knowledge sharing culminates in a parent's active involvement and leadership in the process of helping their own family and feeling valued and appreciated for their contributions. A family support approach based on family systems theory, means that parents are active in identifying and reaching solutions to improve wellbeing and positive outcomes, for their child and family.

Case Study 2

Sarah (age 24) and her son Jack (age 6) present for an occupational therapy assessment. Jack has been having difficulties in school regarding his ability to follow instruction and with challenging behaviour. Jack has been on the waiting list for two years, and Sarah is visibly upset at the appointment.

Sarah explains that Jack is now in school only three half days per week, as the school doesn't have the resources needed to cope with and respond to his challenging behaviour effectively. Sarah is a single parent and lives in a different county from her extended family. Sarah has had to give up her job, as she has no one to help look after Jack, now that his school timetable has been reduced.

Jack is playing with toys on the floor and pauses every few minutes to look at his mother and ask if she's okay. Eventually, Jack gives Sarah a hug and says he's sorry and he will try harder. This prompts Sarah to cry even more. She explains to Jack that it's not his fault, and she knows he is trying really hard in school.

What do you think the key needs of this family are? What needs may be a priority, yet perhaps haven't been shared by Sarah? How would you respond to these needs?

Social Capital Theory

Bhandari and Yasunobu (2009) describe social capital as a communal asset which offers benefits to those who invest. Social capital theory is pertinent to family support for the purpose of creating supportive environments for neurodivergent children and families, as it aims to explore and build upon the social supports surrounding the child and their family. Wall, Ferrazzi, and Schryer (1998) contend that capital is often discussed regarding financial assets invested and acquired. *Social capital* is defined as "the mutual relations, interactions, and networks that emerge among human groups" (Wall et al., 1998).

Pierre Bordieu was instrumental in developing the initial study of social capital and viewed this as a resource for aiding people in reaching their goals, due to the support of others (Field, 2005). Field contends that social capital provides people with opportunities for affection, to discuss matters important to them and to acquire goods and services (Field, 2005). Conversely, an omission of social capital can result in isolation, loneliness and the negative impact such states of being prompt, for individuals and families (Field, 2005). Indeed, Harpham and McKenzie (2006) argue that social capital is clearly visible within social and health policy, which reflects increasing awareness concerning its influence on health and wellbeing. Social capital is viewed as a significant buffer against stress as it provides emotional, social and informational support to those who possess it (Harpham & McKenzie, 2006). A cornerstone study on social capital in 1997 by Kawachi, Kennedy, Lochner and Prothrow-Stith, found that social capital was influential in terms of health outcomes, mortality and life expectancy.

Research to date acknowledges the impact of caring for a neurodivergent child, on the health and wellbeing of parents and families (Weiss, Wingsiong, & Lunsky, 2014; Samadi, McConkey, & Bunting, 2014; Shivers & Resor, 2020; Gunderson & Barrett, 2017). Weiss et al. (2014) contend that social capital for families of autistic children is often limited or nonexistent, resulting in the need for more formal and even emergency services for support, in the event of a crisis. Social support and informal support networks have been found to reduce stress and improve emotional wellbeing, in mothers of autistic children (Sarwar, Panatik, Jameel, Wan Mohd Yunus, & Muhamad, 2022). Sarwar et al. (2022) report that in the absence of availability of access to social capital, parents of neurodivergent children can access desired and needed social support, from online and in-person support groups of other parents of neurodivergent children. Indeed, this is a message I strongly advocate for in my interactions with other parents. The emotional support and understanding we sometimes lack from our family and friends, can be found within peer support. The mechanism of this social support (whether online or in person) is irrelevant, yet it can be instrumental in promoting wellbeing, reducing stress and consequently enhancing coping capacity for parents of neurodivergent children.

Reflection Point!

Parents/caregivers may not be aware of the significance of social capital, pertaining to their wellbeing and levels of stress. Sharing information with parents in the form of research articles, blog posts or links to online/local support groups, can enable parents to feel informed, empowered and enabled to make choices, concerning their social capital. Such information sharing further communicates a partnership approach between practitioners and caregivers, which is a core principle of creating supportive environments for neurodivergent children and their families.

Social capital is considered a pertinent influence on child and family health and wellbeing. Exploring the family's social capital can enable practitioners to evaluate existing social support resources available to parents and neurodivergent children, and consider the impact of such on their emotional wellbeing and general life satisfaction. Evaluating social capital and exploring the capacity of the family to develop this, can empower families to build social capital in a way which is meaningful to them and conducive to their family's and child's unique needs. Yet D'Arcy et al. (2023) report that caregivers of neurodivergent children face barriers in accessing social networks due to their child's needs, in particular concerning challenging behaviours. Participants report feeling isolated in their communities due to the stigma associated with their child's condition and regarding not having sufficient time, due to care responsibilities, to maintain social relationships (D'Arcy et al., 2023). However, social capital which consists of other parents/caregivers of neurodivergent children, reduces the stigma and perceived judgement parents often experience when out in their communities. Concerning creating supportive environments, a social capital perspective lends to the principle of supporting parents to support their child. Enhancing parental wellbeing and coping capacity via empowering parents to establish or engage with existing informal support networks of family and friends, can be life changing (Sarwar et al., 2022).

Social Determinants of Health and Family Support

The social determinants of health are further relevant to consider, when adopting a family support approach to creating supportive environments for neurodivergent children and their families. The social determinants of health are the non-medical and life factors, which impact health and wellbeing (World Health Organisation, 2023). The social determinants of health include factors such as housing, income, education and access to health services, in addition to early child development, social inclusion and employment (WHO, 2023). The WHO (2023) contends that the social determinants of health are more influential than lifestyle choices or healthcare in influencing health and can culminate in substantial disparities concerning life expectancy. To create supportive environments, practitioners must demonstrate knowledge and awareness concerning the family's existing needs and aim to support parents to support their children. Acknowledging the social determinants of health and how the child and family are impacted by these, will enable a more tailored, targeted and appropriate response to the needs of the whole family.

Research concerning the impact of the social determinants of health is well established, and it is widely accepted that where people live, work and interact, has a profound influence on their health, wellbeing and mortality (Townsend, Davidson, & Whitehead, 1992; Preda & Voigt, 2015; Marmot, 2007, 2010). One of the most profound research studies and a cornerstone development concerning understanding of the social determinants of health, relates to the Glasgow effect. Glasgow is a city in Scotland in the UK, which found itself at the centre of global discussions concerning health disparity and the influence of non-medical factors on life expectancy and early mortality (Cowley, Kiely, & Collins, 2016). Research in Glasgow concerning life expectancy and living conditions, demonstrated a stark contrast between postcodes in a relatively small geographical area. The most affluent area had a life expectancy of 20 years higher, than deprived areas just five miles away (Glasgow Centre for Population Health, 2010; Reid, 2011). The most deprived areas had substantially higher rates of deaths relating to addiction, smoking and suicide, and this was attributed to the profound social deprivation within the area (Graham, Walsh, & McCartney, 2012). Such social deprivation within communities negatively impacts mental health and emotional wellbeing, which for some people culminates in alcohol and drug abuse (Reid, 2011; Graham et al., 2012).

Social, health and welfare policy worldwide, further reflects the evolution in understanding concerning the impact of environments, communities and access to health care and education on health and longevity – from employment and working conditions legislation such as the Wages Fair Labor and Standards Act (US Department of Labor, 2023), to policy such as the Supplemental Nutrition Assistance Program (SNAP), which provides food for families on the lowest incomes and living in poverty (US Department of Agriculture, 2023).

The social determinants of health can be profoundly influential, concerning the needs of neurodivergent children and their families. Living conditions, education, community, neighbourhood and housing will influence health and wellbeing outcomes for the child and family. Zuckerman, Lindly, Sinche, and Nicolaidis (2015) conducted research concerning the social determinants of health for families of autistic children and found that parents with lower levels of educational attainment and with the lowest income, were less likely to understand their child's condition, and this impacted their engagement with health care services. Fox, Maribona, Quintero, Lange, and Semidey (2023) argue that social determinants of health impact the ability of families of neurodivergent children, to access health services, in particular due to poverty. Fox et al. (2023) contend that access to transport for attending therapy and medical appointments, lack of access to insurance and housing instability, culminate to further disadvantage children with neurodevelopmental conditions. Effective support initiatives should examine and aim to address the social determinants of health for families to whom they are providing care, in an effort to remove the barriers to accessing health and social care services (Fox et al., 2023).

Given the substantial impact of the social determinants of health on wellbeing and health outcomes, it would be inadequate to assess the needs of neurodivergent children and their families, without exploring how they are impacted by the social determinants of health. If a parent is working in a job where they can't take time off to attend appointments and may risk losing their job if they do, knowing this information can enable practitioners to find a way to meet this family's needs, while remaining cognisant of the impact of health disparities. Equally, if a family is struggling to put food on the table and the parents find themselves frequently hungry as they prioritise their child's meals over their own, this would substantially influence their capacity to engage with services concerning their child's diagnosis. Finally, a family experiencing social exclusion, without social or family support networks and struggling to cope with their child's needs, will be impacted concerning parental wellbeing, perhaps mental health and feelings of loneliness. To create a truly supportive environment, the catalyst of acknowledgement of the family's unique needs, circumstances and barriers to date will enable the practitioner to identify their needs holistically and create an appropriate and distinctive support plan, based on these unique needs. A family support approach advocates for the consideration of the family's needs holistically and comprehensively, in order to plan an adequate and effective practice response.

Each of the examples here illustrate the significant impact of the social determinants of health on the child and their family and further in the context of their capacity to identify, access and utilise services and supports for their neurodivergent child. Consequently, an approach to family support which evaluates the social determinants of health and how the child and family are influenced by these, will enable practitioners to identify unmet needs and additional barriers facing the family. By approaching the family's needs from this perspective, the practitioner is actively aiming to gauge how best they can empower families, based on their unique needs, challenges and circumstances.

Reflection Point!

Can you think of how consideration of the social determinants of health could inform practice with a child and family you have worked with previously?

Assessment of a Family's Needs

Assessment of the family's need for support, is an essential first step in adopting a family support approach to empowering and enabling the families of neurodivergent children. Existing support networks, the unique needs of the neurodivergent child and the wishes and preferences of the family, will dictate the type and extent of supports needed. Remaining cognisant of the interdependency of family members based on a family systems approach, further enables a holistic assessment of their needs (Bowen, 1978).

There are multiple assessment-of-need templates which are utilised in different settings, sectors and countries, to establish the most appropriate way to identify and plan to address the family's needs. For example: in the United Kingdom, a whole family assessment is undertaken to establish how best the family can be supported (Department for Education, 2010). For needs assessments for families with complex needs or when a child is in foster care, a Family Assessment of Needs and Strengths (FANS) can be employed (State of Michigan Department of Health and Human Services, 2021). The Caregiver Burden Inventory is more specific to families of children with medical or developmental diagnoses and aims to evaluate the impact of the child's condition on the family (McStay, Trembath, & Dissanayake, 2014). The state where you practice and the protocols and regulations within your profession and within the organisation where you are employed, will further dictate or inform your approach to assessing the needs of neurodivergent children and their families, from a family support perspective.

Yet ascertaining the family support needs of neurodivergent children and their families, with the aim of creating supportive environments, is concerned with a distinctive knowledge base and nuanced awareness. Underpinned by a family systems approach (Bowen, 1978), Table 12.1 shows family support assessment criteria unique to neurodivergent children and their families, which can be used to inform your practice.

Table 12.1 Criteria for assessing the family support needs of neurodivergent children and their families

Criteria	Questions	Rationale
Health and wellbeing of the whole family	Do parents, siblings and the neurodivergent child have any health or wellbeing issues? Does any family member have a diagnosis of a physical or mental health condition? Do family members live with chronic pain or have mobility issues? Is any member of the family suffering from sleep issues?	The health, wellbeing of the whole family, impacts and is impacted by other family members. Understanding comprehensively the health and wellbeing of each family member, can enable the practitioner to holistically and comprehensively aim to address the family's unique needs effectively.
Access	Does the family have access to healthcare services? Do they have access to financial supports or information about such supports? Have the family been supported to access all of the information they require to meet their child's and family's needs?	Determining the level of access to information, services, supports and resources currently available to the family, will equip the practitioner to create a plan which accurately identifies the family's access needs. Literacy, health, mobility and location, will impact the capacity of the family to access information and support.
Fears	What worries present concern for the family? What does this family fear most (e.g. violent behaviour, mental illness, social work involvement, children removed from the home)?	Providing a safe and open space for families to express their innate fears and worries, is a vital step in helping families to overcome these. Ascertaining the families' fears regarding their child and family, means the practitioner can provide more specific and tailored support to address these fears.
Daily Living Challenges	What are the family's biggest challenges or struggles in their everyday life? What aspects of their family routine cause substantial stress? What difficulties do the family experience daily, which negatively impact individual family members and, subsequently, the family as a whole?	Problem sharing assists in building a partnership between the practitioner and family and clarifies the family's priorities, concerning the support they need most.

Criteria	Questions	Rationale
Strengths	What are the family's strengths? What do this family do really well? How do they get through difficult days?	Ascertaining strengths enhances the practitioner's ability to ascertain what works well for this family and what they can build upon, e.g. the mother is really good at recognising when she needs help. Or a sibling is helpful in resolving conflict which leads to challenging behaviour. Identifying and naming these strengths, communicates to the family that you value them and appreciate their unique insights and expertise concerning their family's needs.
Support	What informal existing support networks does the family have? Do they avail of or interact with any community supports locally? Or do they utilise formal support services?	Gauging the level of existing support, informs the practitioner and family of current support levels and, consequently, where additional supports may be helpful.

Self-Assessment

How would you define family support?

Why is family support relevant concerning creating supportive environments?

What are the key benefits of adopting a family support approach for neurodivergent children and their families?

Chapter Summary

This chapter has introduced a family support approach, to responding to the care and support needs of neurodivergent children and their families. Although not rigidly aligned to one specific theory or perspective, a family support approach can prompt professionals to consider the broader, more holistic support needs of each family. A family support approach further aligns with the principles of creating supportive environments for neurodivergent children and their families. Incorporating a family support approach and adopting some of the strategies associated with this discipline, can enable practitioners to consider and address the broader societal and social support issues which are impacting this family, in terms of planning their support. Theories and perspectives which inform understanding of family function, dynamics and wellbeing, can be utilised by practitioners to inform their practice and support the family from a more insightful and knowledgeable perspective. Practitioners outside specific services providing family support, may be apprehensive in approaching their work from this perspective. Yet such an approach can be complementary alongside more traditional approaches associated with individual disciplines and may culminate in more positive outcomes for neurodivergent children and their families.

References

Allen, K., & Henderson, A. (2016). Family systems theory. In *Family theories* (p. Family Theories, 2016). Hoboken, NJ: John Wiley & Sons, Incorporated.

Barnados. (2023, May 30). *Family support*. Retrieved from www.barnardos.ie/our-services/work-with-families/family-support

Bhandari, H., & Yasunobu, K. (2009). What is social capital? A comprehensive review of the concept. *Asian Journal of Social Science*, *37*(3), 480–510. https://doi.org/10.1163/156853109X436847

Biegel, C., Singer, Biegel, D., & Conway, P. (2012). *Family support and family caregiving across disabilities*. London and New York: Routledge.

Bowen, M. (1978). *Family therapy in clinical practice*. New York, NY: Aronson.

Canavan, J., Dolan, P., & Pinkerton, J. (2000). *Family support: Direction from diversity*. London and Philadelphia: Jessica Kingsley.

Churchill, S., Leo, M., Brennan, E., Sellmaier, C., Kendall, J., & Houck, G. (2018). Longitudinal impact of a randomized clinical trial to improve family function, reduce maternal stress and improve child outcomes in families of children with ADHD. *Maternal and Child Health Journal*, *22*(8), 1172–1182. https://doi.org/10.1007/s10995-018-2502-5

The Community of Practice for Supporting Families of Individuals with Intellectual and Developmental Disabilities. (2023, August 3). *History of supporting families*. Retrieved from https://supportstofamilies.org/about/history/history-of-family-support/

Cowley, J., Kiely, J., & Collins, D. (2016). Unravelling the Glasgow effect: The relationship between accumulative bio- psychosocial stress, stress reactivity and Scotland's health problems. *Preventive Medicine Reports*, *4*, 370–375. https://doi.org/10.1016/j.pmedr.2016.08.004

D'Arcy, E., Burnett, T., Capstick, E., Elder, C., Slee, O., Girlder, S., Scott, M., & Milbourn, B. (2023). The well-being and support needs of Australian caregivers of neurodiverse children. *The Journal of Autism and Developmental Disorders*. https://doi.org/10.1007/s10803-023-05910-1

Department for Education. (2010, August 7). The use of the whole family assessment to identify the needs of families with multiple problems. *UK Government*. Retrieved from https://assets.publishing.service.gov.uk/government/uploads/system/uploads/attachment_data/file/181688/DFE-RR045.pdf

Family Support Network of North Carolina. (2023, August 4). *What is family support?* Retrieved from https://fsnnc.org/what-is-family-support/

Field, J. (2005). *Social capital and lifelong learning*. Bristol: Policy Press.

Fox, K., Maribona, A.S., Quintero, J., Lange, C., & Semidey, K. (2023). Addressing health inequalities in the United States: A case report on Autism Spectrum Disorder (ASD) and social determinants of health. *Cureus*, *15*(7), e4253. https://doi.org/10.7759/cureus.42539

Glasgow Centre for Population Health. (2010, August 8). *Investigating a Glasgow effect. Why do equally deprived UK cities have different outcomes?* Retrieved from www.gcph.co.uk/assets/0000/0801/GCPH_Briefing_Paper_25_for_web.pdf

Graham, P., Walsh, D., & McCartney, G. (2012). Shipyards and sectarianism: How do mortality and deprivation compare in Glasgow and Belfast? *Public Health, 126*(5) 378–385. https://doi.org/10.1016/j.puhe.2012.01.018.

Gunderson, J., & Barrett, A.E. (2017). Emotional cost of emotional support? The association between intensive mothering and psychological well-being in midlife. *Journal of Family Issues, 38*(7), 992–1009. https://doi.org/10.1177/0192513X15579502

Haefner, J. (2014). An application of Bowen family systems theory. *Issues in Mental Health Nursing, 35*(11), 835–841. https://doi.org/10.3109/01612840.2014.921257

Harpham, T., & McKenzie, K. (2006). *Social capital and mental health.* Philadelphia, PA: Jessica Kingsley.

Kadiri, M. (2023). Family social support and children's mental health resilience during COVID-19—Case of Morocco. *Youth, 3*, 541–552. https://doi.org/10.3390/youth3020037

Kawachi, I., Kennedy, B.P., Lochner, K., & Prothrow-Stith, D. (1997). Social capital, income inequality, and mortality. *American Journal of Public Health, 87*, 1491–1498. https://doi.org/10.2105/AJPH.87.9.1491

Li, S., & Xu, Q. (2022). Family support as a protective factor for attitudes toward social distancing and in preserving positive mental health during the COVID-19 pandemic. *Journal of Health Psychology, 27*(4), 858–867. https://doi.org/10.1177/1359105320971697

Marmot, M. (2007). Achieving health equity: From root causes to fair outcomes. *Lancet, 370*, 1153–1163. http://dx.doi.org/10.1016/S0140-6736(07)61385-3

Marmot, M. (2010). *Fair society, healthy lives—The Marmot review* (Strategic review of health inequalities in England post-2010). Retrieved from www.instituteofhealthequity.org/projects/fair-society-healthy-lives-the-marmot-review

McCurdy, K., & Daro, D. (2001). Parent involvement in family support programs: An integrated theory. *Family Relations, 50*, 113–121. https://doi.org/10.1111/j.1741-3729.2001.00113.x

McStay, R.L., Trembath, D., & Dissanayake, C. (2014). Stress and family quality of life in parents of children with autism spectrum disorder: Parent gender and the double ABCX model. *The Journal of Autism and Developmental Disorders, 44*(12), 3101–3118. https://doi.org/10.1007/s10803-014-2178-7. PMID: 24997633

Mullan, A., Boyd, K., & McConkey, R. (2021). The Impact of a brief home-based intervention on families with a child with autism spectrum disorder. *The Journal of Developmental and Physical Disabilities, 33*, 693–708. https://doi.org/10.1007/s10882-020-09768-4

Mullins, L. (2022). *It takes a village. Navigating the journey of parenting your autistic child.* Dublin: Orpen Press.

Pfeiffer, S., & In-Albon, T. (2017). Family systems. In *Reference module in neuroscience and biobehavioral psychology* (p. Reference Module in Neuroscience and Biobehavioral Psychology, 2017). Amsterdam: Elsevier.

Preda, A., & Voigt, K. (2015). The social determinants of health: Why should we care? *The American Journal of Bioethics, 15*(3), 25–36. https://doi.org/10.1080/15265161.2014.998374

Reid, M. (2011). Behind the "Glasgow effect". *Bulletin World Health Organisation*, *89*(10), 706–7. https://doi.org/10.2471/BLT.11.021011.

Samadi, S., McConkey, R., & Bunting, B. (2014). Parental wellbeing of Iranian families with children who have developmental disabilities. *Research in Developmental Disabilities*, *35*(7), 1639–1647. https://doi.org/10.1016/j.ridd.2014.04.001

Sarwar, F., Panatik, S., Jameel, H., Wan Mohd Yunus, W., & Muhamad, S. (2022). Psychological capital, social support and wellbeing in mothers of children with autism spectrum disorder. *SAGE Open*, *12*(3). https://doi.org/10.1177/21582440221121773

Shivers, C., & Resor, J. (2020). Health and life satisfaction among parents of children with physical disabilities. *Journal of Developmental and Physical Disabilities*, *32*(5), 719–733. https://doi.org/10.1007/s10882-019-09716-x

State of Michigan Department of Health and Human Services. (2021, August 7). Family assessment of needs and strengths. *Children's Foster Care Manual*. Retrieved from https://dhhs.michigan.gov/OLMWEB/EX/FO/Public/FOM/722-09A.pdf

Stevenson, C., Wakefield, J.R.H., Kellezi, B., Stack, R.J., & Dogra, S. (2022). Families as support and burden: A mixed methods exploration of the extent to which family identification and support predicts reductions in stress among disadvantaged neighbourhood residents. *Journal of Social and Personal Relationships*, *39*(4), 886–907. https://doi.org/10.1177/02654075211050071

Townsend, P., Davidson, N., & Whitehead, M. (Eds.). (1992). *Inequalities in health: The black report and the health divide*. New York: Penguin.

TUSLA. (2023, May 16). *Family support*. Retrieved from www.tusla.ie/services/family-community-support/family-support/

US Department of Agriculture. (2023, August 8). *Supplemental Nutrition Assistance Program (SNAP)*. Retrieved from www.fns.usda.gov/snap/retailer/faq

US Department of Health and Human Service. (2023, August 8). *Family support services*. Child Welfare Information Gateway. Retrieved from www.childwelfare.gov/topics/supporting/support-services/

US Department of Labor. (2023, August 8). *Wages and fair labor standards Act*. Retrieved from www.dol.gov/agencies/whd/flsa

Wall, E., Ferrazzi, G., & Schryer, F. (1998). Getting the goods on social capital. *Rural Sociology*, *63*(2), 300–322. https://doi.org/10.1111/j.1549-0831.1998.tb00676.x

Weiss, J.A., Wingsiong, A., & Lunsky, Y. (2014). Defining crisis in families of individuals with autism spectrum disorders. *Autism*, *18*(8), 985–995. Retrieved from https://doi.org.nuigalway.idm.oclc.org/10.1177/1362361313508024

World Health Organisation. (2023, August 8). *Social determinants of health*. Retrieved from www.who.int/health-topics/social-determinants-of-health#tab=tab_1

Zeng, S., Hu, X., Zhao, H., & Stone-MacDonald, A. (2020). Examining the relationships of parental stress, family support and family quality of life: A structural equation modelling approach. *Research in Developmental Disabilities*, *96*, 103523. https://doi.org/10.1016/j.ridd.2019.103523

Zuckerman, K.E., Lindly, O.J., Sinche, B.K., & Nicolaidis, C. (2015). Parent health beliefs, social determinants of health, and child health services utilization among U.S. school-age children with autism. *The Journal of Developmental and Behavioral Pediatrics*, *36*(3), 146–157. https://doi.org/10.1097/DBP.0000000000000136

Chapter 13

Reflective Practice

Abbreviations

ADHD: Attention Deficit Hyperactivity Disorder

Introduction

Reflective practice is a core tenet of professional practice within the health and social care sectors and particularly relevant to supporting neurodivergent children and their families. Reflective practice enables practitioners to critically consider their approach to a situation and to continually improve their practice, via reflection. Practice which is reflective in nature communicates a commitment to professional development and the consistent questioning of one's practice, regarding its effectiveness. Reflective practice has been identified as a fundamental principle of creating supportive environments for neurodivergent children and families.

This chapter will examine the key theory which informs the evidence base concerning reflective practice. Methods of incorporating reflective practice into your daily work routine, will be discussed. Case studies and reflective exercises will further be employed, to enable you to grasp the key concepts of reflective practice and how this can empower you to create supportive environments. Finally, this chapter will explore barriers to incorporating reflective practice and proactive methods of overcoming such barriers.

Learning Outcomes

Upon completion of Chapter 13, learners should demonstrate an enhanced understanding concerning:

- Defining reflective practice
- The rationale for continually engaging in reflective practice, while supporting neurodivergent children and their families

DOI: 10.4324/9781003455868-13

- Methods of engaging in reflective practice
- The significance of reflective practice in the context of creating supportive environments

What Is Reflective Practice?

Reflective practice is fast becoming a fundamental element of professional practice, within the health and social care sectors. Yet reflective practice can enhance practice for educators and practitioners, regardless of the setting or sector of employment. John Dewey was an American educator and philosopher and the person most known for their work on reflective practice and thinking critically (Miettinen, 2000). Dewey (1910) argues that critical reflection is a valuable mechanism for learning. He contends that reflective thought is sequential, rather than random, and based on the premise of existing evidence, new experiences and new evidence, and subsequently logical next steps (Dewey, 1910).

Reflective practice is the in-depth and focused analysis of a situation and exploration of your thoughts, feelings and perceptions (Bottomley, Cartney, & Pryjmachuk, 2019). Thompson and Thompson (2018, p. 18) define reflective practice as a very specific type of thinking "that helps us make sense of our practice". Grant, McKimm, and Murphy (2017) argue that reflective practice promotes patient/service user safety, through enhancing the competence of practitioners. Reflective practice entails an intentional and rigorous look at ourselves and our practice (Rolfe, Jasper, & Freshwater, 2011).

In contrast to everyday reflection, which we engage in continuously as we interact with the world around us, critical reflection within a professional practice context relates to in-depth reflection, which culminates in deeper understanding and meaning (Rolfe et al., 2011). Rolfe et al. (2011) contend that the professionalisation of health and social care has further contributed to the emergence of reflective practice and increased accountability of practitioners. Thompson and Thompson (2018) contend that reflective practice is now a central element of professional practice across settings, which aims to improve practice and contribute to continued professional development. Curry and Epley (2022) argue that reflective practice presents practitioners with a greater understanding of themselves and what they bring to the table, when interacting with service users. Reflective practice further enables practitioners to consider the broader context, systems and policies, which impact both themselves and the families for whom they provide support (Curry & Epley, 2022).

Dewey (1910) argues that critical thinking is an essential component of reflective practice and extends beyond mere observation. Critical thinking demonstrates a hesitance in accepting things as they appear or at face value (Dewey, 1910). This hesitation communicates curiosity and a wish to

---

Reflection Point!

Think of a time when you were competitive, at a sports game or tournament, or in a spelling bee or student competition. If you won, what did you do differently next time? If you didn't win, what did you do to increase your chances of winning?

Both scenarios require that you reflect. If it went well, why did it go well and how can you maintain this? If it went badly, you reflect on what went wrong and what you should do differently, to create a more favourable outcome.

---

inquire, confirm and acquire new knowledge and understanding (Dewey, 1910). Dewey contends that each experience we reflect upon is steeped in the multidimensional reflection and interpretation of previous historical time and places. Dewey uses a metaphor which really illuminates the unique interpretative lenses people use for reflection and likens this to viewing a three-dimensional figure from different viewpoints, and each person sees a different angle or perspective (Miettinen, 2000).

It's much like the social media images where people see different colours or even objects, based wholly on the individual's perspective. Dewey (1922) proposes that an act or occurrence has different meanings to different people. It can be both a fact and an interpretation simultaneously, and is further based upon our previous experiences of this subject, act or occurrence and the experiences of others who have previously studied this (Dewey, 1922).

Author Reflection Point!

Reflecting about my time meeting with families in practice and with students in a support or mentoring capacity, I'm inherently always conscious of the power differential. I'm the professional, in a position of insight and oftentimes control over the outcome for the person with whom I'm meeting. I'm also in a position of experience, where I can use my previous insight to enable and empower them to move to a position where they have more power and control over their current situation. So this power dynamic must remain always as a fundamental awareness for me in my reflective practice, as it's ever present and without question is something the person I'm interacting with is acutely aware of. I have a professional practice responsibility to continually reflect on my practice and critique my practice choices, particularly concerning power.

Unconscious Bias

Reflective practice can help practitioners to identify unconscious bias, stereotyping and misinformation, which may inadvertently impact the care and support they provide. Unconscious bias refers to the generalisation of an individual from a subgroup within society and subsequent negative assumptions about them (FitzGerald, Martin, Berner, & Hurst, 2019). Each of us has had a negative interaction in the past which may have upset, distressed or damaged us emotionally or even physically. When we have been hurt by someone, it can cause us subconsciously to perhaps fear or avoid people similar to those who negatively impacted us previously. For example: if you were pickpocketed while walking in Florida Gardens, you may perceive people from there to be dishonest. Logically this doesn't make sense. One person pickpocketed you, and they may not have even been originally from Florida Gardens. Yet when you hear of this location, it invokes these negative emotions of a time when you felt violated or unsafe. This is emitted via prejudice or prejudging someone you meet, or even in discrimination, where you treat them less favourably (Eagly & Koenig, 2021). Therefore, although not consciously, you may be stereotyping people from this area, including families with whom you work.

Bias can further manifest based on wider societal prejudice and acceptance of negative stereotyping, of a certain group of individuals. For example, in Ireland, Irish Travellers (or gypsies) experience persistent and damaging stereotyping, because of their ethnicity. They are often portrayed negatively in the media, and many face prejudice in relation to employment opportunities, access to social venues and even in terms of friendships (Quirke et al., 2022). Negative stereotyping for Travellers has resulted in significant health disparities for this group, culminated in shorter life expectancies, higher rates of infant death and greater suicide rates, compared to members of the general population (Heaslip, Wilson, & Jackson, 2019).

Whether in education, a medical or health care setting or a community organisation, supporting neurodivergent children and families will entail working with families from varied and multiple geographical locations and neighbourhoods, ethnicities, social classes, sexual orientations, religions and abilities. Practicing from a non-biased or prejudiced position is critical not only from a professional practice perspective, but also in terms of maximising the effectiveness of your interactions with this family and subsequently more positive outcomes for the neurodivergent child.

Reflective practice prompts professionals to dig deep and examine what unconscious bias or long-buried prejudice, they are bringing to the table. It's safe to say that most people have experienced bias at some point in their life. Yet uncovering this bias via reflection, naming and exploring this bias and consequently remaining ever mindful concerning this bias, results in a productive, professional and proactive response to inherent bias. The consistent and recurring nature of reflective practice, affords practitioners protected time within which to pause, reflect and reset, and consciously minimise the impact of their bias on the families with whom they work.

Engaging in reflective practice concerning bias, is particularly pertinent in the context of creating supportive environments for neurodivergent children and families. Any bias you feel, although subconsciously, has the capacity to negatively impact your interactions with neurodivergent children and their families. For example: assuming people from a certain area or ethnicity are single parents or are unemployed. Or even generalising a family's needs due to their surname or non-attendance at school or appointments. Such assumptions or even suspicions concerning the family's life and their need for support, cause harm to them and negatively influence the likelihood of creating a supportive environment, where the child and their family feel safe, heard and understood. Acceptance and acknowledgement are key catalysts for creating supportive environments for neurodivergent children and their families. Reflective practice facilitates acknowledgement of unconscious bias, stereotyping and prejudice and empowers practitioners to accept and value the unique attributes of each child and family with whom they interact. Reflection prompts practitioners to check themselves continually for such bias and aims to challenge practitioners to challenge themselves, to ensure such bias does not find its way into the classroom, clinic or community.

Methods of Engaging in Reflective Practice

Reflective practice enables the analysis of one's own practice, rationale, approach and outcome, to ascertain if something can be changed or enhanced. Reflective practice is not only engaged in when a serious incident occurs, but can also assist practitioners to review their everyday practice and make sense of this. By exploring one's practice through reflection, practitioners can develop a deeper understanding of their practice approach and its effectiveness. Each practitioner will identify and engage in a method of reflective practice which works best for them and is conducive to their unique professional development needs. Some practitioners view reflection as a very private and personal experience, which they would not wish to share with other people. Other practitioners may benefit from sharing their reflections with someone else or within a group setting. Many tools and methods can assist practitioners to engage in reflective practice, and three such methods are discussed as follows.

Journaling/Reflective Diary

Using a reflective diary, or journaling, is a method of documenting experiences from which to engage in reflection. Reflective diaries present practitioners with a medium within which to explore the challenges they face within their practice and verbalise their thoughts and feelings about their experiences (Vinjamuri, Warde, & Kolb, 2017).

Olmos-Ochoa et al. (2021) propose that reflective writing is a tool for continuous personal and professional development and increased effectiveness in practice. They contend that reflective writing facilitates the critical interpretation of practice and the identification of areas where skills development might be needed to improve practice (Olmos-Ochoa et al., 2021). The most wonderful aspect of journaling with the aim of facilitating reflective practice, is that this process is for your eyes only and based on your interpretation, practice and development goals and not subject to the views or scrutiny of anyone else. It provides a space where you can be completely honest in your reviews of your own practice and regarding the areas where you feel you could develop or improve upon.

Reflective journaling can promote the conscious analysis of practice experiences, for the specific scrutiny of each situation and how the professional viewed this and responded (Murillo-Llorente, Navarro-Martínez, Valle, & Pérez-Bermejo, 2021). Murillo-Llorente et al. (2021) surmise that journaling contributes to an increased level of practice planning and organisation, which practitioners value in terms of professional development. Reflective journals are as individual as each professional and will likely vary significantly from one person to the next. Yet once this medium of reflection is effective in facilitating true reflective practice and critique of one's practice decisions, then it is an appropriate technique to enable reflection. Reflective journaling can further culminate in increased self-awareness and a culture of continual critique of one's own practice. The private nature of reflective journaling may appeal more to some practitioners compared to supervision, for example, where another person is involved in your reflective efforts. No one aside from you will have access to your reflective journal, and you can revisit your thoughts, views and reflections as they change and evolve over time. Reviewing journal entries from a month ago or five years before, can illuminate the practitioner's professional practice development and chart how their perceptions and experiences have evolved. Consequently, reflective journaling provides practitioners with a personal record of their journey and progress through reflection.

Case Study 1

Jake is a 16-year-old boy with a dual diagnosis of ADHD and dyspraxia. Jake and his mom Zara attend a meeting with school staff (teacher, home/school liaison and deputy principal), Jake's child psychologist and you, his social worker. The purpose of this meeting is to discuss Jake's poor *attendance and truancy. The meeting commences with introductions and the deputy principal highlights the key concerns for Jake's education and overall wellbeing. Zara lists the challenges she has been facing with Jake at home such as aggressive behaviour, slamming doors and staying awake all night playing computer games. Zara shares that she suspects Jake is taking drugs and is at a loss as to what to do with him. You notice Jake looking increasingly uncomfortable and attempt to ask Jake what his views are, but Zara interjects and continues to share negative incidents of Jake's behaviour and how it is impacting her life. At this point (10 minutes into the meeting), Jake walks out of the meeting, telling everyone they can go f**k themselves, and slams the door.*

Stepping back and reflecting on this meeting . . .

- What went wrong?
- What was the trigger or turning point where Jake felt the need to disengage?
- What could have been done differently in terms of the meeting structure?
- What feelings, emotions and motivations did each person bring to this meeting?
- What could have happened prior to the meeting, which may have resulted in a different outcome?
- What action could you have been taken during the meeting, which may have resulted in a different outcome?
- What are your key learning points from this experience?
- How can these learning points inform future practice, in supporting Jake going forward?

Supervision

Supervision is probably best recognised and utilised within the social work and therapy sectors. Yet supervision is both an accessible and highly effective method of facilitating reflective practice, which can be employed across all health, social and educational settings. Formal supervision, also known as clinical supervision, is described as a focused relationship-based interaction which aims to "manage, support, develop and evaluate" the work practices of the supervisee (person in receipt of supervision) (Milne, 2007). Rothwell, Kehoe, Farook, and Illing (2019) argue that formal supervision improves practice and culminates in better outcomes for patients.

Beddoe et al. (2022) contend that formal supervision presents a protected slot of time within which practitioners can reflect on their practice and receive feedback from their supervisor. The practitioner meets in a one-to-one capacity with their supervisor, to discuss their practice, engage in reflection and plan for future practice. Snowdon et al. (2020) found that clinical supervision facilitates shared reflection, where supervisees are encouraged to consider the impact of their own beliefs and values and how these impact their practice and decision making. Reflective practice within supervision contributes to skills development concerning critical thinking, with the additional benefit of having the perspective and expertise of another person (usually a line manager or supervisor within your workplace).

In contrast to formal or clinical supervision, informal supervision affords practitioners an opportunity to garner emotional support and validation, according to Coren and Farber (2017). They found that practitioners sought informal supervision from colleagues, as a means of developing their own understanding of their decision-making processes and interactions with clients (Coren & Farber, 2017). Farber and Hazanov (2014) propose that the accessibility of informal supervision is a distinct advantage, in that it occurs as and when it's needed, as opposed to being limited to pre-agreed times. The frequency of formal supervision may not meet the needs of practitioners, particularly during training or the early career stage (Farber & Hazanov, 2014).

Informal supervision can take place between peers or friends and can be scheduled into the work day, or undertaken more generally within their interactions with one another. While recent developments concerning the use of Zoom and MS Teams creates greater access for engaging in supervision, perhaps with practitioners you no longer work with or who you completed your training alongside. Sometimes speaking to a colleague or friend outside of your immediate workplace, can enable more honest and open reflections on your practice.

Peer supervision is a type of supervision undertaken with a work colleague, as opposed to a supervisor (Rothwell et al., 2019). Rothwell et al. (2019) contend that practitioners having choice regarding their supervisor (and subsequently choosing a peer), can enhance the benefits of supervision for the recipient. Furthermore, peer supervision can be facilitated as a group capacity, meaning that a greater number of practitioners can participate (Rothwell et al., 2019). Peer supervision can be created by staff members, without the formal input of the organisation. It can be within a structured format where you are allocated a peer for shared supervision sessions, or can be undertaken within a group setting. Peer supervision is often bidirectional, where each party shares their reflections and critical consideration of their own practice, and both parties provide feedback and support.

Critical Incident Analysis

Another method of engaging in reflective practice is via critical incident analysis. Bolton (2016) argues that critical incident analysis provides for a structured means of prompting further examination of a practice incident or interaction. Tripp (2012) suggests that a critical incident is anything that happens which you identify as significant. A critical incident is an occurrence that warrants further examination in terms of what happened and how it happened (Tripp, 2012). Tripp (2012) clarifies that most critical incidents are neither major nor dramatic in nature, yet they become critical through the subsequent reflection and analysis of what happened. Critical incident analysis involves examining the why and the how of the event and the ways in which each person was involved, contributed and was impacted (Tripp, 2012).

In a research study regarding medical students and the use of critical incident analysis, findings propose that this method of reflective practice prompted students to explore in more depth their interactions with patients and peers (Gathright, Thrush, Guise, Krain, & Clardy, 2016). Gathright et al. (2016) surmise that the critical analysis of the interactions of other staff members with patients in particular presented learning opportunities for students concerning effective and appropriate practice, versus poor practice. The collation of participants' (students') feedback was deemed transformative, by both students and practitioners within this medical setting (Gathright et al., 2016). Although critical incident analysis is ordinarily personal and not shared with anyone else, this study illuminates the potentially powerful nature of critical incident analysis, in terms of prompting further reflection and subsequently positively impacting practice (Gathright et al., 2016).

Reflection Point!

Reflection is about looking at yourself and what you do. Why do you look in the mirror every day before work or college? What are you aiming to achieve by seeing yourself? Does looking at yourself in the mirror prompt action or change? Why is looking at your reflection important?

Reflective Practice While Supporting Neurodivergent Children and Families

Neurodivergence presents so uniquely for each child and their family. Equally, the family's capacity to cope with and respond to the child's needs and engage with support services, will vary substantially from one family to another. Reflective practice facilitates the critical questioning of one's own practice and that of other practitioners, to promote the best possible outcome for those in receipt of care (Grant et al., 2017). Reflective practice is so momentous in terms of practice with neurodivergent children and families, that it has been identified as a fundamental principle of creating supportive environments. In order to build and maintain a supportive environment, practitioners must continually review and reflect upon their practice. Employing reflective practice acknowledges that as humans, we don't get things right every time. Equally, reflective practice can enable practitioners to identify which elements of their practice are particularly conducive to creating an environment where children and families feel included, valued and that their needs are being addressed. By identifying what works well, practitioners can aim to build upon this success.

No file review or reading material can comprehensively prepare a practitioner to meet the varying and changing needs of a child with ADHD, dyspraxia or who is autistic (or a combination of all). Hence, reflecting on practice presents an exceptional opportunity to examine what's working well and what can be changed or modified, to meet the unique health, education and social care needs of the neurodivergent child. Integrating reflective practice into your practice, communicates that you are actively striving to achieve best practice and create more positive outcomes for neurodivergent children and their families. This demonstrates that you are less likely to become complacent and that you are committed to continually developing as a practitioner. Creating supportive environments is concerned with altering or establishing an environment which meets the unique needs of the neurodivergent child and their family, and one within which they can thrive.

Engaging in reflection further demonstrates an acknowledgement that practice can always be improved upon. The strategies you employ to support families may become less effective, as the needs of the family change. Equally, if a child or family share that the approach taken is unhelpful or even damaging, then it's essential to explore the interactions with this family and identify what went wrong or could have been done differently. As a parent having given negative feedback to professionals providing support to my children at different times, I've always been reassured by their willingness to reflect. No practitioner (myself included) gets it 100% right every time. Even when your practice is progressing well, reflecting on this can enable you to keep evolving as a practitioner and continually become more aware of what works well, compared to what could or should be changed.

Reflective practice is a tool which can prompt practitioners to reflect on the environment and the extent to which this is supportive for the child and family. Practitioner attitudes, partnerships with parents and each and every interaction with families, create and maintain a supportive environment. Hence, critically reflecting on your practice can empower you to explore your approach and its effectiveness, specifically concerning creating supportive environments.

Case Study 2

Shane is an occupational therapist working as part of a multidisciplinary team, providing assessment, diagnosis, therapeutic and family support to autistic children and their families. A new family whose 6-year-old daughter Maya has recently been diagnosed as autistic, have cancelled their last two appointments with Shane. Maya's parents Nigel and Carmel have not provided an explanation for these cancellations. Shane makes a call to Nigel to ascertain if there are any issues or problems he should be aware of or could help with. Nigel responds that both he and his wife felt uncomfortable during their last meeting, when asked about their jobs and educational backgrounds. Nigel advises that they will be looking for another service and abruptly ends the call.

Shane is very upset and shares the issues with his supervisor. Shane advises that he did ask Maya's parents about their jobs and educational backgrounds, as Carmel mentioned some medical terminology, so Shane asked if she was a medical professional. Shane meant no harm and was just making conversation. Yet he feels very sad that the family are no longer engaging due to his actions.

What method of reflection may help Shane to critically consider what happened here?

How could this reflection contribute to a greater depth of understanding concerning the environment and the extent to which this was supportive for Maya, Nigel and Carmel?

How could such reflections and insights into his practice, inform Shane's future practice?

How might engaging in reflective practice regarding this incident, help Shane to process his own feelings and emotions?

The three key catalysts for creating supportive environments for neurodivergent children and families – acknowledgment, access and acceptance – are further realised via engaging in reflective practice.

Acknowledgment requires the practitioner to become deeply aware of the challenges, needs and experiences of the neurodivergent child and their family, due to their specific diagnosis and unique attributes. Reflective practice provides the practitioner with a more focused and determined critique of the extent to which they acknowledge the child's world and consequently how practice can be tailored to their distinctive needs.

Access as a catalyst prompts the practitioner to empower and enable families to be informed and have access to the information they need, to make decisions regarding their child's care. Via employing reflective practice, practitioners are pressed to explore the appropriateness and effectiveness of their efforts to date concerning access and information sharing. Such reflection may prompt the identification of new means of information sharing or access points previously not considered, or alternative ways of increasing ease of access for families.

Acceptance prompts the practitioner to sincerely and openly embrace the uniqueness and presentation of each neurodivergent child and family, and meet them where they are at. Reflective practice can assist in facilitating honest consideration of one's thoughts, views, values and experiences and the extent to which they could be perhaps skewing true acceptance of a family due to subconscious stereotyping, prejudice or misinformation.

Author Reflection Point!

Recently, one of my children had a negative experience in a social setting/ group they are a part of. A staff member singled them out for a forgotten item, and this caused my child substantial distress. For a neurotypical child (with no additional needs), this incident would likely not cause distress at all and, in fact, the child would possibly not even remember it. But three days later, this interaction still upset my child, and they struggled to cope with the overwhelming feelings this presented for them.

I debated whether or not to highlight this issue, as the team there are usually very informed in terms of neurodiversity and inclusion, and my fear was that expressing this negative experience would negatively impact my relationship with them and subsequently my child's experiences in this setting. However, this incident really upset my child and communicated complacency in terms of autism understanding and awareness. So I communicated this to the team.

The team:

- Reviewed what happened
- Discussed why this happened and staff thoughts, views and recollections of this incident
- Reflected on what could have been done differently
- Committed to ensuring this incident or a similar one wouldn't happen again
- Demonstrated new learning and practice, based on the reflection this incident prompted
- Shared the reflection process and outcome with me as the parent

This reaction reassured me as a parent, reassured my child and reduced the anxiety they felt around returning to this setting. This process further reminded staff that continued and conscious awareness of the unique needs of neurodivergent children, needs to remain a priority and that reflection culminates in continued professional growth and positive outcomes for professionals, children and families.

Barriers to Engaging in Reflective Practice

It's important to acknowledge that barriers to engaging in reflective practice exist in some settings and professions, and subsequently explore ideas for overcoming these challenges. Figure 13.1 outlines some common barriers experienced by practitioners, when attempting to implement reflective practice into their role.

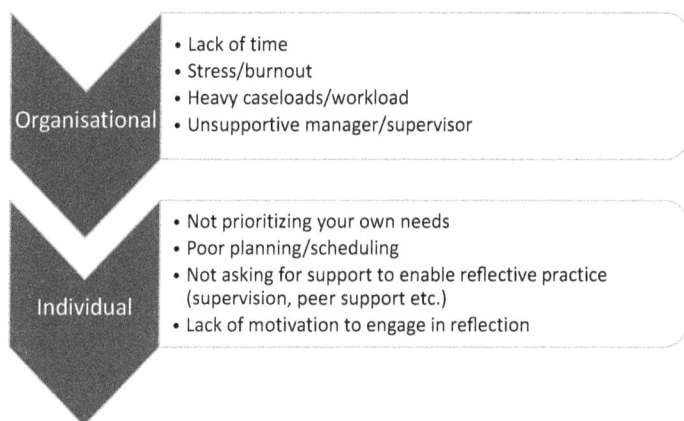

Organisational
- Lack of time
- Stress/burnout
- Heavy caseloads/workload
- Unsupportive manager/supervisor

Individual
- Not prioritizing your own needs
- Poor planning/scheduling
- Not asking for support to enable reflective practice (supervision, peer support etc.)
- Lack of motivation to engage in reflection

Figure 13.1 Barriers to reflective practice

Reflection Point!

As practitioners, evaluations of our practice can be terrifying! We fear hearing that we didn't do well at our jobs or that our practice added to the stress or distress of the people we help. But not evaluating, not asking our clients, patients and students how we're doing, means that our reflection is solely based on our own perspectives. Views and experiences from the people we support in the form of feedback, is a valuable asset in promoting critical reflection on practice and making changes to improve practice going forward. We can't create supportive environments if we don't ask neurodivergent children and their families, if they view and experience these environments as supportive!

Ways of Overcoming Barriers to Engaging in Reflective Practice

There are many ways you can aim to overcome the barriers to engaging in reflective practice. Yet innately, you must be committed to incorporating reflective practice into your role, for such strategies to be effective.

- *Planning your time*: schedule reflective practice as you would another important meeting or work event. If this is visible within your schedule, it presents protected time dedicated solely to engaging in reflection.
- *Ask for help*: sometimes having someone else to prompt, motivate and support you can make adopting a new work practice easier. Ask a peer if they would like to meet fortnightly and discuss your collective reflection and methods which worked best or could be changed.
- *Ask a supervisor or manager to provide formal supervision*: formal supervision can be incorporated into any workplace, regardless of the setting. If this is not available in your workplace, ask! If your manager or supervisor say no, then ask another manager or email the CEO/lead clinician/school board/board of directors. Some organisations will outsource formal supervision or will send staff on training so that they can provide this. Present a case as to why this would be beneficial for you in your role, and subsequently for the children and families with whom you work. The organisation won't change unless you drive this change!
- *Highlight the barriers*: if your workload is insurmountable and you are concerned that you are unable to engage in reflective practice because of this, highlight this within feedback to the organisation. It may prompt troubleshooting to identify methods of reducing workloads or innovative ways of integrating reflective practice into existing workload models.
- Research how other organisations or professionals facilitate reflective practice, to ascertain if such ideas could make reflective practice more feasible where you work.

Self-Assessment

What is reflective practice?

What method of engaging in reflective practice would be applicable/appropriate to your practice?

How can engaging in reflective practice contribute to creating a supportive environment, for neurodivergent children and families?

Chapter Summary

This chapter has introduced the reader to the concept of reflective practice and its significance as a principle of creating supportive environments, for neurodivergent children and their families. Reflective practice promotes a critical review of one's practice, for the purpose of improving future practice and subsequently improving outcomes for neurodivergent children.

Methods of engaging in reflective practice are varied, and practitioners can try multiple strategies to identify which works best for them. Reflective practice enables practitioners to strengthen the three key catalysts for action in creating supportive environments for neurodivergent children and their families, as they facilitate and deepen self-awareness and the identification of unconscious bias. This chapter highlighted the potential barriers within professional practice for engaging in critical reflection. Yet actions for overcoming barriers, illustrate the potential for making engaging in reflective practice a reality, despite the challenges present.

References

Beddoe, L., Ferguson, H., Warwick, L., Disney, T., Leigh, J., & Cooner, T., S. (2022). Supervision in child protection: A space and place for reflection or an excruciating marathon of compliance? *European Journal of Social Work, 25*(3), 525–537. https://doi.org/10.1080/13691457.2021.1964443

Bolton, S. (2016). Critical incident analysis – A reflection. *Veterinary Nursing Journal, 31*(12), 374–377. https://doi.org/10.1080/17415349.2016.1245118

Bottomley, J., Cartney, P., & Pryjmachuk, S. (2019). *Critical thinking skills for your social work degree (critical study skills)*. St Albans: Critical Publishing.

Coren, S., & Farber, B.A. (2019). A qualitative investigation of the nature of "informal supervision" among therapists in training. *Psychotherapy Research, 29*(5), 679–690. https://doi.org/10.1080/10503307.2017.1408974

Curry, A., & Epley, P. (2022). "It makes you a healthier professional": The impact of reflective practice on emerging clinicians' self-care. *Journal of Social Work Education, 58*(2), 291–307. https://doi.org/10.1080/10437797.2020.1817825

Dewey, J. (1910). *How we think*. Lexington: D.C. Health

Dewey, J. (1922). An analysis of reflective thought. *The Journal of Philosophy, 19*(2), 29–38. https://doi.org/10.2307/2939444

Eagly, A.H., & Koenig, A.M. (2021). The vicious cycle linking stereotypes and social roles. *Current Directions in Psychological Science, 30*(4), 343–350. https://doi.org/10.1177/09637214211013775

Farber, B.A., & Hazanov, H. (2014). Informal sources of supervision in clinical training. *Journal of Clinical Psychology, 70*(11), 1062–072. https://doi.org/10.1002/jclp.22127

FitzGerald, C., Martin, A., Berner, D., & Hurst, M. (2019). Interventions designed to reduce implicit prejudices and implicit stereotypes in real world contexts: A systematic review. *BMC Psychology, 7*, 29. https://doi.org/10.1186/s40359-019-0299-7

Gathright, M.M., Thrush, C., Guise, J., Krain, L., & Clardy, J. (2016). What do medical students perceive as meaningful in the psychiatry clerkship learning environment? A content analysis of critical incident narratives. *Acad Psychiatry, 40*, 287–294. https://doi.org/10.1007/s40596-015-0303-3

Grant, A., McKimm, J., & Murphy, F. (2017). *Developing reflective practice a guide for medical students, doctors and teachers*. Chichester: Wiley Blackwell.

Heaslip, V., Wilson, D., & Jackson, D. (2019). Are Gypsy Roma Traveller communities indigenous and would identification as such better address their public health needs? *Public Health, 176*, 43–49. https://doi.org/10.1016/j.puhe.2019.02.020.

Miettinen, R. (2000). The concept of experiential learning and John Dewey's theory of reflective thought and action. *International Journal of Lifelong Education, 19*(1), 54–72. https://doi.org/10.1080/026013700293458

Milne, D. (2007). An empirical definition of clinical supervision. *The British Journal of Clinical Psychology, 46*(4), 437–447. https://doi.org/10.1348/014466507X197415

Murillo-Llorente, M.T., Navarro-Martínez, O., Valle, V.I., & Pérez-Bermejo, M. (2021). Using the reflective journal to improve practical skills integrating affective and self-critical aspects in impoverished international environments. A pilot test. *International Journal of Environmental Research and Public Health, 18*(16), 8876. https://doi.org/10.3390/ijerph18168876.

Olmos-Ochoa, T., Fenwick, K., Ganz, D., Chawla, N., Penney, L., Barnard, J., Miake-Lye, I., Hamilton, A., & Finley, E. (2021). Reflective writing: A tool to support continuous learning and improved effectiveness in implementation facilitators. *Implementation Science Communications, 2*, 98. https://doi.org/10.1186/s43058-021-00203-z

Quirke, B., Heinen, M., Fitzpatrick, P., McKey, S., Malone, K., & Kelleher, C. (2022). Experience of discrimination and engagement with mental health and other services by Travellers in Ireland: Findings from the All Ireland Traveller Health Study (AITHS). *Irish Journal of Psychological Medicine, 39*(2), 185–195. https://doi.org/10.1017/ipm.2020.90

Rolfe, G., Jasper, M., & Freshwater, D. (2011). *Critical reflection in practice: Generating knowledge for care* (2nd ed.). Basingstoke: Palgrave Macmillan.

Rothwell, C., Kehoe, A., Farook, S., & Illing, J. (2019, August 5). *The characteristics of effective clinical and peer supervision in the workplace: A rapid review. Final report*. Newcastle University. Retrieved from www.hcpc-uk.org/globalassets/resources/reports/research/effective-clinical-and-peer-supervision-report.pdf

Snowdon, D.A., Sargent, M., Williams, C.M., Maloney, S., Caspers, K., & Taylor, N.F. (2020). Effective clinical supervision of allied health professionals: A mixed methods study. *BMC Health Services Research, 20*, 2. Retrieved from https://doi.org.nuigalway.idm.oclc.org/10.1186/s12913-019-4873-8

Thompson, S., & Thompson, N. (2018). *The critically reflective practitioner*. London: Red Globe Press.

Tripp, D. (2012). *Critical incidents in teaching: Developing professional judgement* (Classic ed., Routledge education classic edition series). London and New York: Routledge

Vinjamuri, M., Warde, B., & Kolb, P. (2017). The reflective diary: An experiential tool for enhancing social work students' research learning. *Social Work Education, 36*(8), 933–945. https://doi.org/10.1080/02615479.2017.1362379

Chapter 14

Practitioner Self-Care

Abbreviations

ADHD: Attention Deficit Hyperactivity Disorder
US: United States
WHO: World Health Organisation

Introduction

Practitioners supporting neurodivergent children and their families, are often expected to carry a heavy caseload and see families who have been waiting for two years plus for service provision. Practitioners and educators may also be responsible for advising families that there are limited or no services available, to meet their child's needs. Practicing within the confines of limited budgets and resources, while on the frontline of service delivery, can culminate in stress and burnout for healthcare professionals and educational providers. This chapter will discuss self-care for practitioners and how this can be implemented from a personal, to the broader top-down approach within an organisation.

This chapter will explore the significance of self-care in the context of creating supportive environments for neurodivergent children and families, and provide tangible methods and strategies for practitioners to adopt. The challenges and barriers to engaging in self-care will be discussed. Case studies will be provided to prompt reflection and illustrate the value of self-care in the practice context, for both the practitioner and the children and families they support.

Learning Outcomes

On completion of Chapter 14, learners should demonstrate an enhanced understanding concerning:

- The critical role of practitioner self-care, in professional practice with neurodivergent children and families
- Strategies and methods of engaging in self-care

DOI: 10.4324/9781003455868-14

- The significance of practitioner self-care concerning creating supportive environments, for neurodivergent children and families
- The link between self-care, effective communication and conflict resolution capacity

What Is Self-Care?

Self-care is defined as intentional activity to promote one's mental, emotional and physical health (Godfrey et al., 2011). Godfrey et al. (2011) elaborate and explain that self-care is the maintenance of health and wellbeing an individual employs, in between interactions with healthcare services. Mordue, Watson, and Hunter (2020) caution that self-care is so very distinctive, and each person must work in a trial-and-error fashion to establish which methods of self-care are right for them. Self-care is further informed by self-compassion. Neff (2003) explains that self-compassion is concerned with being kind to ourselves, as we would to someone else in the same position. Self-compassion necessitates that we are forgiving of ourselves when we make a mistake and actively aim to alleviate our own suffering (Neff, 2003). Practitioners working in the health and care sectors are known for their care and genuine empathy in their provision of support. Yet practitioners often provide this care, empathy and emotional support to other people, at the expense of their own care and emotional wellbeing needs.

Self-care is a conscious action taken by a practitioner to promote their own health and wellbeing. It aims to replenish depleted energy reserves and nurture your mind and body. A good metaphor for self-care is watering a plant. If the plant doesn't get water and sunlight, it can't grow or thrive. Equally, if we don't feed our body with the fuel and care it needs to function, eventually we will be unable to continue with our work and daily lives. Another metaphor which depicts self-care accurately is putting on an oxygen mask on a plane, should the cabin pressure drop. Cabin crew always advise to put on your own oxygen mask first. This may directly contradict your instincts in that moment, particularly if you are travelling with your children, parents or someone you love dearly, who is looking to you for care and support. Yet if you assist them to put on their oxygen mask first, and pass out due to lack of oxygen yourself, you are then unable to help and support them whatsoever.

Reflection Point!

Think of a time when you made a mistake in your practice or college course work, or failed an assignment or exam . . .

How did you feel? Did you berate yourself? What was your inner voice telling you?

Now compare this to what you would say to a friend or colleague who made the same mistake or failed an exam. Did you show yourself this compassion and care? Did you talk to yourself in the same way as you would someone you care about?

The World Health Organisation (2009) contends that self-care is strongly influenced by the culture and society within which it occurs. For example: working long hours for low pay may be culturally acceptable in developing countries. In contrast, in developed countries there's a greater emphasis on work-life balance. Government legislation and workplace policies, further communicate a focus and appreciation for self-care and staff wellbeing, or lack thereof. A really interesting comparison in terms of the societal and political context within which people practice, is the difference between parental maternity leave when having a baby in the US versus Ireland. The United States Family and Medical Leave Act provides for employees (in companies of over 50 employees) to take 12 weeks of unpaid leave to care for a newborn/cover their maternity period (US Department of Labor, 2023). In Ireland, paid parental/maternity leave is provided for 26 weeks, and the parent has the option to take an additional 16 weeks in an unpaid capacity (Government of Ireland, 1998).

Reflection Point!

Practitioners deserve to feel well and give themselves the same level of care and support they give to other people! Although this book discusses practitioner self-care in the context of creating supportive environments for neurodivergent children, educators and practitioners deserve wellbeing, feelings of positivity and to feel in control of their wellness. Your health matters for you and not just for other people!

It's important to think about self-care in the context of the work you currently do, or will engage in when qualified. Instinctively, as health, social care and education professionals, we want to help people. We want to end any suffering they are experiencing and make things better for them. Yet the reality for many sectors and settings means that you are practicing within the confines of limited resources, possible budget cuts and likely a colossal caseload/number of students. When families ask for your help and you can see the difficulties they are experiencing, you want to do everything in your power to support them. Engaging in self-care is a proactive method of doing this. By caring for yourself, you are creating a more supportive environment from which to provide care and support to other people. Providing care to other people and neglecting the care of yourself, will eventually manifest in a depletion of caregiving/support capacity.

Case Study 1

Sally is a second-grade elementary school teacher with a class of 28 children. Four of Sally's students are suspected of being neurodivergent and are on waiting lists for assessment. Challenging behaviour is a regular occurrence for two of these children awaiting ADHD assessment, as their need for additional support in the classroom remains unmet. Two of the children are struggling with the sensory environment of the classroom, as they await autism assessment.

Sally loves her role and is very well liked by her students and colleagues. She is a conscientious and caring teacher and makes herself available to meet with parents frequently, to ensure the needs of her students are met as much as possible. As parents have no service providers, Sally finds herself assisting parents with referrals, developing classroom support strategies for her suspected neurodivergent students and advocating consistently for additional classroom support.

Sally has been suffering from insomnia and low mood for six months and has tried meditation, yoga and herbal remedies to treat this condition. Yet nothing seems to work. Sally is adamant she won't use medication and has not discussed her symptoms with her doctor, as she is worried she may be diagnosed with a mental health condition. Sally worries that her colleagues and parents of children in her class would see her as less capable in her role, if they thought she was mentally unwell. She never misses work regardless of how unwell she feels, as she worries about the impact of her absence on her students.

What are the key issues within Sally's role which may be impacting her wellbeing?

What could Sally's school do to address these issues?

What broader political and societal issues are impacting Sally in her role?

Who should Sally prioritize?

Burnout

The World Health Organisation (WHO, 2019) defines *burnout* as an occupational phenomenon, as opposed to a medical condition. Burnout is a state of being which manifests due to the work environment and is characterised by exhaustion, negative feelings about one's job and reduced professional effectiveness (WHO, 2019). Work overload, according to Maslach and Leiter (2016), is the primary causal factor in burnout, with professionals increasingly being expected to give more in their work life, often in addition to coping with diminishing resources.

Within this vein, Hossain and Clatty (2021) researched the impact of the Covid-19 pandemic on nurses in their professional practice and found that the moral and ethical dilemmas the pandemic presented were particularly challenging. Nurses found themselves having to make decisions on who should receive treatment or who should have their needs met first, in light of the limited resources available (Hossain & Clatty, 2021). Although this study considers a major and unprecedented public health event, education, health and social care service staff make such decisions on a daily basis. Within disability support and education services, staff often find themselves deciding: which family will receive respite services? Which child will receive in-classroom support? And which family is experiencing the most acute crisis and needs to be seen as a priority?

Reflection Point!

Think of a time in your past when you felt stressed or overwhelmed (exams, break-ups, job stress, etc.). How did this stress impact your sleep? How did this stress affect your social life? How did feeling overwhelmed affect your motivation levels?

Burnout is intrinsically linked to practice within healthcare settings, partially due to the interpersonal nature of the work (Halbesleben, 2008). If you work in a factory manufacturing printers, or in a shop selling vegetables, the working environment will be in stark contrast to that of a social worker, nurse, teacher or physiotherapist. Within health and social care settings, staff interact with and provide direct care and support, seeing, hearing and feeling the impact of this consistently. Wanting to provide the help that people need and perhaps being unable to, due to resource limitations, can culminate in feelings of stress and burnout. Powers and Myers (2020) argue that the more emotional the work is, the higher the increase of burnout for staff. Staff practicing in roles which require practitioners to support other people in processing their emotions in an empathetic capacity, are more likely to be negatively influenced by such emotions and more at risk of burnout (Powers & Myers, 2020). Within health, education and community settings, supporting neurodivergent children and their families, is frequently concerned with the provision of emotional support. Hence, practitioners may be more at risk of burnout and emotional fatigue.

In a large-scale study within a medical setting in New Zealand with 1,487 participants, findings indicate that women under the age of 40 are most at risk of burnout (Chambers, Frampton, Barclay, & McKee, 2016). Chambers et al. (2016) further found that increasing and unsurmountable caseloads contributed to burnout, while self-reported poor health was further deemed to be a risk factor. A US study in 2015 identified that more than 43% of hospital clinicians in their sample of 578 people, reported experiencing emotional exhaustion (Roberts, Shanafelt, Dyrbye, & West, 2014), while 40% of staff surveyed in this study were identified as suffering from depression, based on their screening scores (Roberts et al., 2014). Roberts et al. (2014) surmise that causal factors for the self-reported burnout are associated with the frontline nature of clinicians' work, in addition to low levels of perceived self-accomplishment. A study undertaken by Yürür and Sarikaya (2012) specifically on social work, concluded that supervisor support was a protective factor against staff burnout. This study found that perceived support from one's supervisor, decreased emotional exhaustion and increased feelings of personal accomplishment associated with one's role (Yürür & Sarikaya, 2012).

Barnett and Cooper (2009) explain that practitioners experiencing stress or burnout, may inadvertently have their practice impacted by this. Ongoing burnout which is not addressed, can culminate in a reduced level of competence, objectivity and an ultimate inability to meet the needs of the people they support (Barnett & Cooper, 2009). On a practical level, this could manifest in impatience when communicating with neurodivergent children and families. It may culminate in feeling overwhelmed and unable to manage your workload and the stress associated with this. As an individual, your first priority should always be yourself. This is not selfish; it's self-preservation and an acknowledgement that you matter and deserve to feel well and healthy. Secondary to this, you have both a moral and professional responsibility to maintain your health and wellbeing, as this directly and indirectly impacts your capacity to effectively support the families/children you help within your role.

Resilience

Given the systemic issues which impact negatively the availability of educational, therapeutic and support services available for neurodivergent children, responding to dissatisfaction with service provision will likely be something you experience within your career. Closely linked to burnout, resilience is defined as the ability to bounce back after adverse events and recover (United Nations Office for Disaster Risk Reduction, 2023; Bonanno, 2005). Resilience is concerned with the ability to adjust and evolve, while coping with challenging life experiences (American Psychological

Association, 2023). Resilience for practitioners relates to their capacity to accept, cope with and adjust to challenges presented within their work life. It is further associated with the ability to continue and progress with one's role, while facing adverse circumstances.

Resilience is impacted by individual factors such as coping capacity and the availability and utilisation of social resources and supports (American Psychological Association, 2023). Long, Gardner, Hodgkin, and Lehmann (2023), within their social work profession research, surmise that socialising and spending time with other people from your profession, can assist in building and maintaining resilience regarding your work. Participants from their study reported not interacting with their peers or lone/remote working, as an issue which reduced the level of resilience they experienced within their practice (Long et al., 2023). This is particularly noteworthy post pandemic, as some practitioners continue to work remotely and spend less time on site interacting with their peers.

Bowles and Arnup (2016) argue that resilience in the teaching profession, is promoted by adaptive functioning ability. Adaptive function relates to the ability to cope with adversity and demonstrate an openness to new experiences (Bowles & Arnup, 2016). Bowles and Arnup (2016) surmise that although resilience is an attribute which is difficult to teach, teaching adaptability skills may be an effective method of promoting resilience. Adaptability, according to Ainsworth and Oldfield (2019,) is dependent upon both individual and environmental factors. Individual factors such as self-esteem, emotional intelligence and self-care, were found as notable issues which resulted in resilience for teachers. Environmental factors such as the organisational culture and support from management, were further identified as key factors which impacted resilience for teaching staff (Ainsworth & Oldfield, 2019).

Reflection Point!

What do you think the key causes of burnout are for your profession?

What actions do you think your employer could undertake to reduce burnout in your profession?

What actions could you undertake to promote your wellbeing at work and help prevent burnout?

Strategies and Methods for Self-Care

This section will discuss tangible methods of promoting self-care for practitioners, with the aim of enhancing wellbeing and preventing burnout. It's important to remember that the strategies discussed here are suggestions and ideas, based on the literature and research available on this topic. Work stress, feelings of burnout and being overwhelmed, spill far beyond the boundaries of the place of employment and eventually permeate every aspect of the person's life. Proactive engagement in burnout prevention is the most effective method of maintaining practitioner wellbeing (Otto, Van Ruysseveldt, Hoefsmit, & Van Dam, 2021). However, each person is completely unique, and your methods self-care may not be mentioned here, but are likely to be effectively meeting your individual and distinctive self-care needs.

Physical Activity

Physical exercise was found to be the primary strategy of engaging in self-care, reported in a Swedish study by Hansson, Hillerås and Forsell (2005). The WHO (2022) defines *physical activity* as bodily movement which results in the expenditure of energy, including but not limited to walking, swimming, cycling, dancing, running, etc. Maugeri et al. (2020), in their Italian study on physical activity during the pandemic, found a positive correlation between physical activity and improved self-esteem and wellbeing. Their study further reports that the decrease in physical activity (due to the closure of gyms, sports clubs, etc.) as a result of the pandemic culminated in poorer psychological wellbeing (Maugeri et al., 2020). The WHO (2022) reiterates such findings and proposes that physical activity reduces symptoms of anxiety and depression and further "enhances thinking, learning and judgement skills".

Author Reflection Point!

You may find the idea of physical activity as additional work and not something you would enjoy. Ten years ago, a friend persuaded me to join a group boot-camp class. It was torturous and I assured myself while I was there that I would never be back! BUT after I left, I felt so proud of myself. I slept better and felt a sense of accomplishment. So I tried another class, and slowly but surely I began to enjoy it. Since then it's been a staple within my self-care routine, and the group environment is a great motivator.

Boundaries

Carter and Barnett (2014) suggest creating clear boundaries in terms of your work and home life, to contribute to the maintenance of your self-care.

All of us have been guilty of checking emails and voicemails at home, or even on vacation! I hear myself saying "there's just one email I need to check", and before I know it I've spent an hour working. Carter and Barnett (2014) suggest having a clear work schedule with start, stop and break times included, and maintaining this rigidly.

Mills, Wand, and Fraser (2018) reiterate such views concerning boundaries and stress the importance of clarifying role boundaries and scope, both with colleagues and families in receipt of care. Self-awareness concerning professional boundaries is a vital prerequisite to maintaining self-care for practitioners, i.e. knowing the limitations of their time and resources (Mills et al., 2018). Indeed, for some staff members this may mean reducing work hours to find a greater work/life balance (Mills et al., 2018). The National Institute of Mental Health (2022) suggests that saying no to tasks you don't want to do or don't have the capacity to do, is another expression of self-care. We tend to feel we should, must and have to say yes, when a request is made of us in work. Yet if this additional task or role could further deplete your already diminishing energy or capacity to cope, then saying no is the right decision both for practitioners and for the children and families you support.

Carter and Barnett (2014) propose that creating a schedule to include your out-of-work activities, can assist in maintaining a good self-care routine. We schedule our work meetings, often social events, yet we tend to leave out our weekly yoga class or swimming session, or coffee date with a friend. Then other things overlap and our self-care activities are missed. Carter and Barnett (2014) advise not to wait for personal time to come about, but rather to plan this and make it happen!

Sleep

Mordue et al. (2020, p. 21) describe sleep as "nutrition for the mind" and argue that sleep is a crucial cornerstone, within the realm of self-care for practitioners. If you have ever experienced insomnia, you will know how detrimental this can feel for your overall health and wellbeing. Afonso, Fonseca, and Pires (2017) report that the number of hours someone works, can directly impact their sleep. They conducted a comparative study consisting of two groups: one group working 38 hours per week and the other group working 55 hours per week (Afonso et al., 2017). This study found that 75% of the group working longer hours reported bringing work home regularly, and they were significantly more likely to be impacted by sleep disturbance.

Wolkow et al. (2019) found a direct link between insomnia and sleep difficulties and risk of burnout in a large sample (6,307) of firefighters in North America. Such findings present the question of the chicken and the egg scenario: does sleep disturbance cause burnout? Or does burnout cause sleep disturbance? The research suggests that both may be true. Workload, hours and work stress can impact sleep. Sleep problems such as insomnia impact the individual within their role and their risk for burnout (Wolkow et al., 2019; Afonso et al., 2017; Armon, Shirom, Shapira, & Melamed, 2008).

Social Supports

Ruisoto et al. (2021) report a direct link between social supports and mediating the effects of burnout, for professionals in healthcare settings. Indeed, Foy and colleagues propose that a lack of social support culminates in increased levels of stress for employees (Foy, Dwyer, Nafarrete, Hammoud, & Rockett, 2019). Kiema-Junes et al. (2020) define social support in the workplace as support from a colleague or supervisor, which provides emotional and practical assistance, in addition to feedback. Harris, Winskowski, and Engdahl (2007) expand on understandings of social support in work and further include coaching and career mentoring as within this remit. Social support in the workplace is associated with perceived help should one need it, and the extent to which employees feel like their supervisor/employer values their wellbeing (Kossek, Pichler, Bodner, & Hammer, 2011).

Barnett, Martin, and Garza (2019) found that rather than general social support, workplace-specific social support contributes to lower levels of employment stress. Barnett et al. (2019) further report that the proximity of this social support in the workplace makes it accessible and immediately available, hence reducing stressors at the earliest possible opportunity. Kiema-Junes et al. (2020) argue that social support in the workplace culminates in better work performance, commitment and engagement.

Self-Care and Creating Supportive Environments

The extent to which your workplace is a supportive environment for neurodivergent children and families, will be undoubtedly influenced if you are experiencing burnout. Equally, if you've been suffering from chronic insomnia and are struggling to get through your workday, then this will impact your ability to create and maintain a supportive environment. There exists an inextricable link between your work-related, physical and social wellbeing and the environment within which you interact and support neurodivergent children and families.

Creating and maintaining a supportive environment is concerned with maximising the extent to which neurodivergent children and their families feel valued, included, listened to and understood. A supportive environment is one within which families feel confident in the practitioner's competence, knowledge and professional expertise. A supportive environment communicates the practitioner's commitment to working in partnership with parents/caregivers, to empower and enable them to meet their neurodivergent child's needs. A supportive environment aims to magnify the voices of people marginalised due to disability and actively aims to reduce health inequalities. Such an environment can only be realised when practitioners feel like their voices are heard and their needs are met. Supportive environments are created and maintained when practitioners value and prioritise their own health and wellbeing needs and are practicing within a supportive environment.

Speaking up as a professional is rarely an easy option. Yet the context of creating supportive environments for marginalised families, necessitates the practitioner to use their voice to create a supportive work environment for themselves, and consequently to enable them to competently do the same for those to whom they provide health, social care and education. Self-care is directly and unequivocally linked to creating supportive environments within the surgery, clinic, community or education setting.

Practitioner self-care is a conscious action to promote one's own health and wellbeing, for the purpose of creating supportive environments for neurodivergent children and their families. Self-care is closely linked to the principle of the power of each and every interaction with children and families. Practitioner wellbeing directly contributes to their capacity to make every contact count and to positively influence the child and their family. If you are feeling overwhelmed, burnt out or suffering from insomnia or another health condition due to work stress, this will influence (albeit unintentionally) your interactions with the families you support.

Author Reflection!

If I'm not feeling great, if my sleep is erratic or if I'm feeling unwell or in pain, I'm not able to give 100% in my role. I want to and I try to, but the reality is that if I'm not feeling well, this impacts my ability to do my role as effectively as I normally would. This isn't a failure, and I often try my best to compensate when I'm working and perhaps don't feel my best. Yet it's completely realistic to conclude that my health and wellbeing directly influence my efficacy within my interactions with colleagues and students.

Self-Care and Your Employer

Debate exists regarding whose responsibility it is to prevent burnout and promote practitioner self-care. Is this the employer's or the employee's role?

One could argue that if burnout is the result of excessive workloads, then this is the responsibility of the employer. Yet it could equally be argued that the employee has a moral obligation to maintain their own self-care and prevent burnout.

However, the challenge lies within the culture and complexities of both the profession and organisation. We tend to have an acceptance of increasing caseloads and working extra hours in health and education settings. Yet when everyone else also experiences these increasing workloads, it can become the norm. Equally, the fear of judgement should you put up your hand and say "this is too much" or "I'm not coping" dissuades practitioners from speaking out. Knowing that everyone's workload is the same can further lead to feelings of self-doubt and questioning of why other employees can do this and you can't? But often, everyone is struggling . . . and no one is saying anything! This is how the acceptance of excessive workloads manifests and is maintained. Each practitioner is afraid to say anything, which could potentially make them be perceived as less capable. This is where collective advocacy is a really useful resource to employ. An organisation can respond to an individual practitioner feeling overwhelmed by their workload, as an individual issue. Yet if a team of, or indeed all staff come together to collectively express their increasing stress and burnout due to workload, then the message to the employer is strengthened, and they are more likely to examine and address this issue.

Bakker and de Vries (2021) argue that human resources (HR) play a substantive role both in responding to and preventing burnout for staff in the workplace. Monitoring of staff stress levels and workload coping capacity, can enable HR departments to gauge when burnout is imminent and act proactively to support staff and prevent this (Bakker & de Vries, 2021). Medisauskaite and Kamau (2019) argue that staff being provided with modules and education on the psychology of distress, reported a notable reduction in anxiety, emotional exhaustion and burnout.

Organisations of employment have a significant role in creating supportive work environments for staff, which will promote and nurture their health and wellbeing. Some employers offer health and wellbeing programs for employees and access to information on where to access further supports. Some employers create specific initiatives to enhance employee wellbeing and reduce burnout, based on the unique needs of the staff. For example: Esquivel (2021) reports that nutrition strategies aimed at promoting staff wellbeing and healthy eating, are an effective organisational strategy for reducing burnout. Esquivel (2021) suggests that such efforts must take a systemic approach and facilitate accessibility to healthy food availability and further by influencing policy and information/training on diet and nutrition. Another insightful example is provided by Langran, Mantzourani, Hughes, Hall, and Willis (2022), via their research pertaining to the burnout experienced by pharmacists during the Covid-19 pandemic. They discuss the organisational response to the increased workload and stressors presented to their staff as a result of the pandemic (Langran et al., 2022). Langran et al. (2022) report that the organisational decision to close the pharmacy at lunchtime to offer staff a brief respite from their interactions with patients, was found to be a highly effective strategy for promoting staff wellbeing.

Case Study 2

Kenneth is a social worker on a multidisciplinary team supporting neurodivergent children. Waiting lists mean that families being seen in clinic have had no services for at least two years. Kenneth is increasingly responsible for meeting with parents who are irate and whom other staff feel unable to communicate with effectively. On a particularly tough morning of meeting with two families in distress due to extensive waiting times and lack of services, Kenneth leaves work feeling unwell. Upon visiting his doctor, Kenneth is signed off work for four weeks due to stress.

What Kenneth's colleagues don't know is that Kenneth has been feeling increasingly overwhelmed by his role and the mounting responsibilities associated with this. He dreads opening his emails and finds himself over-thinking each decision he needs to make. Kenneth's appetite has decreased, and he has stopped attending his regular basketball practice, something he used to really enjoy. Kenneth eventually began working at home in the evenings and on weekends, as he felt he just couldn't catch up with his workload or ever get to the bottom of his to-do list.

What are the key issues contributing to Kenneth's burnout?

What boundary issues may have exacerbated this situation?

What work supports or resources could have reduced the likelihood of this situation occurring?

Self-Care, Effective Communication and Conflict Resolution

The responsibility of self-care lies with the individual practitioner, in addition to the organisation of employment. An environment and organisational culture which doesn't encourage and support practitioners to engage in self-care, will undoubtedly experience higher rates of staff sick leave, absenteeism and turnover. An organisation which actively supports staff to prioritise their self-care, is communicating that they value their staff as employees for the work that they do and their wellbeing as people outside of their role. Organisational investments in staff self-care and burnout prevention, are actively aiming to contribute to the capacity of practitioners to create supportive environments for neurodivergent children and their families. A work environment which doesn't provide a supportive environment for practitioners and within which they can realise their wellbeing, cannot expect for such an environment to be provided to families.

Seul Ryu and Shim (2021) found that burnout had a direct impact on patient safety, in their study pertaining to nursing staff. They contend that excessive workload contributed to practitioner fatigue and subsequent burnout, reducing patient safety as an outcome (Seul Ryu & Shim, 2021). Richemond, Needham, and Jean (2022) concur and further propose that burnout and fatigue, negatively influences both patient outcomes and practitioner health and wellbeing. In fact, burnout has been shown to directly impact the practitioner's communication capacity (Salyers, Flanagan, Firmin, & Rollins, 2015). Practitioners report poorer communication, less patience and less energy, when suffering from burnout, according to Salyers et al. (2015). Another study found that staff burnout affects the patient's experience of the practitioner's communication, specifically regarding taking time to listen and communicating with the patient about their condition (Lu, Weygandt, Pinchbeck, Strout, & Cico, 2018). Lu et al. (2018) surmise that overall patient satisfaction was decreased, in their interaction with emergency department staff experiencing burnout. Within the context of creating supportive environments for neurodivergent children and their families, such reduction in the effective communication capacity of the practitioner, would detract from a supportive environment and potentially negatively impact relationships and interactions between practitioners and families.

Given the impact of burnout on both the practitioner and care recipient/child and family, consider the case study about Kenneth. If Kenneth remained in work and continued to meet with families, how might his communication be impacted? Would Kenneth be as effective as he usually is within his role? If a family is in crisis and presenting for immediate intervention, what could the impact of Kenneth's level of wellbeing be for this family, if any? Now imagine Kenneth is responsible for meeting with a parent who is extremely upset as their child has not been provided with a speech and language therapy assessment as promised. How might this interaction further impact Kenneth's wellbeing? How could Kenneth's level of burnout impact his interaction with this parent?

Given the impact of practitioner stress and burnout on the communication capacity of practitioners (Lu et al., 2018; Salyers et al., 2015), it is realistic to assume that practitioners would be less capable to respond effectively to conflict with parents. Preventative strategies to avoid conflict occurring within the context of creating supportive environments for neurodivergent children and families, is strongly informed by the building and maintaining of partnerships with parents. Conflict resolution requires practitioners to demonstrate competent listening and communication skills. Communication capacity is fundamental to both preventing and responding to conflicts. Hence, burnout which negatively influences the practitioner's capacity to communicate effectively, will undoubtedly subsequently impact their ability to prevent and respond to conflict within their practice with children and families.

Self-Assessment

How does burnout present?
    Define self-care.
    Provide three reasons why self-care is essential in practice with neurodivergent children and families?
    Can you identify two methods of enhancing self-care?

Summary

This chapter has discussed the significance of self-care for practitioners, when supporting neurodivergent children and their families. Burnout is a condition which manifests as a result of one's job and is more common within healthcare settings. Burnout can negatively impact the practitioner in all areas of their life, in addition to reducing the quality of their work and subsequent outcomes for the children and families they support. Yet self-care can offset the likelihood of burnout and can empower practitioners to prioritise and maintain their wellbeing. Self-care is individual and should be based on what works well for you. Specific strategies for self-care were explored in this chapter, including the importance of boundaries, social supports, sleep and physical activity. Being aware of your self-care needs and how to identify when you are at risk of burnout, will enable you to be proactive in promoting your wellbeing in work. Organisations further play a significant role in burnout prevention for staff and subsequently reducing risk and potential negative outcomes for neurodivergent children and families, in the context of creating and maintaining supportive environments.

References

Afonso, A., Fonseca, M., & Pires, J.F. (2017). Impact of working hours on sleep and mental health. *Occupational Medicine*, *67*(5), 377–382. https://doi.org/10.1093/occmed/kqx054

Ainsworth, S., & Oldfield, J. (2019). Quantifying teacher resilience: Context matters. *Teaching and Teacher Education*, *82*, 117–128. https://doi.org/10.1016/j.tate.2019.03.012

American Psychological Association. (2023, August 3). *Resilience*. Retrieved from www.apa.org/topics/resilience

Armon, G., Shirom, A., Shapira, I., & Melamed, S. (2008). On the nature of burnout-insomnia relationships: A prospective study of employed adults. *Journal of Psychosomatic Research*, *65*, 5–12. https://doi.org/10.1016/j.jpsychores.2008.01.012

Bakker, A., B., & de Vries, J., D. (2021). Job demands–resources theory and self-regulation: New explanations and remedies for job burnout. *Anxiety, Stress, & Coping*, *34*(1), 1–21. https://doi.org/10.1080/10615806.2020.1797695

Barnett, J., & Cooper, N. (2009). Creating a culture of self-care. *Clinical Psychology (New York, N.Y.)*, *16*(1), 16–20. https://doi.org/10.1111/j.1468–2850.2009.01138.x

Barnett, M.D., Martin, K.J., & Garza, C.J. (2019). Satisfaction with work–family balance mediates the relationship between workplace social support and depression among hospice nurses. *Journal of Nursing Scholarship*, *51*(2), 187–194. https://doi.org/10.1111/jnu.12451

Bonanno, G.A. (2005). Resilience in the face of loss and potential trauma. *Current Directions in Psychological Science*, *14*(3), 135–138. https://doi.org/10.1111/j.0963-7214.2005.00347.x

Bowles, T., & Arnup, J. (2016). Early career teachers' resilience and positive adaptive change capabilities. *Australian Educational Researcher*, *43*(2), 147–164. https://doi.org/10.1007/s13384-015-0192-1

Carter, L., & Barnett, J. (2014). *Self-care for clinicians in training: A guide to psychological wellness for graduate students in psychology*. New York: Oxford University Press.

Chambers, C., N., Frampton, C., M., Barclay, M., & McKee, M. (2016). Burnout prevalence in New Zealand's public hospital senior medical workforce: A cross-sectional mixed methods study. *BMJ Open*, *6*. 10.1136/bmjopen-2016–013947

Esquivel, M.K. (2021). Nutrition strategies for reducing risk of burnout among physicians and health care professionals. *American Journal of Lifestyle Medicine*, *15*(2), 126–129. https://doi.org/10.1177/1559827620976538

Foy, T., Dwyer, R.J., Nafarrete, R., Hammoud, M.S.S., & Rockett, P. (2019). Managing job performance, social support and work-life conflict to reduce workplace stress. *International Journal of Productivity and Performance Management*, *68*(6), 1018–1041.

Godfrey, C.M., Harrison, M.B., Lysaght, R., Lamb, M., Graham, I.D. & Oakley, P. (2011). Care of self – care by other – care of other: The meaning of self-care from research, practice, policy and industry perspectives. *International Journal of Evidence-Based Healthcare*, *9*, 3–24. https://doi.org/10.1111/j.1744-1609.2010.00196.x

Government of Ireland. (1998, May 18). Parental leave Act 1998. *Office of the Attorney General*. Retrieved from www.irishstatutebook.ie/eli/1998/act/30/enacted/en/index.html

Halbesleben, J. (2008). *Handbook of stress and burnout in health care*. New York: Nova Science.

Hansson, A., Hillerås, P., & Forsell, Y. (2005). What kind of self-care strategies do people report using and is there an association with well-being? *Social Indicators Research*, *73*(1), 133–139. https://doi.org/10.1007/s11205-004-0995-3

Harris, J.I., Winskowski, A.M., & Engdahl, B.E. (2007). Types of workplace social support in the prediction of job satisfaction. *The Career Development Quarterly*, *56*, 150–156. https://doi.org/10.1002/j.2161-0045.2007.tb00027.x

Hossain, F., & Clatty, A. (2021). Self-care strategies in response to nurses' moral injury during COVID-19 pandemic. *Nursing Ethics, 28*(1), 23–32. https://doi.org/10.1177/0969733020961

Kiema-Junes, H., Saarinen, A., Muukkonen, H., Väyrynen, S., Ala-Mursula, L., & Hintsanen, M. (2020). Dimensions of social support in the experience of work engagement in middle age: A Northern Finland birth cohort 1966 study. *The Scandinavian Journal of Psychology, 61*, 679–689. https://doi.org/10.1111/sjop.12640

Kossek, E., Pichler, S., Bodner, T., & Hammer, L. (2011). Workplace social support and work family conflict: A meta-analysis clarifying the influence of general and work-family-specific supervisor and organisational support. *Personnel Psychology, 64*(2), 289–313. https://doi.org/10.1111/j.1744-6570.2011.01211.x.

Langran, C., Mantzourani, E., Hughes, L., Hall, K., & Willis, S. (2022). "I'm at breaking point"; Exploring pharmacists' resilience, coping and burnout during the COVID-19 pandemic. *Exploratory Research in Clinical and Social Pharmacy, 5*, 100104. https://doi.org/10.1016/j.rcsop.2022.100104

Long, N., Gardner, F., Hodgkin, S., & Lehmann, J. (2023). Developing social work professional identity resilience: Seven protective factors. *Australian Social Work*, 1–14. https://doi.org/10.1080/0312407X.2022.2160265

Lu, D., Weygandt, P., Pinchbeck, C., Strout, T., & Cico, S. (2018). Emergency medicine trainee burnout is associated with lower patients' satisfaction with their emergency department care. *AEM Education and Training, 2*(2), 86–90. https://doi.org/10.1002/aet2.10094

Maslach, C., & Leiter, M. (2016). Understanding the burnout experience: Recent research and its implications for psychiatry. *World Psychiatry, 15*(2), 103–111. https://doi.org/10.1002/wps.20311

Maugeri, G., Castrogiovanni, P., Battaglia, G., Pippi, R., D'Agata, V., Palma, A., & Musumeci, G. (2020). The impact of physical activity on psychological health during Covid-19 pandemic in Italy. *Heliyon, 6*(6), E04315. https://doi.org/10.1016/j.heliyon.2020.e04315

Medisauskaite, A., & Kamau, C. (2019). Reducing burnout and anxiety among doctors: Randomized controlled trial. *Psychiatry Research, 274*, 383–390. https://doi.org/10.1016/j.psychres.2019.02.075

Mills, J., Wand, T., & Fraser, J. (2018). Exploring the meaning and practice of self-care among palliative care nurses and doctors: A qualitative study. *BMC Palliative Care, 17*(1), 63. https://doi.org/10.1186/s12904-018-0318-0

Mordue, S., Watson, L., & Hunter, S. (2020). *How to thrive in professional practice.* St. Albans: Critical Publishing.

National Institute of Mental Health. (2022, May 18). *Caring for your mental health.* Retrieved from www.nimh.nih.gov/health/topics/caring-for-your-mental-health

Neff, K.D. (2003). Self-compassion: An alternative conceptualization of a healthy attitude toward oneself. *Self and Identity, 2*, 85–102. https://doi.org/10.1080/15298860309032

Otto, M.C.B., Van Ruysseveldt, J., Hoefsmit, N., & Van Dam, K. (2021). Investigating the temporal relationship between proactive burnout prevention and burnout: A four-wave longitudinal study. *Stress and Health, 37*(4), 766–777. https://doi.org/10.1002/smi.3037

Powers, S., & Myers, K. (2020). Work-related emotional communication model of burnout: An analysis of emotions for hire. *Management Communication Quarterly, 34*(2), 155–187. https://doi.org/10.1177/0893318919893

Richemond, D., Needham, M., & Jean, K. (2022). The effects of nurse burnout on patient experiences. *Open Journal of Business and Management (Irvine, CA), 10*(5), 2805–2828. https://doi.org/10.4236/ojbm.2022.105139

Roberts, D.L., Shanafelt, T.D., Dyrbye, L.N., & West, C.P. (2014). A national comparison of burnout and work-life balance among internal medicine hospitalists and outpatient general internists. *The Journal of Hospital Medicine, 9*, 176–181. https://doi.org/10.1002/jhm.2146

Ruisoto, P., Ramírez, M., García, P., Paladines-Costa, B., Vaca, S., & Clemente-Suárez, V. (2021). Social support mediates the effect of burnout on health in health care professionals. *Frontiers in Psychology, 11*, 623587. https://doi.org/10.3389/fpsyg.2020.623587

Salyers, M., Flanagan, M., Firmin, R., & Rollins, A. (2015). Clinicians' perceptions of how burnout affects their work. *Psychiatric Services (Washington, D.C.), 66*(2), 204–207. https://doi.org/10.1176/appi.ps.201400138

Seul Ryu, I., & Shim, J. (2021). The influence of burnout on patient safety management activities of shift nurses: The mediating effect of compassion satisfaction. *International Journal of Environmental Research and Public Health, 18*(22), 12210. https://doi.org/10.3390/ijerph182212210

United States Labor Department. (2023, May 18). *Family and medical leave*. Retrieved from www.dol.gov/general/topic/benefits-leave/fmla#:~:text=The%20Family%20and%20Medical%20Leave,be%20maintained%20during%20the%20leave

United Nations Office for Disaster Risk Reduction. (2023, June 22). *Resilience*. Retrieved from www.undrr.org/terminology/resilience

Wolkow, A.P., Barger, L.K., O'Brien, C.S., Sullivan, J.P., Quadri, S., Lockley, S.W., Czeisler, C.A., & Rajaratnam, S.M.W. (2019). Associations between sleep disturbances, mental health outcomes and burnout in firefighters, and the mediating role of sleep during overnight work: A cross-sectional study. *The Journal of Sleep Research, 28*. https://doi.org/10.1111/jsr.12869

World Health Organisation. (2019, May 18). *Burn-out an "occupational phenomenon". International classification of diseases*. Retrieved from www.who.int/news/item/28-05-2019-burn-out-an-occupational-phenomenon-international-classification-of-diseases#:~:text=It%20is%20characterized%20by%20three,reduced%20professional%20efficacy.

World Health Organisation. (2022, May 16). *Physical activity*. Retrieved from www.who.int/news-room/fact-sheets/detail/physical-activity

World Health Organisation. Regional Office for South-East Asia. (2009). *Self-care in the context of primary health care*. WHO Regional Office for South-East Asia. Retrieved from https://apps.who.int/iris/handle/10665/206352

Yürür, S., & Sarikaya, M. (2012). The effects of workload, role ambiguity, and social support on burnout among social workers in Turkey. *Administration in Social Work, 36*(5), 457–478. https://doi.org/10.1080/03643107.2011.613365

Index

Den Hertog, R. 147
Den Houting, J. 6
Destructive Behaviour Diagnostic
  Observation Schedule (DB-DOS) 52
developmental coordination disorder
  (DCD) 33, 35
Devereaux, P. 144
de Vries, J. D. 240
Dewey, John 214–215
De Wijngaert, P. 42
Dhillon, S. 178, 180
Diagnostic and Statistical Manual
  (DSM-5) 37, 51–52
Diagnostic and Statistical Manual of
  Mental Disorders (DSM) 2, 6, 8, 18
Diaz-Orueta, U. 57
Diener, E. 159
disability movement 1
dyspraxia 33, 35, 149
dyspraxia/DCD 33; assessment and
  diagnosis of 37–38; communication
  and 93; defined 34–35; DSM-5
  37–38; gender 35; impact on family
  39–41; left-handed/ambidextrous
  34; motor and coordination
  problems 34; occupational therapy
  38; perception difficulties 34, 42;
  spatial awareness 34, 42
dyspraxia/DCD in adulthood 41–42;
  employment 41; motor function 42;
  perception issues 42
Dyspraxia Foundation USA 42
dyspraxic child 35–37; balance 35–36;
  caring 41; comorbidities 35;
  handwriting difficulties 36; motor
  function 36, 39; occupational
  therapy 38; problem solving 36;
  speech challenges 37; at sports 36;
  undertaking daily tasks 35–36

Echenne, B. 34
ecological systems theory 78, 188
Ecological Systems Theory of Human
  Development (Bronfenbrenner)
  77–78
education settings, creating supportive
  environments in 75–77
Edwards, A. 131
Edwards, L. 41
Eggenberger, A.L.B. 99
Ellis, P. 150

empathy 132
empowerment 67
Engdahl, B.E. 238
environment 78
Epley, P. 214
Esquivel, M.K. 240
ethnic minority families 180
evidence-based practice: accountability
  151; challenges 151–152; clinical
  expertise 145–146; and creating
  supportive environments 154–155;
  defining 143, 144–145; lack of
  cooperation 151–152; in practice
  151–153; preferences of
  patient/child/family 147–148;
  research 149–150
executive functioning 15–16
exosystem 77

Family Assessment of Needs and
  Strengths (FANS) 207
family support: activities 196–197;
  assessment of family's need 207,
  208–209; defining 195, 196–197;
  neurodivergence and 197; parental
  coping capacity 198; rationale for
  199–200; social determinants of
  health and 204–206; theory and
  approaches 200–204
Family Support Network (FSN) 197
family systems theory 200–202
Farber, B.A. 220
Farmer, M. 34
Farook, S. 219
Farre, A. 4
fear: of advocacy 179, 182, 185;
  contact issues 115–116
feedback 98
Ferrazzi, G. 202
Field, J. 203
Fineout-Overholt, E. 150
Fisher, R. 133, 135
Flora, D. 163
Fong, V. 164, 166
Fong, V.C. 26
Fonseca, M. 237
formal advocacy 185–186
formal supervision 219–220
forms 101
Forsell, Y. 236
Fox, K. 205

For Product Safety Concerns and Information please contact our EU
representative GPSR@taylorandfrancis.com
Taylor & Francis Verlag GmbH, Kaufingerstraße 24, 80331 München, Germany

www.ingramcontent.com/pod-product-compliance
Lightning Source LLC
Chambersburg PA
CBHW050635280326
41932CB00015B/2653

9 781032 593944